Life of Miracles along the Yangtze and Mississippi

Association of Writers & Writing Programs Award for Creative Nonfiction

Life of Miracles along the Yangtze and Mississippi

WANG PING

The University of Georgia Press *Athens*

Athens, Georgia 30602
www.ugapress.org

Designed by Erin Kirk New
Set in Minion Pro
Printed and bound by Thomson-Shore
The paper in this book meets the guidelines for permanence and durability of the Committee on Production Guidelines for Book Longevity of the Council on Library Resources.

Most University of Georgia Press titles are available from popular e-book vendors.

Printed in the United States of America
22 21 20 19 18 P 5 4 3 2 1

Library of Congress Cataloging-in-Publication Data pending
ISBN 9780820353920 (paperback: alk. paper)
ISBN 9780820353937 (ebook)

To Ariel and Leo, sunlight and rainbows on my path

To those who shared their stories of the Yangtze and Mississippi Rivers

To Allen Kornblum, who provided a home for my stories

To the 30 million children crossing oceans with parents or alone, carrying stars in their dreams as they flee from war to war, hunger to hunger

Contents

Acknowledgments

My deepest gratitude to those who read, edited, and gave me invaluable comments on the manuscript: Jim Cihlar, Scott Gannis, Erik Anderson, and others.

The following pieces were previously published:

"The Book War," *Moth*, 2018, *Speakeasy*, 2002
"We Are Water," *Hanging Loose*, spring 2018
"Morning Cloud, Evening Rain," *Trouble the Waters: Tales of the Deep Blue*, Rosarium, 2018
"Allen Ginsberg's Apology for Buddha," *Otter*, 2015, nominated for a Pushcart Prize
"Kelisu Diner," *Hanging Loose*, 2013
"Old Home" and "The Road to Joy," *Black Renaissance*, 2011
"Tough Love," *Riding Shotgun: Women Write about Their Mothers*, an anthology edited by Kathryn Kysar, Minnesota Historic Society / Borealis Books, 2009
"The Chinese Toilet," *Speakeasy*, 1999

Some of the names in the book are changed for protection.

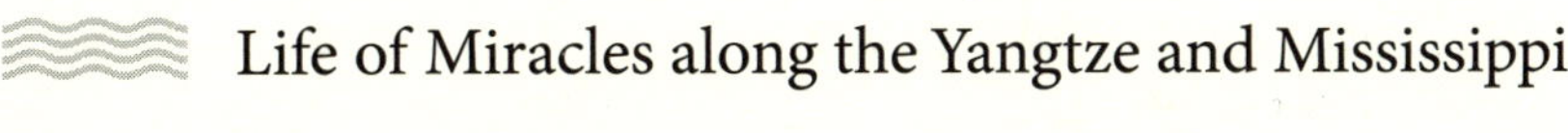

Life of Miracles along the Yangtze and Mississippi

Overture *The Book War*

I was six when the Cultural Revolution began, and it crushed my college dream.

Everything was shut down: factories, stores, schools, libraries. My father was exiled to the deep mountains far away, and my mother was under house arrest for teaching Western music. As the oldest daughter, I took up the duty to feed my grandma, younger sisters, and brother. I grew vegetables in a backyard plowed by bombs, caught insects and worms to raise chickens for eggs and meat, and walked six miles every dawn through minefields, chicken wire, checkpoints, and flying bullets to find food and fuel for my family.

My college dream drifted farther away than Beidou, the Big Dipper. And worse, I couldn't see the yellow star that sits in the sky above the Dipper, like a Buddha. Grandma had taught me how to locate it, the Polaris that forever points to the north. "Know the star, and you'll never get lost," she said.

For two years, the North Star vanished from the sky.

One early morning, I took out the coal stove to light a fire. Every day, this little stove cooked three meals for my family: breakfast, lunch, and dinner, plus all the hot water for tea and washing. When I opened the door, I saw Jiajia, the new girl from Beijing. She was reading Mao's Red Book under a streetlight. She was heaving with sobs, her face smeared with tears and snot, her hair white with frost.

I became curious. Nobody would weep from reading Mao's words anymore, let alone Jiajia, the uppity girl who had just moved to our navy compound on an island in the East China Sea. Dressed in the gray Mao suit like everyone else, she strutted with her chest high as if she were a ballet dancer. Rumor had it that her father was a general in disgrace, waiting for the verdict from the central government: to be sent to Mongolia to die or called back to Beijing in glory.

I tiptoed closer, peeked over her shoulders, and—gasped. The book in her hands had nothing to do with Mao; it was Hans Christian Andersen's fairy tales, and she was reading "The Little Mermaid," the story that ignited my college dream when I first heard it on the radio. I'd begged my mother to start my school a year earlier so that I could read it on my own, and she did, even promised to buy me a copy of Andersen's *Complete Fairy Tales* if I got good grades. Before I finished my first year, the Cultural Revolution broke out. Students became Mao's little Red Guards. They beat up teachers, shaved their hair, made them clean toilets. They rounded up books from homes and libraries, had the teachers and librarians kneel and watch their treasures thrown into bonfires. I'd raked through piles of confiscated books on the streets before burning, even sneaked into sealed libraries, to look for my Little Mermaid. No luck.

Now I found her, wrapped in Mao's red cover, in Jiajia's hands.

Engrossed in the story, Jiajia didn't realize I was reading the story over her shoulders until she heard me weeping for the mermaid's death. She jumped, fairy tales clutched to her chest. Her panic-stricken face said she was ready to fight me to death if I dared to report her. We stared at each other for an eternity. Suddenly, she pointed at my wet face and laughed. She knew she had found a kindred spirit and her secret was safe.

I begged Jiajia to loan me the book, just for three hours. I would read it in the cornfields instead of going to the market. My grandma would beat me for not bringing food home, but it would be worth it. Jiajia shook her head and turned to leave. "Wait, I have something you want!" I said. She snorted mockingly. I didn't blame her. It would be hard to believe I possessed something a princess would want. I was eight years old but looked like a wild, undernourished five-year-old, my thick hair matted and unruly, my face caked with dirt and soot, my self-made shoes gaping with holes. Jiajia chuckled and walked to her apartment. "I have *yi qian ling yi ye*!" I shouted to her back. She stopped and stood still. I walked to my chicken coop, taking my time to retrieve the book from under the roof. I knew she'd wait for me. *Yi qian ling yi ye*, *1001 Nights*, a.k.a. *The Arabian Nights*, was on the top list of banned books and the most difficult to obtain. I'd rescued it from a book pile outside a TB patient's house. He'd thrown it out to be burned, along with other banned books, but nobody wanted to touch anything from a man who'd been coughing blood and pus for years. The book had been rained upon, yellowed by the sun, and smeared with suspicious stains. It reeked of cigarettes. I didn't care. The stories had saved me from many gloomy days.

"*Aaaarabian Niiiights*!" I sang, as I waved the book to Jia's face.

"Oh my God, how on Earth did you get this?" she cried, snatching the book from my hand and thrusting "The Little Mermaid" into mine. I didn't answer her rhetorical question. There was an unwritten rule among secret book traders: Don't ask where the book comes from, where it goes, to ensure the safety of the loaners and borrowers, in case one gets caught.

Jiajia and I agreed to meet again the next morning, at the same spot and same time, to return each other's book. If we needed more time, we would renegotiate.

Our dawn book exchange lasted more than two weeks. I spent most of my days growing, hunting, and preparing food. It was hard to find a safe place to read. I shared a bed with my sisters and brother. My grandma's bed was in the same room. I tried to read in the fields, in trees, and in public bathrooms, but none of the places were safe. Even though soldiers guarded her family's apartment 24/7, Jia fared a bit better because she had her own bedroom. Whenever her father went out for a long walk with his guard, I would sneak into her room, and we would roll around in her bed, read, and tell each other secrets. I told Jiajia how "Little Mermaid" had inspired me to leave the island for college. Jiajia told me how she wanted to dance like the mermaid. I confessed I wanted to sing like her. . . . Our time together flowed endlessly like the Arabian Nights.

When we finished our books, we started daydreaming: Wouldn't it be nice to form an underground book club so that we had more books to read? But we needed more than *The Arabian Nights* and Andersen's fairy tales to start the network.

One of my chores was to feed chickens. I had ten hens and one rooster. My favorite was Silkie. She had silky white feathers and a black face. Grandma said even her blood and bones were black. She was the best brooder for chicks, her meat the best tonic for human blood. So whenever Silkie stopped laying eggs for brooding, my mother would order me to kill her so that she could have her meat. I had managed to stop her brooding just in time to save her. But this time, I knew she was determined to hatch chicks. So I decided to build a semi-underground nest behind the chicken coop, away from foxes and my mother.

After just a few strikes, my pickaxe hit a wooden box. I dug it out, pried it open, and pulled out *The Book of Songs*, *Journey to the West*, Shakespeare,

Huckleberry Finn, and to my ecstasy, *The Complete Fairy Tales of Hans Christian Andersen*, hardbound with a gilded title. On the first page, mother's handwriting: *To my stubborn girl Ping, may you be as courageous as the mermaid.* This was the gift my mother had promised if I finished my first grade with straight As. It contained every story Andersen had written, twice as thick as Jiajia's version, and it had no missing pages. Mother must have buried it under the chicken coop before Red Guards could burn it.

I ran to Jiajia and brought her to the treasure. We cried in each other's arms. We had just hit a jackpot for our book club!

We made membership rules to join our Mermaid Club:

1. You must own at least five forbidden books to become a member.
2. You can trade one book at a time only.
3. You must swear never to betray other members if you get caught.
4. You must replace the loan with your own, if it's confiscated or destroyed.

Jiajia found a few kids, exiled to the island from Beijing with their families, and they each had a cache of "poison." We got together in the woods, cut our wrists, and mixed our blood as a pledge to become a mermaid.

Our club grew quickly and expanded to twenty-five. I devoured books of poetry, philosophy, drama, plants, animals, medicine, math, physics, military training, and more. I was careful. If I got caught, I would jeopardize not only myself but also my family and the club members. Jiajia got ambitious. She wanted to expand the club to one hundred members. I told her to wait, for I had a premonition something bad would happen.

That night, I dreamed of a monster yanking me by my hair and throwing me into a fire pit. I opened my eyes. My mother held Andersen's fairy tales to my face, screaming in a hushed voice: *Where did you get this? How did you get this?*

I remained silent. She knew damn well where it came from. She had inscribed it to me and buried it behind the chicken coop. My question was how SHE had found the book? I had hidden it under my grandma's mattress, the last place my mother would check, because the two of them were constantly at each other's throat. Mother slapped my face with the book, burst my mouth open from inside. I tasted metal. She dropped the book, took out the bamboo whip.

Are you trying to kill me and your father? I'll kill you first! I'll kill you first! she hissed as she whipped me.

I covered my face with my hands. It was burning like fire, swelling like an angry sea. The pain was unbearable, not from the whipping or slapping but from a bleeding heart. I'd never see my "Little Mermaid" again. My mother would burn the book after she was done with the punishment.

And she did. She sat down and ordered me to tear out the pages and burn them in the stove. I heard my mermaid scream in pain as she turned into ash.

"Where are the rest?" she asked. I knew she wanted the rest of the books from her box. They were time bombs, and she must destroy them before they destroyed us. I shook my head. I had sworn to guard my books with my life, and I would.

She threw down her whip and left without a word. She knew if I had decided not to talk, nothing could make me. I knew she was going to comb through the house and the chicken coop to find my cache. Fortunately, half of the books were in the hands of the club members, and I would alert them the next day to halt our trade in the woods; they could hold on to my books until further notice. My heart shriveled as I listened to my mother pull out every drawer, turn over every mattress, and pull up each loose floorboard. Soon, she gathered a pile of books, all dog-eared, heavily perused, missing pages. She set the stove by the open window and watched me rip them up and feed them to the fire.

When all the books were gone, Mother went back to bed. I walked out and sat by the chicken coop. Silkie came to me, along with her chicks, cooing and nudging for food. I looked up. No moon in the sky. No Polaris. The night had entered its darkest hour. When would dawn break? Where was my hope? The whole country was in a bloodbath. No school, no food, only bullets flying over our heads, bombs and cannons exploding outside windows. My book club had been my only hope. Now it was gone. College seemed farther than the most distant galaxy. I was choking with tears when a flicker of neon orange rose from the sea, cutting across the sky and landing on the chicken coop. It bobbed up and down like a buoy in the sea, long hair floating and small feet bleeding. Little Mermaid? Impossible! She sang, her voice a whisper, but clear.

Don't give up, Ping, never give up. They took away your books but not your voice.
Go to the mountains. Tell your story to trees, birds, animals, and human friends.

A smudge of pink and blue appeared at the horizon. Dawn was breaking. I stood up. I knew what I was going to do.

I went about doing my chores that day, feeding the chickens, buying food from the market, cooking, cleaning. When night fell, I went into the woods with Jiajia, empty handed this time. Nobody asked what happened. The welts, cuts, and bruises on my face, arms, and thighs said it all. After a long silence, I started talking. Words flew out of my mouth like seeds and stars, forming the constellation of the Big Dipper. I looked for the Polaris, still invisible in the sky, but I knew it was there and would come out as long as I didn't give up. I smiled and nodded at my hidden star as I told the "Little Mermaid" story, her beauty and courage to go after her dream at any cost, which was now my story. Everyone listened as if they were hearing it for the first time. She had come alive like a flower, between my chapped lips.

So I started my Beidou Star Club, telling stories to the members in the woods, then to my siblings at home, then to neighbors. When the indoors became too small, we moved to the yard, where children and adults gathered night after night, from spring to summer to fall. When snow came, we made fires, each audience member bringing a piece of wood. I told stories of Romeo and Juliet, Tom Sawyer, Huckleberry Finn, Ali Baba . . . and Jiajia told about Red Shoes, Swan Lake, Lady Macbeth. When we exhausted stories from books, we created our own. We were hungry and cold. Our future was bleak without jobs or college, but we had our stories.

On Jiajia's fourteenth birthday, I threw her a party with the biggest bonfire ever. It was her last night at the navy compound. The verdict for her father had finally come: exile to Mongolia. That night, I told the story that had sparked our friendship five years before. Over the blazing fire, I spotted my mother, her eyes glistening like stars. She had tears as she listened to my mermaid story. My voice quivered as joy flowed through my heart like a river.

I might have lost the book battle with her, but I'd won the war.

I looked up. In the night sky, a bright yellow star. My Polaris was back!

And I knew I would leave home soon, to exile myself to the poorest village to work as a farmer, for the one-in-a-million chance to be recommended for college. I also knew I would cross oceans, the East China Sea, the Atlantic, the Pacific, to explore the world. It was still a crazy and dangerous dream, but no longer impossible now that I had the North Star to guide my way.

1

What's in a Miracle?

Life along the Yangtze and Mississippi

It's summer in Minnesota, the land of ten thousand lakes, and everybody is soaking up sunlight by the water under the blue sky. I sit on the floor of a lakeside cabin, surrounded by medical books I've studied for the past eight years: meridians, acupuncture points and prescriptions, microbiology, anatomy and physics, pharmacology, lab analysis. I'm reviewing them all for my eight-hour test.

"Mom, come play with us," shout my sons from the lake.

"I'll join you after I pass the test and graduate with a medical degree. I promise," I shout back to their sailboat.

"Are you out of your mind?" my friends asked when they found out I had signed up for the master's degree in traditional Chinese medicine. "Isn't your plate overflowing? Two kids, full-time teaching, writing, publishing, performing, photography, house, garden, rowing, flamenco, yoga, skating, meditation, and Kinship of Rivers project, its installations and exhibitions.... When do you ever sleep? Where do you get the energy?"

I laughed, and they laughed with me. We all knew that I only sleep 5 hours a day, that once I decided to do something, I became a honey badger, an ocean wave that kept pushing until it reached the shore. But that's not the secret of getting things done. The secret is an appetite to be alive, to take whatever life offers.

"Pain and bitterness are good for your heart," my paternal grandma would tell me. "You can't outrun them anyway. So you might as well turn them into nectar. Yes, that's right. Bitter is the prerequisite of sweet, just as night is the mother of dawn, and joy the child of pain. In fact, life won't be fun unless you've tasted all its flavors. Yes, I know your sister is getting away with things just because she has a sweet face and slippery tongue. And you, people call you dumb and ugly and dump all the chores on you. But wait twenty years, and see who will get the last laughter. Just watch. Her beauty and cleverness will bite her ass after she turns forty. And you, my ugly, dumb girl, will be reaping the harvest from what you're sowing now."

"Life is a river running to the sea, taking in every stream and every drop of rain along its way. A river never picks or judges. It just receives until it becomes the sea," sang my maternal grandma as she beat the laundry with a stick.

They also believed that our body and mind is a mirror image of the universe, yin and yang, water and fire, mountains and rivers, sun and moon, always changing from one into the other. Change is the norm, is life. Stasis is stagnation, is death. Once we embrace change, we no longer fear, and we are free to dream and make dreams real.

"This is the secret of *I-ching, Book of Change*," they said. "Step in the river, child. Find your key."

I was born in Shanghai, the mouth of the Yangtze, grew up on an island where the river ends and the East China Sea begins. Since I turned five, I would get up at 4:00 a.m. and walk five miles to the market to buy food for the day. There was no refrigerator, no stove, no running water, no heat or air conditioning on the island. Everything was rationed at that time: rice, flour, meat, tofu, cooking oil, soap, even matches. All food stands had long lines, except for the seafood. Fishmongers crouched next to mounds of creatures from the sea, shouting, "Fresh sea bass: five cents a pound! Live crabs: three cents! Shrimp: two cents! Squid: one cent!" People say girls from Shanghai and the island are prettier and smarter because of the seafood. It may hold some truth. My mother and sister love fish the way cats love mice, and they were both lauded as beauty queens on the island.

"If you would eat just one morsel of fish a day, you wouldn't be such an eyesore for the family, and your face wouldn't be covered with fungus rings," lamented my mother.

"And perhaps your eyes might grow a little bigger, and you might be a little smarter, like me," laughed my sister.

But I had sworn off seafood, chicken, and pork, the islanders' major protein sources, after I saw the terror in their eyes before slaughter. No, I would rather stay ugly and dumb than eat them. They felt pain like me, so they must have souls like me. Besides, my sister might be prettier but definitely not smarter. Otherwise, she wouldn't have made me do her homework every day, until I gave her a poem that was supposed to praise Chairman Mao, but I slipped in a word that suggested both love and lust. Either my sister didn't bother to read the poem or was too dumb to see the danger, but the next day, the teacher sent her to the principal's office with two charges: plagiarism (because the poem was too good to come from her) and sacrilege of Chairman Mao.

I don't know how she got out of the mess, but my sister never asked me to do her homework again.

As an ugly, dumb child, I roamed the island's mountains and rivers, gorging on juicy yangmei berries from gnarly trees in the monsoon season, dancing with my roosters, howling with typhoons that sweep across the island in July, August, and September, and tiptoeing through the ruins in eerie calmness after the destruction. I breathed the salty mist from the ocean, swam in the waves, and floated with its currents until we merged into one.

At the age of six, I knew I would go to college, an impossible dream at the time, as all schools and libraries were shut, sealed, destroyed. But I formed an underground book club, trading and reading forbidden books. They taught me how to think and write, and soon, I started telling my own stories to a growing audience that included my parents and siblings. After I discovered I could get *Voice of America* on my little radio, I started listening to Mark Twain, Edgar Allan Poe, Jack London, in a secret cave. Listening to *Voice of America* could have gotten me a life sentence in jail. I studied English for a month from a navy officer, who offered to give me lessons every morning in a wheat field, until the day he grabbed my hand and put it in his pants. Before my fifteenth birthday, the college reopened, admitting soldiers, factory workers, and peasants. I tried to join the army but got rejected because I looked like a twelve-year-old. My heart pounded 120 beats per minute from lying to the army recruiter that I was eighteen years old. I tried to find a job in a factory, but my family wanted to save the quota for my sister. So the only route was to move myself to the countryside as a farmer, and in three years, I might have a small chance to go to college. This route was packed with backbreaking labor, briberies, rapes, unwanted pregnancies, and forced marriages. And I was the only fool who showed up at the registration office. But even that officer rejected me. The minimum age to go to the countryside was sixteen, and I wasn't even fifteen. I pleaded with the man for three days. When he realized I would not leave him alone until my wish was fulfilled, he changed my age to sixteen and sent me to the village with a red stamp.

With a body still waiting for its first period and a heart set for college, I left home at the age of fourteen and never looked back.

In the mountain village by the sea, I learned how to get food from the soil, water, seasons, and ocean. I planted, weeded, fertilized, and harvested rice, wheat, yams, potatoes, taro, hemp, trees . . . I raised hens and ducks and fished with the nets I wove. I cussed and wrestled with peasants to make our 15-hours-a-day 365-days-a-year work go faster. I planted rice until my back felt like it would break but kept bending and trudging in the mud. At the age of sixteen, I joined the Communist Party, the highest achievement for Chinese citizens at the time, a path to glory and power for the ambitious. But for me, it meant the open door to college.

The next year, I left the village and went to Hangzhou Foreign Language School to study English. After three years of labor in the fields, I had lost my canine tooth and suffered from chronic diarrhea, a heart murmur, and swollen joints from rheumatoid fever. But I grew taller and got my first period, and my dream had come halfway true. The village had recommended me to study English in Hangzhou University. At the last moment, I was bumped into a secondary language school to be trained as an English teacher. It turned out a blessing in disguise because, four years later, I passed the college entrance exams and got in to China's best college, Beijing University.

It's a miracle I got out of the village with only a missing tooth and swollen joints. All the girls I knew had to sleep their way back to the city with village leaders. And if they got pregnant, they would either get abortions or marry. "Don't make babies here, at any cost," warned the girls who settled in the village. I know how they wept for their parents in Shanghai as they nursed their children and listened to their husbands snore away in bedchambers. There was no pill available to prevent pregnancy, only abortions performed by barefoot doctors, who practiced medicine after a few weeks of training. Once, I had to get a penicillin shot for my pneumonia. The "doctor" hit my sciatic nerve, and I couldn't walk for a month. As the girls talked, I listened, smiled, and nodded. I had no interest in sex, menstruation, or baby talk. My eyes were on one thing only: college.

Peasants liked to have wrestling matches with me because I fought like a honey badger, ruthless, wild, cunning, never giving up until my opponent raised their arms in exhaustion. Sometimes, things would go awry, especially when they pinned me down and tried to strip me. After all my tactics failed, kicking, biting, spitting, I would look into their eyes, and for some reason, they would go limp, cuss, and let me go.

One day, Uncle Bao, the party secretary of the village, barged into my room and started tearing my clothes. I wrestled with him in silence. He was apparently too drunk to reason with. I was hoping he would lose his stamina soon and give up, but he was persistent.

"Oh my God, how old are you, girl? You're not eighteen? No way!" he shouted, looking down on my half-naked body, still hairless. I told him about my college dream, why I lied to come to the village. He left without a word. The next day, his wife invited me to eat with the family. They had three daughters, eighteen, seventeen, and sixteen, all stunningly beautiful. I became their fourth, the ugly duckling again, but they were kind to me. He never touched me again and never let any villager touch me either. Three years later, he fought tooth and nail to get me into the language school in Hangzhou.

Besides "The Little Mermaid," "Angel" is my other favorite tale by Hans Christian Andersen. There was no image in the book. But I could conjure her up in my mind any time I needed her. Together we would walk through the fields, gathering flowers to soothe the pain of the lost souls, and in doing so, I felt soothed myself. I didn't need the visual. Her fragrant breath and feathery wings were enough to keep me safe and alive through the hunger that killed millions in China, the Cultural Revolution that annihilated even more, the daily punishment for reading books, the hard labor in the village. . . .

In 1986, I said goodbye to Beijing University in the north and my Yangtze River in the south and arrived at JFK with twenty-six dollars in my pocket. That night, the Mets won the World Series, and Queens became a carnival. All night long, people drank, shouted, danced, and threw bottles at windows. Alone in the basement, I wept, my heart filled with terror. I thought I knew English well, but I couldn't understand a word from the streets or why the hairy Americans went crazy over a little leather ball. I thought my angel had abandoned me because she had not appeared in the basement in Flushing. Early the next morning, my sponsor drove me to work in his antique store at Union Square. We crossed the East River. I had never seen so many bridges sparkling like jewels hanging from the sky. "Oh, wait until you see the other river, the Hudson, bigger and more bridges than this side," said my sponsor.

My heart settled. I would not lose my way on this peninsula, blessed by two rivers that flowed to the sea. Yes, the sea, I could smell her sweet brine in the morning exhaust.

During my thirteen years in NYC, I often took subways and ferries to Staten Island whenever I felt lonely, homesick, hungry. As the ship crossed the bay and the setting sun blazed the water into a sheet of shimmering gold, I could hear the murmur along the line where the river met the sea, the air mixing oxygen and carbon and nitrogen, and I would be back home again, on the island where the Yangtze meets the East China Sea.

The angel that kept me safe in China continued to bless me in NYC. With the twenty-six dollars I brought with me, I earned an MA from Long Island University, then a PhD from NYU. I walked into a writing workshop by chance, sat down, and wrote my first story. That led me to the Poetry Project at St. Mark's Church, Allen Ginsberg, Gary Snyder, John Ashbery, Anne Waldman . . . I was always starving during my first three years in the city, on the verge of being homeless, almost moved to Montreal to marry and study business at McGill University, but something always happened that led me to food, shelter, jobs, a green card, NEA fellowship, my first book with Coffee House Press, my first son . . .

On my son's first birthday in 1998, I had a banquet to say goodbye to my friends: Paul Auster, Allen Ginsberg, Ed Friedman, Lewis Warsh, Chuck Wachtell, Bob and Donna Hershon, and many others. We were crammed in the empty apartment, eating, sweating, and joking about Minnesota winters. I had shipped all my furniture to St. Paul. After the party, we hopped in the van and drove, following rivers and mountains through New England and Canada, all the way to the loft overlooking downtown St. Paul on the bank of the Mississippi. Everyone predicted I would go back to NYC before Minnesota froze my head off, but I fell in love with the brutal winters and the wild Mississippi, its beauty still taking my breath away daily. At night, I fall asleep to her sound, accentuated by the distant rumbling of freight trains. At sunrise, I watch the mist galloping like wild horses along the frozen mirror of the Mississippi.

It is through the Mississippi that I felt the awe Zhuangzi had described about wild mountains, rivers, and oceans. Through the Mississippi, I felt the essence of the Yangtze, and the island spirit in the East China Sea.

I decided to study Chinese medicine, as a way to go home, to live with two homes on two continents, two cultures, and swim in two rivers simultaneously.

Chinese medicine is about discipline, knowledge, and philosophy—how we know ourselves, body and mind; how we position our microworlds in the macrouniverse, connecting and moving with the five elements: wood, fire, earth, metal, water that circle within and outside us; how we control our action and reaction through this awareness and discipline: eat, work, rest, love, forgive, reconcile. If we are not in sync with the cycles, we become sick. If we move in sync, we maintain our balance, health, and energy.

Our body flows like a river. Where there's stagnation, there's trouble. Where the blood is blocked like a dammed river, cancer grows.

Movement is the key. Movement with awareness is another key. Movement with discipline and devotion is the final key.

When we have all three keys in hand, we step into the river, into the way, free, fearless, fun.

When spring breaks the ice in the Mississippi River, I get up at 5:00 a.m. to row. The river is veiled with mist, and the water foams and whirls with driftwoods after a heavy rain. I sit in my red single, spine straight, shoulders relaxed. I raise my oars, drop them in the water. Whoosh, the boat dashes like a long-legged insect, cutting the water in a straight line. I breathe, knees up and down, arms in and out, chest open and close, open and close . . . I row like a Tibetan pilgrim on her yearlong prostration to Lhasa. It's my thousand prayers each morning along the national park, my gratitude to live in the paradise. The river coos and laughs under me, around me, and within me. Around the bend, on a piece of driftwood, a heron and coyote bathe in the morning light.

"Good morning, handsome," I greet the coyote as I flow by.

"Hey, our lady of the Miss," I bow to the great blue heron gazing into the water.

This is our river temple, where peace and harmony reside.

A bald eagle appears, circling above, then heads upstream, signaling me to follow, to Lake Itasca, the source of the Mississippi.

I often think of the trip there with my writing class, how we paddled its winding path graced with wild rice, cattails, ducks, snakes, eagles, and Jan's spirit. Jan, my mentor at Macalester College, requested to have her ashes scattered there. She wants to sing, dance, and rest in the young water that grows into the longest and mightiest river in North America. My students didn't know the story, but they felt it. Thomas, a freshman from Albany, New York, said, "Someone is watching from the woods and reeds, someone firm and warm, gentle and fierce, a warrior, a goddess. I'll be safe sleeping in the woods, Ping. Good spirits are watching us."

Easter Sunday 2017, Academy of American Acupuncture and Oriental Medicine, Roseville, Minnesota.

I walk to the podium, a black candle in my hand. Dr. Tian lights the candle and hands me the master's degree of traditional Chinese medicine.

I raise the candle and the certificate. I've earned many degrees in my life: bachelor's from Beijing University, master's from Long Island University, master's and PhD from NYU, but this is the first time I'm attending the graduation. Why? Because Dr. Tian, my teacher and friend for the past eight years, asked. Dr. Gong, the president of the academy, asked. My classmates asked. For eight years, the academy had been my home for knowledge, healing, and joy.

The crowd cheers. In the crowd, my sons, my former students, friends.

The black candle symbolizes life: dark, heavy, fragile. But if one is willing to light it, its tiny flame can brighten the whole universe.

Lai and Xiong hand me a card. "From student to teacher, from teacher to student. You believed in us, we believe in you, another degree, another cycle of wonders."

The college told me I'm the worst teacher ever.

But students travel from Asia, Africa, and Europe to study with me. Their trust runs like a river through my meridians, transforming toxin into kindness, kindness into blood, feeding heart, lungs, liver, kidney, brain, limbs. Put a needle in *baihui*, the apex of the head, where the yang energy meets, I can lift my spirits and sharpen the mind. Needle *dantian*, two inches below the navel, I awaken the natal power from Mother. When the season changes from summer to fall, a needle in *zusanli* strengthens *qi* for the coming winter.

Yin and yang, light and dark, pain and joy—energy that cannot be made or destroyed, only transformed for the next cycle.

This is my magic, also Lai's and Xiong's, also yours, our river of life.

Miracles live within us, if we allow it. And good spirits are watching over us.

2

The Chinese Toilet

A week after birth, my son Wei already suffered from constipation. I sniffed his bottom and stuck my fingers into his diaper every five minutes. Nothing there. Finally, I took him to his pediatrician. Dr. Greenbaun inserted a Vaselined Q-tip into his rectum and dug out bullets of poop.

"See, not that hard to do," she said as she washed her hands in the sink.

I know many disorders are genetically inherited. My grandma loved to tell me how she would pin me on her lap for hours trying to make me go, how I struggled and cried but nothing would happen until she slipped in a piece of soap and bloody bullets fell out.

I also heard this embarrassing problem is more psychological than physical. Definitely true in my case. I suffered in my kindergarten because I couldn't go according to the teacher's schedule. At 8:00 a.m., we would bring in portable toilets and line up along the wall of the dining room, also used as our playroom and classroom. Children, including the two-year-olds, queued up, each holding a piece of toilet paper. Nobody seemed bothered by the smell or grunts from the toilets. When it was my turn, I refused to go. A teacher pulled me over by the ear and pressed me firmly on the toilet. "Do it now," she said, "if you don't want to soil your pants, because your next bathroom time is after lunch." An hour passed by. I was the only one left there, sitting on the toilet like an orphaned chick. The teacher came over, shaking her head in disbelief. "Get up, you stubborn girl. No snack for you until you learn how to use the toilet."

Missing the afternoon snack was a severe punishment during China's three-year hunger. I was starved all the time. Our rice porridge with dried, shredded yam seemed more watery with each meal, a skinny pickle floating like driftwood. Our teacher told us that we were lucky to have anything to eat at all. People all over the country were chewing tree bark and grass, even soil. At 2:30 p.m., a bucket of corn bread was brought in. The smell made my stomach growl with pain. I sneaked out and roamed the campus. Our kindergarten used to be a nunnery. Nuns were parasites, our teacher told us. They did not work but made a comfortable living by sucking blood from others. The older nuns went back home to work in the fields or factories. The younger, prettier ones married the peasants assigned by the government. The bloodsucking parasites must have loved trees. Old gnarly mulberries and Chinese scholar trees dotted the campus, all stark naked, no bark on their trunks or leaves on the tops. At the far end of the woods stood some pine trees, untouched because no one had found a way to eat them. Under the shade stood a thatched hut with mud walls: the latrine pit for teachers and grown-ups. It had three linked wooden seats that reached my chest. I peeked into the deep hole. Long, bloody napkins floated upon the brown ooze. I picked a clean seat and climbed onto it, gripping the board on both sides to balance myself. Through the glassless window, I could see the pine trees, the blue sky. I squatted there until the bell rang from the classroom for the choir practice.

I grew up with public bathrooms. The first one stood on a hill, about a quarter mile away from the navy compound where my family lived, its red brick walls and gray tile roof shadowed by old firs. The women's section had five stalls with three missing doors. It was still my favorite because most public bathrooms had no walls, just an open ditch where people squatted next to each other. Because of its distance from our residence compound, we hardly smelled anything except on windy days or when the truck came to empty the pit. Every night, after I finished the chores and my parents went to bed, I would walk up to the hill, a book tucked under my shirt. From a distance, the bathroom, with its curved eaves glowing in the moonlight, looked like a temple. My heart would start thumping with excitement, as if I were entering a cave with buried treasure. Behind the latched door, I read. The only sound came from the wind or crickets chirping in tall grass. When I finished a story or a poem, I'd look up at the moon and stars through the hole in the roof, the treetops trembling with silver dew, and I was the happiest girl on Earth.

In the small hours, when everyone in the navy compound was sound asleep, I would meet and trade books with my club members. Once I traded three of my Russian novels for *Lady Chatterley's Lover*, the "hottest" and "dirtiest" book that was circling underground. The owner swore it would poison my mind and make me sin. I did shed a few tears for Lady Chatterley, but my flesh did not feel any of the changes I had been promised. Perhaps I was too young and innocent to understand what was going on, or my mind had already been poisoned beyond redemption by the stories from the Ming and Qing dynasties. People knew how to party then. Disguised in men's clothes, women became champion scholars, high officials, even generals. Men pierced their ears, bound their feet, and entered the forbidden inner chambers or nunneries to play with girls and women. How passionately they loved and made love, with their neighbors and strangers they encountered over walls or through bathroom wall cracks. When their parents forced them to marry someone else, they would elope or cut off their noses, ears, or cheeks or hang themselves to preserve their virtue. Some jumped into wells, ponds, or latrine pits, probably because they couldn't walk far with their bound feet.

One of my favorites told the story of an old scholar who had failed in each official exam. On his fiftieth birthday, he decided to try his luck one more time, even though his fortune-teller told him he had no chance. On his way to the capital, he found a bag of gold in a latrine pit. He could start a business with the found treasure or spend it on wine and women. Instead, he decided to wait on the roadside. Soon, a sweating merchant came by and asked the scholar if he had found a bag in the latrine. The scholar returned the gold. The merchant prostrated in gratitude and said he would have had to kill himself if he had lost the money his family had borrowed from relatives and moneylenders at a high interest rate. He offered the scholar a reward, but the scholar declined and continued his trip to the capital. To everyone's surprise, he aced the exams and was appointed as a governor. He returned home in glory. When the fortune-teller saw him again, he cried out and asked him what he had done to change his luck. He told the latrine story. "Congratulations! You were doomed to fail and live in poverty because of the misdeeds from your previous life. But you redeemed yourself with that bag of gold and reversed your fate."

Each time I read the story, I would sigh. I had never seen gold in my life. The biggest money I had ever handled was a one-yuan note. And the only time I had found money was a five-fen coin floating in the pit. My sister had found it. She dragged me there, begging me to retrieve it. I walked away in disgust. The next day, it was gone. "We could have bought two packs of candies with that coin," whined my sister.

Our water taps were built near the public bathroom so that we could clean it with used water. Grandma would curse loudly as she carried buckets of soapy water uphill, puffing and limping on her bound feet. Everyone complained, but thcy all did it because nobody wanted a bathroom flooded in excrement. I spent a lot of time at the tap washing food, clothing, and dishes. In winter, the icy water bit into my frostbitten hands like hungry rats. I still liked it there. I was in the open air, away from Grandma and Mother's nagging. I could daydream, listen to gossip, or watch my sister play.

Every afternoon, my sister would gather a crowd of children on the slope outside the bathroom. At nine, she was already known for her beauty and cleverness. Even boys took her orders willingly. They rolled glass marbles from hole to hole, jumped rubber band ropes, and flipped cigarette wrappers folded in triangles or octagons. The winners would get marbles, wrappers, candies, cigarette butts. I watched as I beat dirty laundry with a stick. Nobody wanted me on their team because I seemed to lose every game except for cartwheels. Once I did fifteen in a row and gave the prize to my sister. She pulled me into the bathroom and handed me a piece of toilet paper. "Hold it," she said, digging out some cigarette butts from her pocket. She tore them one by one, poured the tobacco onto the paper, and rolled it into a thick, long cigarette. "Want a smoke?" she handed it to me after a deep drag. I took the roll and blew into it like a whistle. It died instantly. My sister gave me a pitiful look. "First time, eh?"

People used chamber pots to avoid going uphill for the bathroom in the middle of the night. My mother had one from Shanghai. It had a peony bush on its white enamel body, a red flower dotted with golden pollen blooming on the cover. It was my job to clean my family's chamber pots in the morning. I stacked them together, with Mother's on the top because it had a cover. Neighbors passed by, mostly mothers with chamber pots in their hands. "Morning, little Ping, have you had your breakfast yet?" they greeted me. I grunted, red from holding my breath, wishing people would stop greeting one another with "have you eaten" when they carried their nightly waste in their hands.

I grew a vegetable garden in the back of our compound. My grandma taught me how to fertilize vegetables with human waste. "Only the fermented manure from the latrine pit. Safer and cleaner," she said, ignoring my silent protest as she tied a bamboo stick to the ladle. She changed her mind only after a peasant boy fell in the pit and drowned. "Just thin the urine with water and pour it a foot away from the roots so they won't burn," she said. "If there's something other than piss, throw it away." She didn't say why, just gave me a look that made me shiver in disgust. I followed her instructions until the day Mother yanked a handful of hair off of my scalp for breaking her prized teacup. In the morning, I found a turd in her chamber pot. I buried it near a cauliflower. A month later, Mother broke a mop handle beating my sister for talking back. I cut the cauliflower and sautéed it with sliced pork, her favorite dish. I added an extra spoonful of lard and MSG. She gobbled everything down without suspicion, even giving me a friendly pat on the head. I winced, my triumphant bubble popped by shame. If I could never tell anybody, if she didn't know what she was eating, what good was my revenge then?

Many Chinese sayings come out of latrines: shit, dog shit, shit eater, a mouth full of shit, fart, dog fart. *A flower in cow dung* describes a beauty married to an ugly man. Pig-headed people are called "rocks in a latrine pit—hard and stinky." For newly appointed officials with fake integrity, we say "a new chamber pot with three days of fragrance." In describing a bully, we say he's "a latrine pit in July, the more you stir it, the smellier it gets." Every Chinese knows Mao's famous poem: "We regard the mighty no more than muck." The most vicious curse for a woman is "may you bear a son without an asshole." Once my sister called Mother "dog fart." She was slapped so hard her eardrum ruptured. Since then, my sister would fart uncontrollably whenever she saw Mother.

They say wisdom and truth are buried in old sayings. A cedar chamber pot may indeed smell good before use. My grandma from Shanghai loved chamber pots, like all Shanghai people. She placed hers next to her bed behind a curtain, where she hid her treasures: dry fruit, nuts, cookies, cakes, candies. Toward the afternoon, the pot began to fill up. Each time someone lifted the cover, I held my breath until I turned blue. I couldn't understand how my aunts and uncles could continue eating and chatting with the person who was sprinkling and splashing three feet away, behind the curtain.

As my face turned blue from severe constipation, my grandma would comfort me with her chamber pot story. When she married my grandpa, her father gave her a chamber pot carved and gilded with dragons and phoenixes. It matched the bed the bridegroom's family provided. The bed resembled a house with steps. Women guests at the wedding stuck their heads inside the chamber pot, sniffing and sighing with jealousy. "Wish you could see it," said Grandma. "But your grandpa sold it, together with the bed and his land to pay his debt! It turned out to be a blessing in disguise. If he hadn't gambled his wealth away, we would have been branded as capitalists after the liberation and exiled to the countryside." She shuddered. My grandma was a city snob.

She considered Shanghai the center of civilization and everywhere else barbarous. She was still mad at my mother for moving out of Shanghai to an island with her husband.

Every morning, Uncle Shan pulled his manure cart into the lane exactly at 6:30. "Hurry up, and be careful," my grandma would say from her pillow as soon as his bell rang in the lane. I took the pot down the dark, narrow staircase and waited in line with other women. After Uncle Shan poured the waste into his cart for me, I cleaned the pot with a bamboo brush then sprinkled it with the "Stinky Liquid," a deodorant every family used. All the chamber pots lined along the lane like an army. The sound of brushing was loud and chaotic in the beginning but soon synced into an odd harmony.

I hated chamber pots as much as I hated the portable toilets at school. Every day, I would walk ten blocks to use the public toilet.

One day, my father came home unexpectedly early, shaking a set of keys above his head. "I got it," he shouted, "our own bathroom, our own shower!" Mother shrieked and jumped on top of him. Together they chanted, "Goodbye, public toilet. Goodbye, sponge bath." When my sister told me we were assigned a new apartment with modern facilities, I was in tears. "Goodbye, portable toilets," I chanted silently.

A week later, we moved. The new apartment indeed had a private squat toilet and a cold shower. Soon we discovered that the water pressure was too low to flush, and we had to save laundry water in a jar for the cleaning. Mother quickly switched back to her chamber pot, claiming squatting gave her dizzy spells.

The private bathroom didn't change my life. In fact, things got worse. I had no more excuses to get away from the house. And my grandma constantly pounded on the bathroom door, asking if I had drowned myself in the foot-deep hole. It occurred to me one morning, as I carried Mother's chamber pot to the new garden, that the vegetables I ate were all fertilized by her pee. She had her final revenge, as always.

Two years later, my father was demoted for siding with the wrong faction. We had to move into a crowded compound in the old town. It was built for a warlord's concubine and their servants but now was inhabited by at least thirty families. The apartments were old, the walls peeling, and the stairways crumbling. There was always a line outside the two-stall bathroom. Every day, a bully took his radio there, bolting the door to listen to the story broadcasting from 12:00 to 1:00, despite the pounding and cursing outside. I abandoned reading in that bathroom. Besides the long line, the stench and dirt were intolerable.

My sister fell ill soon after we moved. First, blue spots appeared on her arms, legs, and thighs. Then her nose, stomach, and uterus started bleeding, and doctors couldn't figure out the reason. She had to be hospitalized so often and for so long that we moved her desk and chair to her ward.

"What do you expect, when you have a public bathroom in the middle of the living quarters? It's bad feng shui, bad, bad, bad!" My paternal grandma would scream.

I got my own bathroom when I moved to the countryside. Peasants put tall buckets in pigsties as toilets. Once a week, they carried them on a yoke to the community manure pit. Each family could save two buckets a month for their own vegetable plot. Apparently, it wasn't enough because many were caught stealing manure from the community pit. Since I had no pigs to raise, villagers built me a shed next to my neighbor's sty, placing a new pinewood bucket and bundles of rice straw inside. The straw was for wiping. I spread it in the bucket to cover maggots and prevent splashes. For some reason, I didn't mind the bucket as much as the portable toilets or chamber pots. Perhaps because I didn't have to share it with others. As my grandma often said, "Other people's crap stinks to death; your own droppings smell like perfume." Perhaps I got used to it from spreading manure in the fields with bare hands. The stench seeped into the pores, and nothing could wash it off. Sometimes, as I sat in the fields eating lunch with my stinky hands, I would think of my fuss about the chamber pots and portable toilets, and my petty revenge on Mother. It all seemed so far away and trivial. Three months after I became a peasant, the only trace of my city upbringing was the toilet paper I stacked neatly in a basket. Whenever my girlfriend helped me carry out the bucket, she would ask why I wasted money on the paper made of straw, why I couldn't just use the straw for heaven's sake. She said it was like "taking off one's pants to fart."

Villagers collected excrement like treasure. Even children carried baskets when they went out to pick up cow dung on the road. Bloody feuds could erupt between villages over the right to collect manure from public bathrooms in town. But they feared it as they feared pregnant and menstruating women. Women used to give birth in pigsties. The stench could prevent jealous gods from going there and harming babies, especially boys, and prevent the birth blood from bringing bad luck to the house. Nowadays, peasants give birth in hospitals just like city women. They still believe that a pregnant woman's accidental touch can cure a stiff neck and her urine can revive a person from convulsion or coma.

Such attitudes are hard to sustain in the city. Worms, flies, stench, dirt, stories of infants found in pits, of little girls molested in men's rooms, all these associate public bathrooms as places filthy and unspeakable. Bathrooms used to be controlled by *fenba*—feces lords—as lucrative businesses, just as garbage collecting, begging, gambling, and prostitution were controlled by underground societies. In Mao's era, garbage and manure collecting were respected professions like teaching and governing. A bathroom cleaner, Shi Tianxiang, became a national hero. Still, when my parents found me a job in the Sanitation Bureau so that I didn't have to go to the countryside, I thanked them and said I had already moved my city residence to the village, which would lead to a decent job in the city for my sister. I didn't tell them I would rather die than work as a feces collector.

When I got my visa for America, my first thought was *toilet*—my own private toilet. I'd turn it into a cozy haven. The reality, however, was a different story. Since I couldn't afford my own apartment, I had to share the bathroom with three waiters from Hong Kong who refused to flush or lift the seat. I had no choice but to squat on the toilet.

Appalled by the amount of perfectly good water going down the drain, I put rocks in the toilet tank to save water and reduced my bathing to twice a week. Still, I felt shame for the weakness of my flesh whenever I stepped into the water treated with Aveeno moisturizer. I thought about how everything was recycled in China over and over until it couldn't be used. What would happen now that everybody is imitating the American way? My mother had moved into a new apartment with a sitting toilet, leaving the old apartment to my brother and his family. Even my chamber pot–loving grandma had saved enough money to install a flush toilet in her one-room apartment because she was too old to carry the pot downstairs. I offered to pay for a cleaning woman. She said maids nowadays wouldn't clean chamber pots. Besides, Uncle Shan had died without a successor, and peasants no longer came to cities to collect manure. They had learned to use fertilizers.

Lying in the bath, I imagined the pit under my grandma's building overflowing with human waste. With modern facilities spreading far and wide, China would have to pump more water from underground, increase the water pressure so that toilets would flush, and open more sewers to carry out the waste. To where, though?

I laughed when I thought about the flashlight Aiden had dropped into a Tibetan latrine pit. Before our trip to China, he bought a copy of *Lonely Planet*.

The more he studied it, the more concerned he became, especially about toilets that bubble up noxious vapors from deep holes in the ground. When he got to the chapter that described how Tibetan toilets would make those Chinese toilets look like little bowels of heaven, he panicked and started talking about going to Israel instead. I told him we were going to Tibet as planned. So he drove to Home Depot and asked for the most powerful flashlight. The salesperson handed him a nineteen-inch Maglight and a pack of size-D Duracells.

The first night in Lhasa, Aiden took out his "weapon," waving its beam into the dark sky. "I can see everything with this," he said and strode to the bathroom at the back of the hotel. Three minutes later, he returned, speechless, shaking. I asked him what had happened. He pointed toward the toilet. I ran over. From the bottom of the muck, the red Maglight shot its light all the way up to the thatched ceiling. We watched then burst out laughing. The next day, I bought him a Chinese flashlight, cheaper and lighter, but it worked just as well. He used it throughout the trip and brought it back to America as a souvenir.

I often wonder if the Maglight is still lighting from the bottom of the latrine pit in Lhasa. The salesman promised that it would last forever with its size-D Duracell power.

3

Aurora Borealis

For a New Yorker, the city is the center of the world, the only civilized place to be. Pennsylvania, New Jersey, Connecticut, Massachusetts, and Vermont, even New York state, circle around Manhattan as planets move around the sun. Rhode Island, Ontario, Quebec, and the rest are nothing but satellites and asteroids. And people from those places? Country bumpkins! Aliens!

Well, this was MY New York attitude at that time. Born in Shanghai and brought up by my very metropolitan grandma and aunt, I believed that Shanghai was the only place to be, and Shanghai girls were the most beautiful, sophisticated, and seductive on earth. My grandma mourned when my father's navy base moved from Shanghai to the island on the East China Sea and my mother decided to follow her husband. "Oh, my daughter and granddaughters are exiled," she wailed in her operatic chanting. "Oh, they'll live as country bumpkins forever on the far sea, like dogs, pigs, shrimp, and crabs." She was pleased when I left the island and went to Beijing University, though she would have been more pleased if I had chosen Fudan University in Shanghai. When I left China for New York, she threw me a giant party.

"New York is pretty good, almost as fashionable as Shanghai," she said.

We all laughed. "Grandma, New York is the real center of everything."

"Just wait," she said. "In ten years, Shanghai will surpass New York and become the number one city in the world. I'll live to see that, I know."

She did live to see that. Shanghai boomed like crazy and became the hottest place to invest, work, and live. In the 1920s and 1930s, it had been the "Eastern Paradise" for the Western adventurers, until Mao threw them out of the country in 1949. Now, it has become a paradise for adventurers again.

Well, that's the seed that my grandma had planted when I came to New York City. No matter how poor I was, living in a cockroach-infested room with Taiwanese, Malaysians, Filipinos, and Koreans, moving from Queens to Brooklyn to Bronx to Harlem for a cheaper place, eating ramen noodles, and working twelve hours a day for rent and tuition, I was still a proud New Yorker. For my first tour to D.C. and Philadelphia on a Chinatown bus, my friend Mi Young and I nibbled our stale bread and eyed the mansions on the green slopes along the highway: What kind of losers would live in such isolated places? What do they do all day and night? What do they eat? Grass? Laughing, we vowed to each other that we would never, ever move away from NYC and live like cows and horses on a pasture.

In 1998, after a decade of being a New Yorker, my partner, Aiden, and I decided to move to Minnesota with our son, Wei. We didn't have much of a choice. Wei was about to turn one, and we were quickly outgrowing the small apartment in Prospect Park, Brooklyn. I was trying to finish my dissertation at NYU, while taking care of the baby and teaching Chinese as an adjunct professor. The rent for the small apartment ate up my savings as well as Aiden's salary. Aiden's father had been nagging him to return home to take over his publishing business. We discussed this option many times and just couldn't bring ourselves to make a decision until Wei fell down the narrow staircase and nearly broke his neck. That incident made us realize that NYC, no matter how glorious and civilized, was perhaps not the best place to raise a child.

Aiden's friend Jon helped us secure a two-thousand-square-foot loft overlooking the Mississippi River in downtown St. Paul. The contract only had my name on it, since the building subsided exclusively for artists. The rent was $700 a month.

"Imagine the space, five times bigger, overlooking the Mississippi and downtown St. Paul, a space filled with sunlight and joy. You'll never want to leave once you see it," Aiden said. "And if you don't like it, we'll come back to NYC within three years, maximum."

My eyes lit up. I had been dreaming of living in such a place since I came to NYC. But what was a loft in the middle of nowhere? Where would I practice my flamenco, skating, and martial art? What about literary events, art openings, operas, theater? Where could I get the fresh seafood and vegetables? Was there a Chinatown in the middle of a prairie? And most importantly, where would I find a teaching job? I didn't need a PhD to be a stay-at-home mom.

Aiden laughed. "Are you kidding me? In the Twin Cities, you'll find an ice rink and colleges every ten blocks. Minnesota is big on hockey and education.

You'll find everything there, except for Chinatown. But you complain about Chinatown anyway: crowded, loud, stinky, dirty, disorienting. I know you'll miss the food. I'll take you to NYC for dim sum twice a year, how's that? I promise."

That settled it. We shipped our furniture to St. Paul. I threw a huge party for Wei's first birthday, with over forty poets, writers, artists, journalists, and friends—all crammed in our railway apartment on the hottest day of that summer, sitting on the floor, eating "Ping's last meal" with teary eyes. I kept telling my guests to visit me in the Midwest, and I would cook them even more delicious food. But nobody seemed to be convinced, especially myself. Where would I shop for the best meat, seafood, Chinese vegetables, and spices in the "twin towns" on the banks of the Mississippi, home to the Mall of America and Target? Besides, why on Earth would any of these New Yorkers ever visit a small town on the prairie?

The next day, we put everything in the van and drove all night through New England until we reached Maine. Our plan was to ferry across the bay to Canada, then camp our way through Nova Scotia, Quebec, Thunder Bay and enter Minnesota through the Pigeon River and stay in Grand Marais—"to be acclimatized" according to Aiden. If we could survive two weeks of wildness in Canada with a one-year-old, then we would have a good chance of surviving barren Minnesota.

We barely made it. The old van didn't like bumpy dirt roads at all. Neither did its passengers as it trudged farther away from our beloved NYC. One morning, Aiden backed the van into a fire pit, bending the metal grill, puncturing a tire, then crashing into a neighboring trailer. A beefy man rushed out shouting. A huge argument ensued then escalated into a fistfight. Aiden and I bickered like an old couple over everything and nothing: searching for a good campground, setting up the tent, making a fire, cooking, pulling down the tent, and rolling it up. All these things were new, but I learned fast and became a gourmet campfire chef. Pretty soon, I took over making the fire entirely. That didn't go well with Aiden. He liked to think of himself as a fire master. He wasn't bad, if everything was dry. One evening, however, we arrived late in a pouring rain, and the fire wouldn't start. Aiden cursed as he scratched the matches like mad. When I saw there was only one left, I grabbed it from his hand, lit the fire, and grilled the last steak for his dinner. Aiden chomped down the steak in fury. "Don't you steal my fire again, ever," he shouted. I tried to reason with him, citing the hungry baby, the darkening evening, and the last match in the box, but it seemed only to pour oil into a raging fire.

We were at peace with each other, however, when we hiked along the river. Almost all the hiking trails Aiden picked in Canada followed the water. We took turns carrying Wei strapped on our backs and walked along the narrow path in a single line, breathing the fragrance of pines and firs, listening to the sounds of a singing stream, a roaring waterfall, and singing birds, stopping from time to time to take in the beauty around us. Wei was napping most of the time. As a baby, the only time he would sleep soundly was in a car, a moving stroller, or a walking backpack. And he slept exceptionally well in the forests. We would walk for hours without stopping, without exchanging a word, content with the rivers and ourselves.

Wei took his very first step on the Canadian side of Lake Superior.

The line at the Canadian and American border stretched long. Aiden seemed patient and relaxed as we inched forward. Once we crossed the gate, we would be only one day away from our new home. Our plan was to camp one night at Grand Marais, or somewhere on the Gun Flint trail near the Boundary Waters, then drive southward and into St. Paul, where a loft in the Tilsner Artist Building on the bank of the Mississippi waited for us. Aiden had been using it to calm me down whenever I felt depressed. "Just wait until you see your dream loft," he would say, nodding his head to confirm his conviction.

Suddenly Aiden jumped in his seat and yanked a pouch out of the glove compartment. "Oh shit, what am I going to do with this!" he moaned. I asked him what it was, but he did not hear me. The leather pouch seemed very weathered, a pipe sticking out from its opening. It looked like a tobacco bag but smelled funny. Strange that I had never seen him smoke. Why was he so worried? Aiden opened the window trying to throw the bag into the ditch, but we noticed the custom officer looking at us through his window. Aiden spun the car and drove away from the gate. He stopped at the bend and jumped out, kicking into the dirt with his hiking boots.

"Would you please tell me what the heck is going on?" I demanded.

"I need to get rid of this." He kept digging.

I looked up and saw a car coming out of customs, lights flashing. I knew Aiden absolutely hated cops. No use to make him feel even more panicked. I grabbed the pouch out of his hand and dropped it into the storm gutter through its metal grate.

"What the fuck are you doing?" Aiden screamed and lunged for it, but it had already gone into the dark hole.

"Look up, Aiden."

His face turned ashen at the coming car.

"Go in the field and go to bathroom," I ordered.

He went without a word. The car stopped five feet away from us. An officer came out and saluted me.

"Good afternoon, ma'am. I saw you turn away from customs. What's up?"

I pointed at Aiden squatting in the tall grass, head between his knees.

"He had an accident, officer. Food poisoning from a restaurant in Thunder Bay."

He looked at Aiden, me, and the baby sleeping in the back seat and then pressed the dirt road with the tip of his cowboy boot. "Sorry to hear that. You could have just used our bathroom."

"Thanks, officer. But he didn't want to stink up your place. It was a mess, if you know what I mean."

The officer wrinkled his nose as he sniffed the air. Aiden must have been having one of his IBS flares.

"He'll be okay. We'll clean up and return to the border shortly. We need to reach home before it gets dark."

He smiled and waved. "I'll see you there on the other side."

Aiden climbed into the van after the patrol car was gone. "Pig," he mumbled.

"What's in the pouch? Please don't tell me that I won't understand."

He turned red. "It's just part of being an American, okay? You'll never understand, coming from China."

Didn't I just save his ass, literally? Was being an ungrateful jerk part of the American culture?

"At least tell me why you didn't want me to drop the pouch in the gutter. I thought you wanted to get rid of it."

"I was hoping to get it back someday. I got this kit in Israel when I was fifteen."

"Hmmmm, had I known . . . but you would have been caught and lost it anyway. That officer wasn't a fool, you know."

"You are right, Pdubs," he called my nickname. "Thank you for saving my ass. I guess it's about time I let it go. I'm a father now." He looked back at Wei and squeezed my thigh, another gesture to show his affection.

"You betcha," I imitated *Fargo*, and we laughed. But the question was still bugging me like mad: What on Earth was in the pouch? If it was illegal, would it put me in danger? Would it prevent me from reentering America?

We were held for three hours at the border, not because of Aiden's "suspicious act" but because of my "alien" status. The officer who had chased us down the highway greeted us with a funny smile and made a joke about Aiden's "accident" as he checked his driver's license. I handed him my Chinese passport and green card. As soon as he saw the brown colored passport, he called his colleagues over and signaled us to drive into the back of the building. They searched the van inside and out, opened every bag, inspected each baby diaper. Wei had woken up since we pulled in and had been howling like a fiend. No toy or milk could pacify him. But that didn't stop their thorough examination.

I thanked heaven that I had dropped Aiden's pouch into the drain.

By the time we were allowed to cross the border, it was close to 6:00 p.m. Aiden decided to check into the national park campground nearby. It was a Thursday night. Every park was full, except for the Devil's Kettle. The sun had already set when we pulled in. We just had enough time to set up the tent and grab some firewood in the forest before it got dark. There were only two potatoes and one ear of corn left. I wrapped them in tinfoil and threw everything in the flame. Wei had the last jar of applesauce and fell asleep nursing. We sat by the fire in silence. The search at the border depressed me. Aiden got chased for his "pouch," yet they searched me for three hours, just because . . . The officer didn't even bother to open my passport before he pulled us in for the search. Was this the way of Minnesota? Aiden had nibbled the corncob to the "bone." The potatoes were only half cooked in the ash, but he had taken one out and was now throwing it up and down to cool it, his mouth salivating like a dog. I laughed then started weeping. I missed NYC. I wasn't sure how I was going to survive in Minnesota.

"Want a bite?" Aiden offered the half-eaten potato.

I shook my head. "You eat. I'm not hungry."

He looked at me, tried to say something, but took a bite of the potato instead. It scorched his mouth. He dropped it in the ash. He stamped his feet, cussing loudly.

"Can we go back to NYC after a year?"

He looked at me, his face clouded with apprehension. "We can try. My father is getting old, you know. The business transaction takes time. A year goes by very fast."

I hung my head. How long could I endure my life away from NYC?

"Pdubs, look, look, oh my God!" Aiden screamed, tugging my hand. I looked up, and my mouth dropped. The sky blazed with a mirage of lights, lighting up the vast forest of northern pines in neon orange. Above this horizon, ribbons of neon green danced across the night.

“What is it? It can’t be Disney, right?” I asked.

“Oh no, how could you say that! It’s the Aurora Borealis. Do you know how many times I’ve camped here but never seen it until now? It’s a lucky sign. We’re going to be okay, Pdubs.”

I’d seen the Aurora Borealis from advertisements in the *New York Times* for tour trips to Alaska. It cost thousands of dollars just to have a glimpse, if you were lucky. It was the rich New Yorkers’ dream, now gifted to me on my first night in Minnesota.

The Eskimos believed the pulsing lights were the torches carried by travelers to their afterlife. So the spirits, my ancestors, were pointing the way for me, for us? Or was it Buddha? Suddenly, I realized who was dancing in the sky—Green Tara, Allen Ginsberg’s Tara.

I bowed. We’d be okay, better than okay, in the land of Aurora Borealis, Goddess of Dawn.

4

Ten Bodies

"No, Mother, no!" Aiden roars at the sound of the alarm, sits up, then goes back to sleep. I turn off the alarm. Di still asleep, cheeks in and out in sucking motion. Grunts, rubs his eyes with fists, legs up in the air, farts. Nudges to my breast, mouth open for milk. A kiss on his fuzzy forehead and sit up. He's been nursing all night in my arms. Hide the clock in the sock drawer, so it won't break someone's toes. Knead breasts, push and pull. Milk gushes into the bottle. Di needs three bottles while I teach. He's awake now, stuffing his left foot in his mouth, gurgling happiness.

The sky reveals a sliver of blue gray along the horizon. Lately, water floods my dreams. Children strapped to chairs float past adults at cocktail parties, their black gowns dancing in white water. No one seems to hear the cry of the drowned.

Milk begins to trickle, then stops. Yank and squeeze. Nothing. The bottle only half full. Try later, after tea and toast. Di throws his legs down, arches his back, filling the room with baby poop smell. Take off his pants, lay the dirty diaper on the floor, and hold him between my legs. He groans and grunts, his pee shooting up to my face, soaking my knees and feet. Look in his diaper. Good Di. Six months old, already regular like a clock. With Wei, it's been a daily battle. Prune juice, pear nectar, water, suppository, Q-tips, and belly massages, still have to dig it out with fingers.

Di squirms and kicks, chest puffing in and out as he hollers into his father's ear. Aiden groans and rolls to the side. Wipe his tootsie with Kleenex. Give him a snorter to chew. Wash his eyes, face, hands, feet, and bottom. Baby moisturizer on his cheeks, Vaseline on his penis, then diaper and clothes. His stomach and thighs fold and dimple with baby fat. I pinch and tickle. He curls with laughter, pulling my finger into his mouth.

"No, Little, Mama has dirty hands." Insert the snorter into his mouth again and bring the bucket and dirty diaper to the sink. Dump the water, wash the cloth, put them back in the corner. Clean hands with soap. Everyone had stomach flu. First throw up, then diarrhea. Only Di hasn't caught it yet. When Wei soiled his fifteenth diaper within six hours and his stool turned pink, I called the hospital. The nurse said no food for twenty-four hours. Pray that Di will never get it. If he's sick, I'll have to take days off from teaching. The babysitter can't handle two sick babies. Would the college allow me that? I started teaching three weeks after Di was born, barely able to walk. I asked for a later class so that I didn't have to get up at 5:00 a.m. to pump milk. I was told to suck it up.

Wei calls from his room. "Go home, Mommy, go home." Run to his bed. Wei jumps into my arms. "Milk," he says. Carry him next to Di. Pour a bottle of organic juice. Heat it in the microwave for ten seconds. Wei calls juice "milk," and likes his drinks at room temperature, including ice cream and watermelon. Fill the kettle and turn on the stove. Turn on the morning news. Floods continue in Mozambique. A mother gave birth to a daughter in a tree before a helicopter rescued them. The American pilot flipped his thumb as a triumphant gesture, not knowing it means something obscene in Africa.

Both boys lie in bed drinking. Di looks proud holding his own bottle. Take off Wei's diaper. He has two potties. He stands on them to wash his hands and brush his teeth. Occasionally, he'll sit on one with his pants on. Two and a half years old, still terrified of the monster in the hole. "Just let him soil his pants, and he'll want to use the potty," said his step-grandma. Tried once, but stopped when I saw the shame in his eyes. Run to his room. Turn off his humidifier. Take out his pants, shirt, socks. Change his clothes while he sucks his bottle. Weather report: upper seventies today, thirty-nine degrees higher than normal. A six-year-old boy shot his classmate at school. Found his uncle's gun in a shoebox.

Wei hands me the empty bottle and pulls me to his train set. We play. He screams whenever the trains run off the track, blue veins bulging on the sides of his neck. Quick tempered like me. We're both Leos, plus Di, our birthdays only a week apart. A den of proud cats. Di cooing and kicking in bed. The kettle whistles. Run to the stove. Make a pot of Pau d'Arco tea, a pot of organic decaffeinated Earl Grey. Both Wei and Di are screaming. Run to Di. Face down, he's turned over, sprawling on the bed. Sit him up and surround him with pillows and toys. Di grabs an airplane and puts it in his mouth. Wei throws the trains and tracks in the air. Take his hand and walk to the easel. Open cans of paint. Dips brushes into silver, black, and blue. His paintings pile high on top of the piano, numbered and dated. For his sixty-fifth birthday, Aiden's father asked for an aftershave. Couldn't believe he wanted such an unimaginative gift. Framed Wei's best art in golden wood. The old man snorted and asked why we bothered asking him what he wanted if we wouldn't give him what he requested. Good point!

Six thirty. Take-out pizza and chicken to thaw. Wei loves pizza for lunch in his Pitter-Patter Room at the Jewish Community Center in St. Paul. Calls his teacher Svetlana Stetlana, Tubbytubby for Telytubby, snakes for snacks, bubbles for grapes, Bread for Fred, black Cheerio for tire swing . . . For nine months, I had knelt on the floor going though dictionaries, Chinese and English, searching for a perfect name. Settled on Wei, after Wang Wei, the finest poet, musician, and painter of the Tang dynasty. His first sentence was "sky is burning," as he looked up from nursing, pointing at the sunset.

I pick up the bottles from the floor and wash them. Detergent stings. Fungus eats away my fingers. Scars from cleavers, falling objects, hot grease, fire. Grew up watching Grandmas soak their fungi feet in vinegar. Swore I'd never let it happen to me. It did, when I got pregnant with Di while nursing Wei. Fungus turned every nail into powder. "Cure is impossible," said the podiatrist as he examined my deformed fingernails and toenails. "You can take the pills that may damage your liver, $800, at your own cost. Insurance won't cover it. You can't do it until you're no longer pregnant or nursing."

"Other choice?" I asked.

"You can remove them permanently," he said.

"You mean permanently?" I asked.

"Yep, and you'll never have powdery nails again."

"No, thanks, I'll keep my nails, fungus or no fungus." I hobbled out of his office. Along the Nicollet Mall, men and women in business suits passed by. They looked at me, looked away, looked at me again. In a shop window, I saw my watermelon size stomach, belly button poking through the thin summer dress. Di started his routine somersaults. I put my hands on the dome, feeling his fists and feet poking and stretching my skin. "Hello, Little," I greeted my son. "I'll see you soon. And you won't mind my fungus nails, right?" I lifted my chest and walked, passing by the Lerner Books Building. Aiden was working away in his air-conditioned office under his favorite painting by his favorite artist, my birthday present for him. The July sun was melting me into the asphalt. A ride home would be nice. But Aiden wanted me to learn how to drive before the baby was born, before I started teaching full-time. He had a point. I no longer lived in NYC. Buses took too long to get anywhere and were dangerously hot in the summer and cold in the winter. I must get my driver's license before August 10, Di's due date. I wiped the sweat off my face and trudged to the bus stop.

Open a jar of apples and bananas for Di. Grind pear and add brown rice powder. Wash grapes and strawberries. Cut the watermelon. Di is crying. Sprawling on the bed again. He wants to crawl, but his limbs can't support his trunk yet. When he's down, he becomes furious. I pick up Di and call Aiden.

"It's past 7:00. Time to get up."

"Daddy is still tired," he moans and covers his head with the blanket.

"Sorry to hear that. Now get up, please."

"Mother, Mother," he moans loudly, his hands flailing in the air. "Daddy is not feeling well. He's still weak from diarrhea. Help, Mother, help."

"Stop being a sissy."

He sits up instantly, flexing his arms. "Look at these muscles! How could you call me a sissy? How could you ever doubt . . ."

"Good," I laugh, thrusting Di in his arms. "Use those man muscles, now."

Am I too harsh on him? I turn on the fish tank light, unplug the heater, sprinkle flakes into the tank. Aiden does look pale, his eyes puffy from the diarrhea. Should I let him sleep more? But who pities me? Who sees me running like a headless hen, eyes dry, ears buzzing from dizziness, heart flutters from exhaustion?

"But you're the mother, the professional," Aiden says. Wei climbs on the bed. Bugato, Daddy. Aiden scoops him into his arm and sings. "Daddy's twooooooo boys."

I open the refrigerator. Confucius said that a full stomach leads to a lustful mind. What would he say about a stuffed refrigerator? Cow milk, rice milk, soymilk, prune juice, apple cider, ginseng tea, half an apple, a jar of baby food, three bottles of human milk on the top shelf. Bags of bread in the middle, three boxes of tofu, two bags of smoked tofu, pickles, preserved mustard greens, bean sprouts, Napa cabbage, bowls of leftover rice, pasta, and salmon on top of one another to save space. Eggs, fruit, soda, and vegetables are stuffed at the bottom. The freezer. Every time I open it, things fly out like bombs: fish, chicken, ribs, dumplings, spring rolls, sausages, smashing me like bricks.

I need a full refrigerator to feel safe. I starved too much growing up in China.

Breakfast on the table: nine-grain bread, crackers, Cheerios, breadsticks, baby food, cut fruit. Jam, almond butter, all organic. Pay triple prices at Whole Foods. Aiden calls it Whole Paycheck. When I chop them on the cutting board, I chant "You better be worth it, worth it, worth it."

Aiden puts Di in the crib and walks around picking up rags, toys, food, and crumpled Kleenex from the floor. He can't eat or sleep unless everything is back in order and cleaned. His Virgo obsession keeps the apartment tidy.

He picks up a Cheerio and pops it into his mouth. Crunch crunch.

Once he found an Oreo under the bed and popped it into his mouth, then ran to the bathroom gagging and brushing teeth frantically. Wouldn't tell me why but finally confessed that the cookie was Wei's ball of poop. It had slipped out of his diaper. Someone stepped on it, flattened it into something that looked like an Oreo . . .

Things we do as parents.

Wei is hungry. Put him in the highchair. Bring a knife, water, cups, and the teapot to the table. Put a bib around his neck. The toaster jumps. Rush to get the toasts. Bump into Aiden. Arms around my shoulders. "What about some tender loving care for Daddy?" he says. Peck him on the cheek and thrust the toast into his hands. "Butter please."

Pizza melting on the counter. Scrape off the cheese with chopsticks. "What are you doing?" Aiden asks.

"Wei is allergic to dairy products."

"Nonsense. I grew up eating pizza and ice cream. This is the American way. How can he grow big without dairy?"

"It didn't seem to help you or your brother that much."

"What do you mean?" he growls. "I'm huge. Right, son?"

Wei flexes his arms like his father. "Yes, we're huge, huge girls like mommy."

"No, 'boys!'" Aiden hastens to correct him.

I laugh. "But Wei *is* allergic to milk. It makes him constipated and vomit, his nose congested. American kids have the highest rate of ear infection because of dairy. You're also allergic to it. That's why you're so gassy. Cow milk is for calves, not humans."

"You can say whatever you want, but I'm not quitting ice cream. If it were that bad, they'd have told us, right, son? Shall we sing the song: 'You scream, I scream, and we all scream for . . .'" he pauses and Wei joins him from the high-chair, "ICE CREAM."

"That's tragic," I mutter and plant three chunks of Chinese beef stew into the pizza. Wei and Di will grow up as Americans. That's inevitable. But I can sneak in some Chinese. The easiest way is through the mouth. They'll love dumplings, noodles, tofu, bok choi, and rice along with hot dogs, pizza, and ice cream.

Turn on the oven to 450 and slide the pizza in. Di screams and shakes the crib as he tries to stand. Pick him up and put him on the maple wood highchair, $198 from Treasure Island. When we saw the price, we went to Toys R Us. The plastic chairs looked nasty. We looked at each other. I remembered how my friend Lisa's husband wouldn't buy toys for his son because he was afraid the plastic might turn him gay. Told Aiden the story. We had a good laugh. The next day Aiden got the wood chair from Treasure Island.

Put a bib on Di. Plastic. It's twenty-first century. Plastic rules. Di pounds the board for food. Throw down some puffed rice and a strawberry. He stuffs them in his mouth. Crushes with his tongue. Tries to swallow. Coughs. Spits. Cries. Give him water. Sneak a spoonful of apple and banana sauce in his mouth. Wei eats the toast, watching *Dragon Tales* on PBS. Peel grape skin for Di, to take off the pesticide on the surface.

"For you, Mother," Aiden hands me the buttered toast.

"Thanks. But stop calling me Mother, please."

"But you are the mother," he looks up. "What else should I call you?"

A sip of Pau d'Arco tea. I used to have a name. Tea scorching my mouth. Suck in air to cool lips. Learned how to tolerate heat and cold since I was a little girl. Learned to cook since six, how to lift a sizzling wok off the stove with bare hands, how to pick vegetables, chop wood, wash clothes in icy water, how to soothe blisters and frostbites. Aiden frowns, curling his lips to mock my sucking. He boasts his burping and farting, discusses his bowel movements during a meal in detail, and puts his half-eaten food back on the serving plate if he doesn't like the taste. But he can't stand the sound of slurping.

"You need to learn table manners," he told me once after we dined with his parents in a Chinese restaurant. I laughed and pointed at his shirt. It was stained with chicken, shrimp, vegetables, and noodles from the dinner.

The tea is supposed to kill the *Candida* yeast in my intestines that cause fungus nails, said Simone, Aiden's Russian cousin. When antibiotics and junk food kill the good bacteria in the body, *Candida* comes in, producing toxins that cause fatigue, headache, depression, yeast infection, obesity, arthritis . . . I must take the tea four times a day, plus vitamins, mineral oils from Shaklee.

Once *Candida* goes, so will everything else: my powdery nails, gas pain, memory loss, fatigue, constipation, diarrhea, and joint swelling.

"And no cheating, if you want your health back," warned Simone. "*Candida* is very stubborn."

I did it for a month. My stomach growled and churned. Wind passed constantly. I complained that it was becoming a torture to sit in front of my students.

"Great!" shouted Simone. "The dying *Candida* is making toxins. Stick to it. It will get better."

I did, until the bill came. I cut the pills from three to one a day. It's not right to pay $400 a month for a promise that I might have normal nails. I didn't tell Simone about the reduction. But she called after a month asking if I'd been forgetting the pills. She was the sales person who processed my weekly orders. I told her the truth. She pointed out that my *Candida* had made a full comeback. I must resume the full dosage. Absolutely no cheating this time. I hung up gently. I don't have the means to pay for the pills. My salary is so low it is off the chart completely, like a premature baby. Barely covers the bills for food and babysitter. Strange. I'm one of their most published professors, with five books and many awards. No surprise, though, from the way they told me to suck it up when I requested for an easier teaching schedule for my infant.

Di's food is all gone. He ate some, spat out some, crushed most of it, and swept the rest on the floor. Now he roars like a warrior, watermelon juice dripping from his chin, fists, arms. Wei finishes his toast too. He looks like a fox with his jam whiskers. Unfasten the bibs. Take Wei to the sink to wash up. Screams that I get his mouth and nose wet. Dry him with a paper towel. Take Di to the sink. Wet his shirt but he loves it. He's taken many baths in the metal kitchen sink since his birth. Change his diaper. Screams and squirms. Pin the thrashing body down with one hand and handle the diaper with the other. Whistle to distract him. Di reaches up to my lips to catch the sound. Secure the diaper.

Put him on the floor, next to Wei, in front of the toy basket. Wei builds a tower with alphabet blocks. Di grabs one and stuffs it in his mouth. Wei snatches it and hits him on the head. "That's my A. A is for airplane. Fly me to Florida."

Di turns to me, his lips pulled down by the sorrow. I scoop him up.

"Weiwei, my child, please don't hit your brother. Please share your toys."

Silence. Gives the tower a push, and brings it down to the floor, his eyes fastened on the television. Barney sings, "I love you, you love me. We're a happy family," his green belly swaying, arms on the shoulders of the grinning children. I shake my head and take Di to the bed. Open my shirt to comfort him with milk.

Di asleep. Nipple in his mouth. Hands up in relaxed fists. Quivering eyelashes and pink cheeks. Did my mother ever regret not nursing her four kids? Did she ever feel remorse for leaving us to her mother? In her late fifties, she taught herself how to tell fortunes from the *Book of Change*. She flipped coins every night and read her own fate. She was not supposed to have any children.

"What about us?" I asked.

She pointed to the coins. "A total mistake."

Put Di down in the stroller. Squirms. Mouth open. Insert a bottle. Made four vows when my first period came: If I die childless, I'll never forgive myself; I'll never hit my children; I'll never tell them how much they owe me for bringing them up; I'll love them without condition. Push the stroller back and forth. Scrawny wrists. Lost so much weight since I started nursing and teaching.

Di sleeping again, a dimple in his cheek.

Sit down to my toast. In the glider, Wei watches Teletubbies. Aiden bought it when Wei was born, $400.

Too much, I complained.

"For you and the baby, nothing is too expensive," he waved his credit card.

"Finally, all done," Aiden says across the table. I nod, head buzzing from this sudden quietness. Wash the bread down with Earl Grey. "How come you're not talking?" he asks, glancing up from the newspaper. "I hope you're not depressed."

"I'm just tired. Can you tell the difference?"

"Calm down," he says. "You should learn how to relax."

"You're right," I laugh. "When I have time, I'll work on it."

He puts down his paper. "Why don't you stay home today? Your cough seems worse. Perhaps you can take the kids to the hospital. Di feels warm. And Wei seems to have lost some weight from the diarrhea."

I stared at him. I just learned how to drive a month ago. I hate sitting behind the wheel, hate parking, hate driving to a new place . . . Now he wants me to drive an infant and toddler to the hospital in the downtown maze where I almost hit a pedestrian last week? And what for? To get more antibiotics? Dr. Wegman is against it anyway unless the infection gets out of control. He said that all fathers should stay home with kids for a week by themselves, to see what it's like.

"Great idea," I said, laughing. When I get really mad at Aiden, I just say, "May you be a woman in your next life!" and watch his face turn gray.

My grandma said a body has thirty-two spirits. They take turns going out. When they have too much fun and forget to return, the body gets sick. The spirits have to be summoned with songs, wine, and food. They fly around intoxicated, get caught in the fluttering strings on a pole carved with dragons and clouds, thus return to the body.

My grandma also said only man's body has spirits. A woman has only bodies but no soul; therefore, she's just as difficult and unpredictable as children. She lamented that we must have done something terrible in our previous life to be born a woman, that we must work hard to redeem ourselves in order to be born as a man in the next life.

In yoga, I learn that each person has ten bodies and souls, nine of which are hidden but can be cultivated through practice. Whenever I sit on the floor working on the first body that starts from the rectum, the symbol of the earth, I can't help multiplying it with my thirty-two soulless bodies. I chuckle as I imagine the day when they return at the same time, 320 spirits and bodies in all, screeching with joy over the fire, spilling wine, scattering rice, messing up the strings, and making men very upset.

Aiden wants to know what's so funny. That's a secret, I tell him.

Aiden cleans the crumbs off the table and takes the empty cups to the sink before he takes a shower. Pick up the pink plastic comb from the dresser and loosen my braid. Hair sticking out and falling over my face. My colleague Eleanor said I looked windblown when I passed by her office. That's how I feel: windblown. Only my breasts remain heavy with milk. Once I dated a professor at NYU who commented I was so lucky my breasts hadn't sagged for my age. I thanked him and said they hadn't sagged because they were small like lemons, which was a major grievance of my previous lover, who wished I had breasts like cantaloupes, or at least pears.

"Don't ever let them grow into pears or cantaloupes," said the professor sternly. "They mush your brains, and make you prosy, like my ex-wife, after she had our baby."

In the mirror, I look at my haggard face and milk stains. I've aged at least ten years since I started teaching three weeks after giving birth, still healing from the ripped birth canal, milk oozing out of my triple-padded bras through my shirt as I stumbled from class to class Monday/Wednesday/Friday, 8:30 a.m. to 3:00 p.m. "Endure, Ping, just endure," said my kindhearted chair, and it would take me eighteen years to understand what that means.

I squat and pick up the hair around my feet. Every time I pull hair out of the sink, toilet, I hear Mother shout: "Cut it off, cut it off," as she chases me with scissors.

I've kept my hair long, for reasons I can't explain.

Wei slides off the glider and shuffles his feet around the carpet imitating Tinky Winky. Jerry Falwell denounced the show as obscene because he thinks Tinky Winky is gay with his purple body and red handbag. Whenever he appears on the screen, Aiden shouts "Aha!" and asks Wei who this is. Catch Wei and change his diaper. Wipe his nose. Watch him fall on the carpet kicking his legs up like Tinky Winky. Di falls on top of him blowing his tummy. Take out the pizza and put it in the lunch bag, with pretzels and chips.

Aiden returns smelling of Old Spice. I frown. Bought him odorless deodorant for Hanukah. He tried it for a week and gave up when his father wrote in his annual job review that he needed to eliminate his body odor.

"Do I really stink?" he asks.

"Of course not! Your dad wants you to smell like the Old Spice that comes from every businessman's armpits. He wants you to be his good son."

"Come on, don't take it so personal," he says, leaning close to the mirror as he rubs on the deodorant. I bang the bathroom door behind me.

"Could you keep an eye on Wei and Di? I need to get ready for school." Walk into the office converted from the bedroom. We sleep in the living room that also serves as a kitchen, dining room, and playroom. My office has two big windows facing the Mississippi. Walk past the desk to get to the closet. My oak desk has passed through many school principals' hands. Found it on Canal Street and Broadway, the edge of Chinatown. When we moved to St. Paul, Aiden's brother offered to buy it. But I wouldn't part with it. One of the movers slipped as they took it down the staircase. The desk rolled and broke a railing. The landlord jumped out of his apartment and demanded $700 in compensation. He nodded and smiled whenever we complained about clogged toilets or broken handles and came up to do the repairs immediately. We had never imagined him as a union leader until we saw him on TV, leading a group of Chinese garment factory women picketing in front of the city hall. We hadn't seen him much since his wife left for a better job in Hong Kong. Now, he was so angry at the broken banister, his mouth foaming like a crab. We told him we didn't have cash on us, which was true, and wrote him a check, knowing with some guilt that it would bounce. But it seemed the only way to get away from Mr. Cheng's frothing mouth. Much of the furniture arrived with broken legs or damaged drawers. I told Aiden it was our retribution for writing the bad check. He snorted and walked away. But, deep down, I think he agreed with me.

My desk arrived in St. Paul with just a few scratches.

The closet is open, clothing and shoes spilling out. Aiden used to plead with me to close things. Always promised but never remembered. He used to get mad. Now, he just laughs when he walks in and immediately shuts drawers, cabinets, and closets with exaggerated banging. Sigh as I pick a pair of gray velvet jeans and a gray T-shirt off the hangers. Sober color but good for hiding stains.

"Someday you'll be able to buy a house in Edina or Eden Prairie, the nicest suburbs in the area," Simone said, looking away as I lifted my shirt to nurse Di. "And you'll want to go to the Mall of America to buy yourself a nice dress."

I nodded, dizzy from her perfume, her golden blouse shimmering over the purple skirt and silver high heels. "You betcha," I said and sneezed.

From my office, I watch tugboats pushing barges down the Mississippi. In winter, I watch steam running amok over the frozen river and ice cracking with hushed roars. My friends in New York and its streets seem so far away and unreachable, like the spider webs hanging from the ceiling. Dust on the manuscript waiting to be proofread. *Aching for Beauty*. Deadline in two weeks. Stack of writing waiting to be graded. "My Dad Is a Hero," the student from Sudan writes in bold letters. What does it take for a mother to become a hero? How can I convince her that divinity can be embodied in daily routines, like changing diapers, wiping noses, making meals? Haven't written a word for months. Part of me not living.

Di crying. Hop over to Di while putting on socks. Always wanted an office of my own. Now, I have two but have no time to sit in either. Wei is dumping the trash can out of the window but can't get it through the bars. Aiden yelling, stomping. Lean out the window. Broom, drumsticks, paintbrushes, books, and toys scatter along Kellogg Boulevard. This is Wei's new adventure, throwing things from the sixth floor. He once got into my office and flung my Chinese dictionary out of the window. That night, a snowstorm came and covered Wei's "crime scene." I spent days looking for my dictionary until I looked out my window and saw it, half buried in the melting snow on Kellogg Boulevard that runs parallel along the Mississippi. I ran down. The cover had fallen off, crushed by cars. Its body was drenched but still holding together. Wei brings a chair and wants to examine the casualty. Pick him up.

"See what you did?" I ask, hoping he's mortified.

"I did, I did," he shouts with pride.

"What shall we do?" Aiden asks. "I think a spanking will make him remember."

"Perhaps. But he'll also remember you hit him. Do you want that?"

He throws up his hands in despair.

"Just close the window and be patient."

Dress Wei for school. He kicks and rolls on the floor, screaming he wants to stay home today. Was I willful like this? Mother believes that rods make a filial son. When I moved to the countryside at fourteen, I took the bamboo stick she had used as a whip and hung it on the bedroom wall, as a reminder that I'd never ever hit my children.

I squat and hold Wei's little hands, enticing him with his favorite lunch for school—pizza with beef stew. Jumps up and wants to eat it now. Sit him in my lap and put on the socks. He pulls off one sock when I put on a sneaker for him. Put the sock back and put on the other sneaker. Kicks with his rubber sole. "Cut it out," I shout. He freezes, and I tie his laces with a double knot. Aiden sits down at the piano with Di. Wei climbs on the bench. They bang on the piano and sing "Row, row, row your boat, life is but a dream."

At 7:55, our babysitter comes in, a big smile on her rested face. Scoops Di into her arms and consoles Wei weeping over the keyboard saying he wants to sing more. Aiden has returned to his office to put on his tie and suit. I rush to the bathroom. Brush teeth. Rinse face with water. Brush hair. Sunken eye sockets, the lines snaking from the nostrils to the mouth, and the Y chiseled deep between the brows. Is this my face? This noise from the fluorescent light, buzzing out of the cathode like evening prayer of a sleepless child. Pause, hands frozen above the hair, waiting to touch the words flying like a trillion bees or angels. No. We never touch words. They touch us, striking the chosen ones with their electric rods.

Bang on the door. "It's 8:00. Let's get going."

Just a second, I shout from the sink. Put chapstick on cracked lips. "Only good things come from your mouth," said a student from NYC. Not true. When Aiden's father asked why, with a full-time babysitter, I had no time for his family meetings. I told him after work, my only desire is to come home to be with the kids.

"What if there's an emergency? You're not the only one who has children."

"My only emergencies are my children," I want to say but keep silent. Once a word leaves your lips, nothing can chase it back. "Watch your mouth,"

Mother said, whacking me with chopsticks. "Speak up, girl, speak louder," yell Americans.

Yet, he's right about this: How do other mothers do it? A mother needs more than ten bodies, one for each of her children, one for her significant other, one for the household, one for the work, and whatever is left goes to her mind and spirit.

A poet said he writes with his blood; I with my body, ten bodies.

Banging again. Coming, I shout, and open the door to the hallway to Wei carrying his lunch bag across his chest and Di waving. Kiss him goodbye. Di bites nose, slams cheeks with sticky palms, shouting Aaaaah, his first word that will bloom into thousands.

"Who's this?" Wei shouts, leaning against my thighs, his chubby finger pointing at Aiden. "It's Daddy," he answers his own question, a daily ritual he loves since he learned to talk. "And who's that, that, and that?" he points at Di, the babysitter, himself.

"Now, who is this?" he looks up, his hand on my stomach, where the Caesarian keloid stands like a mountain range.

"It's MOM! WOW!" he roars.

5

Tough Love

From the Tiger Leaping Gorge of the upper Yangtze, I called my mother in Shanghai.

"Hello?"

"Are you in Shanghai or America? Are you coming home this time?"

"I'll be in Shanghai tomorrow morning and fly back to Minnesota the next day. I have nothing planned except for a visit to Chongming Island. Have you been there? It's an amazing place. We can meet at the airport at 10:00 then take a cab to the ferry. We can hang out on the island and eat hairy crabs. It's not the season, but we'll find some."

Mother loves Chongming hairy crabs. A brief silence, then she said, "See you tomorrow."

"Happy New Year, Mother," I said. But she was gone.

I began to descend the steep mountain of the upper Yangtze in Yunnan Province. I must reach the ferry and cross the Golden Sand River before sunset then climb to the mountaintop where a four-wheel truck would be waiting to take me back to Lijiang Airport for my early morning flight. It would be a long journey.

Tomorrow, Mother and I would meet again. We had parted in New York ten years ago, angry with each other, and I thought I would never see her thereafter. I thought I had finally heeded my sister's warning: "Mother's a tiger, you're a chicken. A tiger's nature is to devour chickens. So, the farther away from her, the safer you'll be."

I've wanted to talk to my mother all my life. I fantasize about us sitting close, my head on her shoulder, chatting, laughing, and crying like a normal mother and daughter. I've got my entire life bottled up inside—my desire to love and be loved. But whenever I face her, I'm tongue-tied.

"Why do you pull a long face as if someone wronged you?" my late Shanghai grandma would chide. "You scowl like an orphan, and you'll end up like one. Smile and talk sweet if you want to be loved."

I tried. I pulled my mouth from ear to ear, a smile that could conquer the world like Mother's. After a few hours' practice, my father slapped me on the head and told me to "cut out the monkey grimace." So I picked up singing. "Just forget it," shouted my father. "No one can sing like your mother except for your sister." True, Mother was known on the island as the queen of beauty, fashion, and wit. When she was not around, the house felt empty, and Father moved listlessly as if he had lost his soul. When she came home, smiling with her pearly teeth shining in the sunset, her white and black polka-dot dress billowing like a flower, Father's eyes lit up.

Mother was seventeen when she met my father in Shanghai. She was a glamorous singer and pianist teaching music at an elementary school. He was a glorious navy officer. Born in a poor peasant family, he ran away at sixteen to join Mao's army. After fighting the Japanese, then the Guomindang Nationalists, he had risen from an illiterate peasant boy to a battalion commander then captain of a minesweeping ship in the East China Sea. It was love at first sight, but their engagement was met with vehement opposition from both sides. My maternal grandmother called my father a country bumpkin. My paternal grandmother called my mother a husband stealer.

Back at home in Shandong, my father had a fiancée, a peasant girl picked by my grandma. She was hoping for a grandson when my father turned sixteen. But he ran away instead, and the girl moved in to help my grandma in the house and fields. After twelve years of waiting, the fiancée got a letter from my father asking her to dissolve the arranged engagement. She vowed that she would stay home and take care of her aging mother-in-law for the rest of her life—the only choice for a twenty-nine-year-old spinster at the time. My grandma, who had never traveled away from her village, took three buses and a two-day boat ride to Shanghai to plead with her son to marry the good girl at home. When he refused, she went to his boss. Perhaps his adultery would get him dismissed from the navy and he would come home. There, she met her future in-law, who was screaming at the navy commander that his young captain had raped her underage daughter and gotten her pregnant.

The two ladies had a spit fight that ended with scratched faces and torn hair in the navy office.

Under normal circumstances, my father would have been discharged with dishonor. An engagement, arranged or voluntary, was a commitment. But people worshiped the young Communist Party and its army with religious fervor at that time. Every girl wanted to date a People's Liberation Army soldier decorated with medals, and many officers, taking advantage of China's new marriage law, started divorcing their old wives back home, causing disruptions in the Communist old base in the north. The army finally issued an order that soldiers must carry out the revolutionary morality by remaining faithful to their lifelong companions. But due to revolutionary demands, officers above the rank of battalion commander could get a divorce and remarry with the Party's permission.

My father was one of those lucky officers. At the age of twenty-seven, he married a Shanghai girl ten years younger, who loved to sing, dance, laugh, and make love.

I was their firstborn, an ugly child with small eyes on a pudgy face and spiky hair. "You look more like your wet nurse," my mother lamented often. A month after my birth, she went back to her merry life at the navy base, leaving me with her mother in a one-room apartment inhabited by eight people: my grandparents, two uncles, two aunts, me, and my wet nurse, a peasant my grandma hired. "You're just like her," my grandma said laughing, "quiet and stubborn, strong like a cow." I broke bowls, burnt rice, forgot to sweep the corners or mop under the bed. I couldn't bargain at the market or cut in lines to get meat, tofu, and other rationed goods. My mother would hit me with a special bamboo stick she kept behind the door. She hit all of her four kids, but somehow, I fired her temper. She called me lazy, sullen, stubborn, a dead ghost, an abacus that moved only when pushed around. She beat me with the smile that enchanted every beholder.

"Your mother is a tigress," my Shandong grandma would mutter. "She's devoured your father and is devouring all of us."

Before I turned fifteen, I moved my city residency registration to the countryside, a suicidal act at that time. Once a peasant, forever a peasant. The chance to return to the city was almost zero. But I had to get away from Mother. I had tried to join the army, the only chance for young people to get a job. I told the recruiter I was eighteen, even though I was thirteen and looked ten. The nurse measured my pulse and told me to go home. I glanced at the chart. My pulse was 120 beats a minute. I wasn't surprised. My heart had been burning with the desire for college. It was the wildest of all wild dreams. I had no formal education. The Cultural Revolution had closed all schools for years. When they finally opened, we studied Mao's words 70 percent of the time, the rest of the time was spent beating up teachers and other students. I had no math, chemistry, physics, geography, or history. But it didn't stop me from dreaming. Colleges had just reopened that year and started admitting three kinds of people: soldiers, workers, and peasants. Since I couldn't be a soldier or worker, I would be a peasant, so I could be recommended to college as a reeducated youth. It was a one-in-a-million chance, my only chance. I would never achieve my sister's beauty or my mother's charisma, but I would earn a college degree, with my hands and brain.

I got one from Beijing University, after twelve years working in the fields and schools, then two master's degrees in New York, then a PhD, while writing poetry and novels on the side. I should have been happy, and I was, for about a day after each book, award, degree, before I became restless again and my eyes wandered off to the next goal.

"Why don't you spend some time with your mother? Just talk to her, cook with her . . . Create an atmosphere where you could be a daughter," said my friend.

I got a sublet in the East Village and invited Mother. We would enjoy a three-month mother-daughter reunion. I would be whole again, just like the days in the womb.

"Are you sure you want to do this?" my sister called from Germany. "I have consulted fortune-tellers. Each said it would end badly. You're not meant to be close."

I said I had to try this one more time.

"Try not to kill each other," she said and hung up.

Winter 1996, I picked up Mother at JFK Airport. We greeted each other as if we hadn't been apart for seven years. She had aged and put on weight but still walked with rigor toward the exit. She knew where to go, even in a foreign land. I followed with her baggage cart.

"Your dad is gone almost seven years. Now I'm ready to date," she said in the cab. "Lots of men have been running after me. But I have no appetite. Your dad was an ocean that made all other men dirty puddles. And who will ever hold me up that high? I heard Americans are different. They love Asian women. They treat them like queens."

"So you want to date Americans only, Mother?"

She laughed. "If you put it that way, yes."

"I know a lot of poets, writers, students—most of them married, and the rest have no jobs and live in studio apartments infested with rats."

"You mean you've squandered twelve years and haven't built a pool of prospective men for your future? You're heading toward forty-something, not young anymore. When are you going to get serious about life?" she raised her voice.

"I've been writing my dissertation, Mom. I just got two books published and a third coming out."

She waved her hand. "Well, poets are for the young and romantic. I'm almost sixty, need to be practical. Don't you know anyone who actually has a job?"

I counted every man I know, first Americans, then Chinese. "Yes, Dr. Zhang!"

"How much does he make a month?" She didn't seem to mind the Chinese name. "What kind of a doctor? No gynecologist, please. I don't want someone who peeks into vaginas every day."

"He does acupressure. Strong hands that can break bones. His treatment hurts like hell, but you feel like a newborn afterward. Imagine all the free treatments you'll get."

Her lips pulled down. "You mean he gives massages for a living? You want your mother to date a duck?"

"He's not a duck."

"A duck for a man is a chicken for a woman. Where have you been all these years? *Duck* means gigolo, as *chicken* means hooker, the lowest of the low!"

"He's not a gigolo, Mom, he's a masseuse, no, an acupressure doctor, a well-respected trade. This is America. A masseuse is not a synonym for gigolo or hooker. Besides, Dr. Zhang is almost sixty."

"Call him whatever you want, but he's a massage man. How much did you say he brings home every month?"

"I don't know. I pay him $30 a shot. If he has ten patients a day, that'll be $300."

"Set me up, then," she said. "Remember, my visa expires in three months."

Now I got worried. Dr. Zhang was not only my friend but also my painkiller. Once a week, he came to my apartment, loosening my stiff body with his steely hands. When I screamed in pain, he just smiled his Buddha smile and said, "A little pain is good for the heart." He told me stories about his life in China,

Taiwan, and New York: married three times, had many girlfriends, but none worked out. Women only wanted three things from him: money, green cards, and free massages.

"I guess I don't have luck with them," he smiled. "But at least I have health."

Would he have better luck with my mother? According to my sister, there was only emptiness in our mother's zodiac. Whoever lived with her would die prematurely, like our father. She was not supposed to have a husband, not supposed to have kids at all. I asked if it meant we would all die young or have bad luck for the rest of our lives.

"It means our mother has only the empty names of wife and mother but none of the benefits," she snapped. "She's destined to be alone."

That's exactly what Mother complained about: she had worked like a horse, yet still pinched pennies to get by in her old age.

What if she didn't like Dr. Zhang? What if she chewed him up the way she chewed my father alive? If things went bad, I'd lose Dr. Zhang.

I made a dinner for them. Mother was polite and proper, talking about her life as a high-ranking officer's wife, a teacher, and singer. Dr. Zhang sweated and popped his knuckles. Without his homemade baby-blue doctor's uniform, he looked out of place.

I thought the dinner had failed, but a few days later, Mother announced she was going on a bus tour to Niagara Falls. I asked if she needed any more money; she winked and said everything was taken care of. I was shocked. She had never said "no" to money. In her mind, I could never give enough for all the pains she had gone through. Three days after her arrival in New York, I wrote a $400 check out of my student stipend, along with a registration form for a bus tour to D.C., Virginia, and Philadelphia. I needed to buy some time alone for my dissertation. When I was working at my desk, she would sit next to me, drinking tea and chatting whenever she felt like.

"Can't you take a break from the books," she would say. "They don't really make you smarter or richer, you know."

She would go quiet for five minutes after my plea then start again. "The screen will make you go blind, and the radiation will shrivel your breasts, make you lose your hair and eyebrows. Then, you'll have no hope ever to find a date, let alone a husband."

She had pocketed the check and showed no sign of leaving after a week passed by. When I asked if she had signed up with Golden Luck Travel, she said she had put the check in her savings account. "Tour bus is not for me. I would rather die than spend a week with a group of quacking old ladies."

So, what suddenly made her want to go to Niagara Falls?

"Have you seen Dr. Zhang lately?" I asked.

She smiled. "He might turn out to be a real gentleman. We'll see."

I called Dr. Zhang. He admitted they had hung out a few times in parks and restaurants. "Hope you don't mind if I take your mother away for a few days."

"Take her as long as you want, Dr. Zhang."

The first day she was gone, I couldn't write a word. I missed her terribly, though I wished she'd be away longer, three weeks instead of three days. Perhaps she and Dr. Zhang would marry quickly. On the third day, when I finally wrote a paragraph on the pain of footbinding, I heard stomping footsteps.

"What a monster you have introduced me to!" she cried as she burst in.

"Monster?" I murmured and turned to her with a stiff neck.

"A sex fiend, worse than your father," she sang, cheeks flushed like a crazed girl.

I dodged her eyes. How could I dampen her urge to talk about Father's virility this time? For the past three weeks, she had been telling me stories about their sex life in graphic details. When I begged her to stop, she shouted, "What are you ashamed of? Your father was a man. He wanted me every day, twice, three times a day. But I was too young to appreciate him and too busy with four kids and a demanding job. I don't know why he started drinking and smoking in his late forties. I guess he never got the promotions he deserved in the navy, and the five-year exile in the deep mountains really got him. He came home as a wreck, two-thirds of his stomach cut off, hepatitis C, broken eardrums. Depression or deformation, his desire for me never waned."

"How was Viagra—excuse me, Niagara, Mother?" I asked.

"Good, good. I would have enjoyed it more had I not been so tired. Dr. Zhang kept me up all night long."

"Oh!"

"Do you know why he had three divorces? They couldn't keep up with him, those poor women. After he came to New York, he got wild, living with three women from the mainland. They had two queen-size mattresses on the floor and had orgies day and night."

"Did you stop at the casino, Mother? Did you play slot machines?"

She looked annoyed. "I don't care for gambling. I thought you knew."

"What about the glass factory, the most famous one in America?"

"Not bad. I wanted to buy some souvenirs, but the tour guide threatened to leave without me. That little bitch! She had the nerve to ask for tips at the end of the tour."

"So he's a real gentleman, then."

"A gentleman on the surface, a sex fiend in the bones. Our first night at the hotel . . ."

"What did you talk about on the bus, Mother?" I shouted.

"Oh, I asked him how much he had in the bank as soon as we boarded the bus. Why frowning, Daughter? It's good to get the business cleared before you start a romance. He looked frazzled but kept a good front. He has $50,000 saved in his retirement plan. That won't even last a year, I snapped. He laughed, and explained he had no debt, no mortgage payment on his two-bedroom condo in Flushing, and he was making good money doing acupressure, about $2,000 a month, cash. I asked him what one could do in New York with $2,000 a month."

"A lot," I burst out. "Especially if you don't have to pay rent."

She looked at me. "Your mother is too old to live like you, pinching pennies like a miser in a rat hole."

I inhaled. Breathe, Ping, just breathe.

"With $2,000 a month, you don't have to pinch pennies or dollars, Mom."

"That's what he said, but I know better. I've been walking around in Manhattan, Central Park, and the Upper East Side. Two thousand couldn't even buy a jacket. Your mother may not speak English, but she's not stupid."

I stared at her, speechless. What kind of husband was she looking for? And how did she get to those fancy places from the East Village? Bus, subway, taxi, or simply walking? I'd taken her to Chinatown only once to open a savings account for her. Thinking she would be terrified of the underground maze like most new immigrants, I had showed her around my neighborhood so she could walk to parks.

"You're not supposed to ask people how much they make, Mother," I finally said. "This is America, not China."

"Dr. Zhang is Chinese, not American. He didn't seem to mind at all. In fact, he immediately suggested I should meet a patient of his, a retired congressman from Taiwan. He's a bit old, a bit fragile, but loaded with money."

"And you still spent two nights with Dr. Zhang?"

"This is America, not China!" She laughed at her own quick wit. "Besides, I didn't let him touch me. Oh no! I practice qigong. Sex will weaken my qi."

"But you said he's a sex fiend who kept you up all night long."

"You are obsessed with sex, aren't you? What made you think that two people spending a night in the same room have to sleep together?"

But you did sleep together, two nights, and you said he's a sex fiend who kept you up all night long, I wanted to say, but I kept it to myself, and of course, she read my mind.

"We just talked about sex, okay? He told me his stories and I told him about your father and my lovers."

My chest tightened. My mother had quite a few male friends when Father was in exile. One of them, Uncle Qi, was good looking and friendly. A bit too friendly. When Father returned home, he made a stink about Mother's relationship with Uncle Qi. My sister said that Father would have been promoted to a much higher rank if not for her affairs with the navy officers.

"You know what killed your father?" Mother asked, her face two inches away from mine.

"What?" I twitched.

"Not enough sex. In his last two years, I was fed up by his lust. So I kicked him out of the bedroom. If only I had known that all the fire had no outlet and started to burn his liver. Yeah, the fire singed his mind. Once, he cooked a chicken and hid it under the bed. When I saw the half-eaten chicken, I sprayed it with DDT. Just a little. He broke my heart, you know. The old man had always saved the best morsel of food for me, the best everything. I don't know what happened—he didn't leave me a penny in his will. All his pension, military benefits, and savings went to your sister. What a slap in the face! We were husband and wife for over thirty years."

I suggested that DDT might have caused the cancer in his liver.

"Nonsense! I sprayed just a little, not enough to kill a mosquito. I just wanted to wake him up from his stupor. It's the drinking and smoking that killed him, not DDT."

"I thought it was the lack of sex."

"That too," she laughed again. "That's why I can't go with Dr. Zhang. He'll kill me, like your father. I've had more than enough sex for my lifetime. Now, I must preserve my qi, and you should do the same, my daughter. You've been squandering your precious youth. Had you just concentrated on your work and on one man, you would have finished your PhD, gotten married, and had a bunch of kids. Now, you're almost forty, still a poor student living in a dungeon. When are you ever going to do something real? Like helping me with my patients? By the way, I need the apartment for a week, starting tomorrow. I'll treat a boy with brain cancer. His father is bringing him from Canada. They don't have paperwork, so they'll have to cross the border illegally at Niagara Falls. They have no money either, so they'll stay here during the treatment. You can hang around if you have nothing better to do. Perhaps you can be my assistant. Together, we can make loads of money. I'll buy a building, one floor for my business, the other for renting."

"Mom, you just told me to finish my dissertation, so I won't be a pathetic student forever. How can I do my work if you turn my apartment into a hospital?"

"Never mind, then, thou art a rotten log that can't be carved. By the way, I consulted the *Book of Change* a few times for you. If you don't get married before you turn forty, you won't have another chance until you reach sixty."

I'm climbing the "Sky Ladder," made of steel cable with wooden rungs, hanging on the cliff like a snake. Why am I here on this high mountain where nothing grows but giant rocks and white water running through them? The Golden Sand River, where the Chinese sturgeons come every year to spawn and raise their young before they return to the sea. This has been their way of life for millions of years, since before the dinosaurs. Now, they are doomed because of the pollution and dams. They hurl themselves against the concrete over and over until the water turns red. They refuse to settle behind the dam.

Below me, the ferryboat bobs across the riverbank like driftwood, and its owner, Mr. Chen, squats on a rock, smaller than an ant. The silk ribbon of the Golden Sand River flows by, seemingly gentle and quiet. But I know how it roars, rushing through the narrow gorge with a power that moves mountains. I know because I've been here three times, flying across the Pacific to Shanghai, from Shanghai to Chengdu, taking trains and trucks to the Golden Sand River, the upper Yangtze. Of all the great places on Earth, why am I drawn to this place? Is it the river? The sturgeon? Or just my stubbornness?

I look up but cannot see the end of the ladder. I'm terrified of heights. Once, I climbed a tree to rescue a hen, and we both got stuck in the top. Mother put a ladder under my feet. Just look ahead, one rung at a time, she ordered.

An eagle soars above me, so close I can grab its talons and take a ride in the sky.

Mother waits in Shanghai. We'll go to the island, the end of this mighty river and beginning of the sea. We're going to talk.

I focus, one rung at a time.

The day Mother arrived in New York, I started pissing blood. She scraped my spine with a rhino horn until purple blisters popped up. She ordered me to close my eyes, palms in front of my chest. "Fingers grow longer, longer, now shrink shorter, shorter, shorter," she chanted. When my fingers refused to obey, she got angry. "You won't tell me, but I know what you've done. You can fool others but not me. I'm your mother."

After the trip to Niagara Falls, Dr. Zhang arranged for her to meet the retired congressman from Taiwan. It lasted only fifteen minutes. The first thing she told the old man and his daughter was that she had no intention to be a nurse or a maid, nor did she want to be housebound. She was a free spirit, traveling the world to practice qi and heal the sick.

Dr. Zhang apologized for the disastrous meeting.

Mother was furious. She had spent fifty dollars on a dress for the congressman.

After that date, she joined Oriental Fox and Western Stud, a dating club for white men to meet Asian women. Mother bought Global Harmony, a $200 translation gadget, for her first date with a retired engineer from New Jersey. She left in jubilation, telling me not to stay up waiting for her return. By 10:00 p.m., she came home, looking depressed. After much prodding, she said, "American men are cheap!"

I felt like punching my own head. I'd forgotten to warn her of the "go-Dutch" custom. Still, I agreed with mother: the man should have paid for the meal!

"I'm done with cheap American bastards," announced Mother.

Meanwhile, her qigong service was flourishing. Some of my friends returned for more qi healing after she made their fingers grow and shrink. They found her laughter infectious, her communication with her body very amusing, and she only charged them ten dollars. One poet saw her twice a week until he had an enormous seizure on the kitchen floor, and my mother revived him by digging her nail into his renzhong, the tender spot under his nose. She remained calm throughout the emergency, but that night, I heard her tossing around. The next day, she got up early and went to Chinatown. At supper, she announced she was tired of giving away her precious qi to lunatics. She wanted to do something else. She had found a job teaching three kids Chinese, math, and music in Kansas City. Two thousand a month, cash, plus food and lodging and one-way bus fare.

I wept and pleaded. How could she travel to the middle of nowhere with no English, no friends? What if the family treated her badly?

"No need to cry," she said. "I must leave for our own good. We're not meant to be together. Our energies clash. Besides, I need to make some money to buy an apartment in Shanghai. I'm tired of being treated as a country bumpkin by my mother and sisters. And I want to see more of America, especially the Midwest. I saw a painting once, a house floating in tall grass, like a boat in a golden sea. I learned it was prairie, once an ocean, then ruled by buffalos. I want to see the place. I know you can't pay for my flight, so I'll travel by Greyhound. Don't worry. If I could handle the East Village jungle, Kansas City will be a piece of cake. Besides, I have my Global Harmony. I'm fed up with this dump, worse than Shanghai. No good for people like me. You should finish your dissertation so you can get a job somewhere. Your hair is turning gray. Time to quit hiding in college."

Mr. Chen greets me like an old friend but insists I pay before the crossing. He trusts me because I've taken his ferry a few times, he said, but some clients have refused to pay after the crossing, so he needs to stick to the rule. The sun is setting, casting a blue shadow on the yellow water. Under the quiet surface, the river rumbles with whirlpools.

After the ferry, we start climbing back to the mountaintop. Mr. Chen walks on the blue slabs he paved, bending down to pull weeds or kicking a rock off the road here and there, his small body steady against the impossibly high mountain. He borrowed two hundred thousand yuan to open the new ferry on the river and was losing money every day. Why still do this? I want to ask but keep quiet. Certain things can't be explained, like the sturgeons' instinct to go home, like my need to come here. My sack is getting heavy. It contains a bottle of water, a camera, a package of Wisconsin ginseng, and *The Magic Whip*, my book of poetry. I've carried it across the ocean, hiked with it along the river, up and down, down and up.

As a child, I longed to talk to Mother, but every time I saw her, I just choked with fear. So I started writing stories to carry the conversations I could never have with her. Yet, I had to write in English, so that she couldn't read it, because I was terrified of her reactions. When my first book came out, I sent her a copy. Finally, her dumb child had done something with her dim wits. She wrote back fast. "Ungrateful beast, is this how you thank your mother who sacrificed everything for you?"

My shrinks believed my mother had borderline personality disorder. They lent me books, but the more I read them, the less I felt assured. I had more borderline personality symptoms than my mother. To be born in a period of such turbulence and change, who would not be borderline? Between my mother and me, we'd gone through the Japanese invasion, the civil war, the Mao era—riddled with the Land Reform, the Great Leap Forward, and the

Cultural Revolution—and now the economic reform that is uprooting China's five-thousand-year-old traditions.

I wonder what would have happened if she lived in my era, had my opportunities.

After she lived in America for two years, the maximum time allowed by immigration law at that time, she returned home and bought a two-bedroom condo in Taiwan Village, a three-hour bus ride from Shanghai. She had wanted an apartment in the city but couldn't afford it with the nanny money she had earned in America. There, she lived with her granddaughter, helping her with homework and teaching her piano. She continued to practice qigong and started teaching singing to a group of retirees who called her Professor Shen. She also joined a cycling club, planned a ten-thousand-mile bike trip to Xinjiang and Mongolia. Last year, she had two major operations. For years, her uterus had dropped through her vagina. When she had to wear a diaper, she went to the doctor. They took out her uterus and every other reproductive organ, including half of her damaged bladder. I called her hospital, our first conversation since New York.

"Ah, the operation was a great success," she laughed on the phone. "I won't need to wear diapers anymore, thank heavens. My doctor is super kind and skillful. He knew your father, too. So are the nurses. Two of them wanted to be my goddaughters. I have adopted children all over China. I heard you've left New York and have two kids?"

Soon after her discharge from the hospital, she fell off her bike and broke a hip. She took two long-distance buses to see her trusted doctor on the island. This time, she had to stay in bed for three months until the crushed hip healed. "It's killing me. I can't move, can't eat. Lost fifty pounds," she said on the phone, laughing. "You should see the loose skin on my stomach. Your mother is getting old." Then she started counting the days for her recovery. "People here love me. They can't wait for me to start teaching choir again. They hate the substitute. We're planning a ten-thousand-mile bike tour for the sixty-year-olds. Oh, the operation fees are twenty thousand yuan. Send me the money ASAP."

The Magic Whip, my second book of poetry, weighs like a mountain on me. Should I give it to her tomorrow?

≈≈≈

We meet finally, on Chongming Island, the end of the Yangtze, beginning of the sea.

She starts walking toward me, with a cane. So she didn't lie to extract money, as my sister warned. So she does have seven rods to hold her hip together. How did she get herself on the bus? How did she travel across America with no English? How did she go through her life with such laughter? I watch her come toward me, aged and shrunken, yet her eyes still spark with life. She breaks into a smile.

"You look good and strong, my child," she says.

My heart quivers. I'm not used to her wrinkles. "We'll find hairy crabs on the island, Mother. It's not the season, but I'll find some for you." This is all I can do—repeating myself like a dumb child.

She laughs, gutsy, loud, and wild.

The wind blows from the ocean. We stand on the bank, watching the wetland stretch into the horizon. The watch deck seems afloat over the sea of rustling reeds. The island, rising above the water in the eighth century from the Yangtze sediment, is Asia's largest resting ground for birds between Siberia and Alaska. The water here used to be the estuary for the Chinese sturgeon before they swim upstream to spawn in the Golden Sand River, their home since the Ice Age. Now, they're dying off behind the Three Gorges Dam.

"How are the kids?"

"They're growing big and too fast."

"I know. How's Minnesota?"

"Good. It seems to be the right place for me."

"I know."

It occurred to me she knew ten years ago, before I heard of the state. As she nannied her way through America, a month in Philadelphia, another in Michigan, Ohio, Alabama, Kansas, she would send me a postcard from each place. Her last one was from Blue Mounds, Minnesota. Across the golden prairie, she wrote:

"Once an ocean, always an ocean. Here, we'll meet again."

I kept that card and took it with me to Minnesota. It was all coming back, with the light of forty-six years of our lives together and apart.

So my mother has been talking with me, just as I've been trying to talk to her.

An eagle swoops down from the sky, startling flocks of birds out of the dry reeds.

I take out the ginseng and *The Magic Whip*.

"For you, Mother." I hand her the gifts in both hands.

She traces the lips on the high-gloss cover, the fingers braiding hair into a million whips, a million wings. We have the same hands: rough, stubby, and stubborn.

"I carried you an extra month in my womb," Mother said. "You came out with full, raven black hair. I knew I had to train you for your flight. I knew you would travel far."

Her voice seems to come from the ocean, an island far away but close to my heart. I look across the sea of reeds, then at my mother. She's smiling, wrinkles at the corners of her eyes, but I no longer tremble with fear. She looks like a friend I met long ago.

"My child, I met your master at the Puji Temple in Ningbo. Remember him, the monk you met on Putuo Island twenty-six years ago? He sent you his blessing."

"Master, blessing . . ." I echo Mother's words. Every detail is coming back to me, like a dream. "How's he doing? Why is he in Ningbo?"

"He was transferred to Puji Temple. You know he was the most revered and highest-ranked monk in China, right? He passed away last year, soon after he gave you his blessings. He said he would see you in the west when you complete your work."

Tears flow down my cheeks. I haven't cried in front of my mother since I was five, a vow I've kept after she thrashed me with a bamboo stick.

"How did he know you are my mother?"

She smiles. She has aged so, but never have I found her more beautiful.

"Because you are my child."

The salty wind blows again, sending reeds this way, that way. Each stem broadcasts my gratitude. She hears it. Tears roll down her face.

"Forgive me, Jing Ping," she calls my Buddhist name. "Your mother is getting old."

6

Allen Ginsberg's Apology for Buddha

Some say life is a fluke. To this day, I still wonder what force or karma led me astray into Lewis Warsh's Long Island University writing workshop, which led me to poetry to Allen Ginsberg to Buddha to Tibet to Everest, and changed my life completely.

It was my second year in NYC. That day, I walked into a classroom, thinking it was my required eighteenth-century British literature class. The professor had long hair, two shirts, both buttoned wrong, his jeans covered with paint, his nose running down the chin, and he was borrowing Kleenex from a student. I started laughing. He laughed too and gestured at me to sit down. Soon, I realized it was the creative writing workshop I had wanted to take. My advisor, however, had told me to take the British lit. Creative writing was a waste of money and time, especially the one taught by Lewis Warsh, the hipster joker. Well, I liked the joker professor. I'll do the first assignment before I go back to Tristan Shandy and Clarissa, I told myself. So I wrote a story about the Cultural Revolution. It came back with the comment: "You should start writing a novel, now!!!"

Lightning struck me. How did he know my longing since I was five? I kept it a secret so nobody would laugh at me. Writing is sacred in China. Who am I to even imagine I could write poems or stories? But Professor Warsh seemed confident I could do it. His words opened a window. Light poured in. Yes, this is why I came to America: to tell my story in English.

I ditched Clarissa and stayed with Professor Warsh. I wrote a bunch of stories that became part of *American Visa* and *Foreign Devil* five years later.

Semester ended. Christmas came and went. I was about to graduate and go back to China, unless I could find a job to extend my visa. Professor Warsh called me one night.

"Allen Ginsberg is looking for a translator. He's bringing Misty School poets for the first Chinese poetry festival in America. He needs someone to translate their poems into English, to work with his secretary three months prior to the festival. It's a big commitment, no payment. But you get to travel and meet the best American poets like Gary Snyder, John Ashbery, Bob Creeley, Kenneth Koch, and, of course, Allen. What do you think?"

I was stunned. A cluster of stars had just fallen into my lap, literally!

The Chinese poets Lewis mentioned rose to stardom after the Cultural Revolution: Bei Dao, Gu Chen, Yang Lian, Jiang He, Shu Ting. They were revered as gods and goddesses after ten years' ban on poetry. Now, I was going to travel across America with them? And all the American poets I admired?

"If you're worried about money," Lewis mumbled on the phone. "Maybe I could negotiate something with Allen. I know you're not allowed to work as a foreign student. Maybe they can feed you when you work in their office."

"Oh, no!" I jumped. "I mean yes, I will take the job. I'm just worried about my English. Do you think I could . . . I never wrote poetry in your workshop. Only stories. And English is my second language . . ."

"You're a poet, Ping," said Lewis. "Who cares about grammar? Bob, Allen's assistant, will help you with that. You have the soul of poetry. It shines through your stories. Go for it. You won't get another chance like that!"

Late fall, 1989, we gathered at Allen Ginsberg's apartment on the Lower East Side of Manhattan, celebrating the end of the first Chinese and American Poetry Festival since Nixon met Chairman Mao in Beijing. It was a smashing success. Big gatherings in every city we performed: NYC, Chicago, Detroit, San Francisco. Allen's small apartment was bursting with good wine and food and laughter. Everyone was drinking and talking loudly. I stood next to Allen, translating for him and Bei Dao. I was smiling and laughing too, but in the back of my mind, I kept wondering where I would sleep that night, after the party was over. I had lost my apartment after I quit waiting tables to volunteer for Allen.

We strolled into his bedroom. Above his bed hung a portrait of a green maiden, dancing with flowers in her hands. She was standing on a lotus flower on one leg, yet her body seemed to be floating in midair.

"What's this?" asked Bei Dao, pointing to the maiden.

Allen pushed down his finger. "Green Tara," he said, his palm up and open, his head bowed. "Goddess of enlightenment, the great emptiness."

Bei Dao looked a bit embarrassed. He asked Allen how long he had been practicing Buddhism. Allen started with the Beatniks, Chögyam Trungpa Rinpoche, and the Jack Kerouac School of Disembodied Poetics, then Tibet, the sacred land of Shangri-La, the great temples destroyed by the Chinese government and the master teachers and monks imprisoned, exiled, killed . . . He swung his arms as if fighting an invisible giant.

"Things are much better now," Bei Dao murmured. "No more arrests or destructions. In fact, the government is putting a lot of money into repairing destroyed temples and cities, especially Lhasa."

"What the fuck do you know, Ping?" Allen erupted, his trembling finger inches away from my eyes. "What the fuck do you know about what's going on there?"

I wiped his saliva off my face. How his eyes bled with anger!

"Allen, I'm just translating for you guys. I'm just doing my job," I whispered to him, my stomach twisting in pain. How could he treat me like this? Did he know I was starving and homeless working for him without pay?

As if he heard my thoughts, Allen shut up and lowered his head. Bob led him out of the room. Bei Dao fled with them. I stood alone in the bedroom, tears in my eyes. Green Tara on the wall beckoned, inviting me to dance. I took a step, then another; my arms rose on their own, right palm to the sky, left palm to the earth. My knees bent, my center closer to the Earth. As my left foot grasped the floor, my right foot lifted. Green Tara watched and smiled from the wall as I moved from one posture to another.

Someone coughed behind me. I turned around. Allen held a pile of books in his arms. "I, I don't mean to interrupt. But how did you know the Flying Sky dance? Who's your master? How long have you been in training?"

I put my right foot down. The floor felt cool against my burning sole. "I, I don't know, Allen. I guess I must have seen it somewhere in China. But no, I've never danced."

Then I remembered. I did dance ten years ago at Putuo Island, an island at the eastern part of Zhoushan archipelago, the crown jewel of the 1,339 islands and reefs in the East China Sea, one of the four most sacred places for Buddhists around the world. That summer, I was admitted into Beijing University, my lifelong dream finally fulfilled. My best friend, Ning, wanted to see the sacred island, so I took her there, since I grew up on the big island of Dinghai, about thirty kilometers away. We visited Puji, a temple dated from the Song dynasty (960–1279). I peeked in from the threshold. An old monk in a tattered robe sat under the lotus seat of Bodhisattva, Goddess of Mercy. Men and women prostrated in front of him, up and down, up and down. They seemed floating in peace as they kowtowed, after a decade's ban to worship in temples. An old lady got up and wrote something in a book, asked if she could be reinitiated. The old monk waved without opening his eyes. She grunted and went back to her mat. I looked up at Guanyin. She looked worn and tattered after years of neglect; yet, she filled my heart with a mysterious peace. Tears started filling my eyes as Ning tugged at my sleeve. She wanted to go to the famous Golden Sand Beach, but my feet felt glued to the temple ground.

Someone yanked me inside. The room was dim and empty except for a low table with a bell and a seated Buddha on it. An old monk sat on a mat.

"Where have you been?" he asked, as if I were his child late for dinner.

I pointed to the west. I had no idea why. I had left home when I was fourteen, wandering from place to place for one goal: college. Now, my dream had come true. My new home would be Beijing University, in the capital, the north of China.

"I've been waiting for you, my child," he said, gesturing me down next to him, under the goddess's seat. He opened the drawer and took out an old book.

"This is you," he opened to the first page. "Welcome home, Jing Ping."

I saw 静屏 written in black ink on the yellowed page. All my life, I've wondered why on Earth my parents named me 屏 Ping—obstacles, screens, roadblocks. I blamed my hard life on the name. Would Jing Ping, clear obstacles, make life a bit easier?

The monk put his hands in front of his chest.

"Jing Ping, my child, you've been traveling. But your journey has just begun. I know you feel battered with pain. That's why you're here. You'll feel like a newborn from now on. You must walk your path like a newborn, with your new eyes, ears, nose, mouth, limbs. You'll eat more pain and bitterness but take it with laughter and turn it into nectar to fuel your journey. We'll watch you from home. So feel no fear or shame, my child, and have fun, no matter what. Never forget to laugh, even in front of death."

My heart sank upon hearing more bitterness and pain, but my spirits felt high, even though I didn't understand what it all meant. I raised my hands to my chest, palms together, and bowed, my forehead touching the floor.

The old monk closed the book.

"Keep clearing the path, my child. Keep dancing, no matter how your feet hurt. I'll see you again soon." He picked up his stick and tapped my head.

"Oh, there you are!" Ning received me into her arms as I tumbled down the steps of the temple. She was sweating a torrent as if she had been running. "Where have you been? I searched the whole island, thought you had drowned. I was about to report you to the police."

"What for? I was in there only for a few minutes." My ears still buzzed from the tap. Something had shifted in my head.

Her eyes were wide open. "A few minutes? You disappeared for three hours. We were talking about if we should enter the temple and bow to Guanyin. You said you'd never bow to anyone. I laughed, knowing you, and then, you just vanished. I thought you must have gone to the beach but couldn't find you anywhere. Where on Earth . . ."

"There," I pointed to the dark interior of the temple, the broken, peeling Goddess of Mercy, the dozing monk, and the prostrating crowd. "Into a dream," I added.

Ning looked at me as if I had gone mad. She grabbed my hand and pulled me to the beach. The island was known for its sand, the best kind for sculpture. People from different countries used to gather here for the international sand-sculpture festival. It had been empty since the Cultural Revolution. As soon as my feet touched the hot sand, a river opened inside, flowing from the soles, through the legs, abdomen, the heart, the eyes. I started to turn and twist my torso this way and that, to the music that seemed to come from the sky, the wind, the sea. My limbs rippled like the waves, my body dissolved into the water and air. I was floating like foam, drifting like a cloud, whistling like wind. I was foam, cloud, and wind.

I stopped. A crowd had gathered around me. No one spoke. We stared at one another until an old man whispered in tears: "Oh, the Flying Sky Maiden."

Ning took my hand and led me away from the crowd.

"I didn't know you dance," she said when we were alone.

"I didn't know either."

We returned to the big island without saying a word.

"I learned the dance from a dream," I said to Allen.

He laughed, put the pile on the table, took my hand and kissed it gently. Then, he opened his books one by one and drew on each. He drew Buddha, stars, and lotus blossoms. "My apologies for yelling about Buddha. AAAAH!" He wrote.

I stroked the cloth-bound books, each a limited edition, each wafting ink fragrance. I looked at Allen, at Green Tara over his bed. "Allen, I'll go to Tibet as soon as I get my green card. I'll find out what's happening there."

He laughed again, his beard shaking with joy.

In the summer of 1992, I flew to Shanghai with my temporary green card, my first trip home since I left in 1986. I visited my father on the island first. He was fighting a war with liver cancer, getting up at 5:00 every morning to practice qigong and climb mountains to search for *linzhi*, the magic mushroom that could bring the dead back to life. He told me he was not ready to leave this world yet, not before he had a chance to visit America. He was going to heal himself through herbs and exercise.

I practiced qigong with him for a week then flew to Lhasa.

The old Russian plane shook and roared as it went over the Himalaya mountain ranges. It dipped suddenly, about to crash into the snow-covered peaks before lifting up like a hawk. Kids cried. Tibetans chanted mantra with eyes closed. I glued my face to the window, entranced by the magnificent blue-white landscape underneath. It wouldn't be a bad thing to crash into this awe-inspiring place, I thought to myself, but we arrived safely. The Lhasa Airport was small and old, built in the Russian style in the early 1950s. Workers pulled a mobile stairway to our plane. Passengers grabbed their bags and left quickly. I stood on top of the stairway and scanned the snowcapped mountains. So close to the sky. A rush of euphoria overwhelmed me. I felt light. If I just opened my arms, I could fly into the sky. Lhasa's altitude is 11,450 feet, 3 miles high. I breathed deep and long; yet, my lungs felt empty, as if they had lost the gravity and floated out of my chest. Was this what Allen described as "great emptiness" or "disembodiment"?

I saw Allen frequently after our "fight" over Tibet, in his apartment, on the streets, in our favorite noodle place, at St. Mark's Church poetry readings. The night before my departure to Tibet, we met again at Philip Glass's house. It was packed with people chanting Heart Sutra. I spotted Allen in the crowd. During the pizza break, I told him I was flying to Tibet soon.

"Please light incense for me in the temples," he said. "I wish I could go too. I wish my doctor would give me the permission to visit the land before I die."

I knew he had diabetes and a heart condition. He had brought Jack, a young man he had met during his visit in China, to live in his apartment. Jack was supposed to cook his meals with organic ingredients, no red meat, no oil, no salt, no frying, only steaming. Jack rarely followed the order, as he thought this diet was good only for pigs.

"Perhaps next year, Allen," I whispered. The chanting had already resumed. He nodded and sat down with the crowd.

I scanned the mountaintops and shouted, "I'm in Tibet, Allen. It's just awesome!"

Lao Han, a poet of Tibetan, Mongolian, and Kazakhstan descents, waited at the bottom of the stairway. He put a white *hada*, a greeting scarf, around my neck then scooped me into his thick arms. "Baby steps and baby breaths," he said, laughing. "You've got good lungs and a good heart, right? Just sync to the rhythm of our land. Let your lungs and heart do the work."

The road to Lhasa zigzagged along a wide, shallow river. I pointed to the cranes, ducks, and geese foraging in the pebbled riverbed.

"Oh, that's nothing," said Lao Han. "In another week, the Yaluzangbu River will be covered with migrating birds. You can't even see the riverbed. They come from all over the world to eat and rest here, some of them from the Mississippi River, I heard." He stopped the car. "I know you want to get into the river. Go ahead, but walk slowly."

I baby-stepped down the riverbank, the only way I could move. At this altitude, the air had less than 40 percent oxygen. I gasped at each step, my legs heavier than mountains, my body creaking like a thousand-year-old crone. The birds didn't seem to care. Some even made room for me to get closer to the water. I knelt on the riverbed. The stones gripped my knees, shins, and feet like tiny hands. I was touching the ancient sea floor. I could feel its magnetic pull. In the water, my face danced with the darting smelts. I scooped up a handful of the river and drank. It tasted of snow, mountains, fish, birds, rocks, and sky. The liquid traveled down my esophagus, into my heart, stomach, veins.

You're part of the river now, Jing Ping, part of the mountains and sky.

The voice sounded near and far, young and old. It was the old monk from Putuo Island. I looked down. Only birds and fish. I looked up. Clouds floated over the mountains. I lowered myself further until my face touched the water. My prostration to Tibet.

I had come to Tibet with my life at a crossroad. I was about to move to Montreal to marry Danny, a business professor at McGill University, and start my MBA degree. "Forget about writing," said my Canadian fiancé. "It's impossible to get published, especially with your sixth-grade English. In fact, it'd be easier to reach heaven than publish your poetry and stories."

So everything had been arranged: my visa, my train ticket . . . I had given notice to my landlady in Flushing, who immediately found a new immigrant from Taiwan to take my room. I had no valuable belongings except for two plates from the Ming dynasty, gifts from my friend when I left Beijing for New York. "They're invaluable and will be worth more and more," he said. "So keep them unless you're in an emergency." I had kept them no matter how hungry I was during my first two years in NYC. Danny couldn't keep his hands off the plates the minute he saw them. He made long speeches about how thieves could break into my room in Flushing and steal the plates, until I finally let him lock the plates inside his cabinet in his Montreal home.

"You will be happy in Montreal: a nice home, a nice degree from a nice university, a nice job with a nice salary," he repeated his mantra during our phone conversations.

Would I? Yes, I would graduate from McGill and make good money. I would make Danny and my mother and everyone else happy, except for myself. No, making loads of money for the sake of making money would never make me happy. But what would make me happy? Staying in NYC and writing and getting published? I knew every publishing house was swarmed with wannabe authors. Their manuscripts never got read. How was I going to make a living in NYC? I didn't even have a place to stay after this trip. Danny locked up my precious Ming antiques. He would not return them to me if I broke off the engagement.

And my father? Would he survive his cancer? Would I have time to get to know him before he passed away?

The sky was an immaculate blue. No cloud or bird cast shadows on the giant canvas. Under the sky flowed the river, the artery of the Earth, dancing along its blue path. If I followed its path, I could reach all the way to Shanghai, my birthplace, to the East China Sea, where I grew up, where my father was fighting for his life.

I dipped my face in the river. The glacier water jolted me like electric shocks, opening a new path between my eyes, down my throat, my navel. All the swirling doubts and worries vanished. I looked up and breathed. "Baby breaths and baby steps in Tibet, Ping." Lao Han's words echoed in my ears. "One at a time."

I breathed, the only thing I could do in this thin air, the only thing that mattered.

I looked back to the mountains. Lhasa Highway snaked around their waists. On the road, pilgrims prostrated in a single line toward Lhasa. They had been on the road for years, their wooden gloves paper thin from sliding on the concrete every three steps, their kneepads torn, their hair matted, but the light in their eyes made my heart jump. When one touched the land and water for thousands of miles, something magical would happen.

Lao Han waited patiently on the side of the highway, his head almost touching the sky, cigarette smoke rising between his fingers. Behind him, a Buddha, carved out of the mountaintop, watched through his closed eyes. Suddenly, I understood why Allen asked me to go into the river as soon as I arrived in Lhasa, why he wanted me to visit every temple for him and for all those who couldn't make it to Tibet.

I understood why he yelled for Buddha.

Everything became clear: I would leave Danny, the wedding, and MBA. I would stay in NYC. I had no green card, no husband, no job. I would starve but be alive doing what my heart wanted to do: tell my story through poetry and stories, with my sixth-grade English. I might never get published, as Danny warned. But when I exiled myself to the countryside for a chance to go to college, I knew it was an impossible dream, and I went anyway.

Millions of prayer flags fluttered from mountaintop to mountaintop. "Every flap in the wind, a prayer is uttered and sent to the sky," Lao Han had explained in the car ride.

How many prayers a second, a minute, a day, a year?

Floating in the sea of prayers, I made a vow: I'll be back to Tibet, as a kin and messenger, to spread peace and love from river to river, mountain to mountain, continent to continent.

An eagle flew over the mountaintop. I waved.

"Thank you for pointing my way home, Allen."

II

Into the Three Gorges

7

The Biggest Dam on Earth

In May 2006, I traveled to Sichuan with Evan, my colleague from Macalester, to study migrants displaced by the Three Gorges Dam. Built in the midsection of the Yangtze, from Yichang to Chongqing, it was, still is, the biggest dam on Earth, one of China's most ambitious projects since the Great Wall and Grand Canal.

The Yangtze starts in Tibet, falling 22,000 feet and flowing 4,000 miles to reach Shanghai, then spilling into the East China Sea. Its watershed encompasses 700,000 square miles—a fifth of China's land—and irrigates over one-third of its agricultural output that feeds half of the nation's population. Standing more than 600 feet high and nearly a mile and a half across, the dam contains a reservoir 370 miles long, equivalent to Lake Superior, and produces the electricity of 18 nuclear plants combined—18,200 megawatts. The raised water level supports vessels ten times bigger, boosting economic growth along China's most productive and resource-rich land.

The price for the dam? Almost a quarter million acres of fertile land is submerged under the water, and nearly two million people, half of them farmers, have lost their homes. The government claims that 40 percent of the total funding for the dam went to the displaced people. Each migrant should have enough money to move into a new house, to be trained for a new job, to learn a new dialect, open a new business . . . .

We flew to Chongqing, a mountain city known for its hot fondue and beautiful girls. The dam ended here, so did many displaced peasants. We learned quickly that foreigners were not allowed to interview dam migrants. I was Chinese, but Evan had blond hair and blue eyes. So we went upstream disguised as tourists.

The new settlements rose like mushrooms along the riverbanks. Where an old town went underwater, a new town rose a few hundred meters above or across the river. They all looked the same, from Ghost Town Fengdu to Poetry City Fengjie and Port Wanzhou—matchbox structures of concrete, steel, and glass, in imitation of the White House and New York's Fifth Avenue.

For three days, however, we couldn't find a single migrant. According to the official, about 1.5 million people moved and resettled, the largest exodus in Chinese history. Where did they go?

Xiao Family Village

At a travel agency in Chongqing, we met Mr. Zhu, who agreed to drive us into the Three Gorges along the river for about $400. We would visit the cities of Hechuan, Fengdu, Wanzhou by car then take a boat all the way down to the Three Gorges Dam. It was the route of the submerged towns, fields, and migrants.

"Once you're there, you'll see migrants everywhere," assured the agent, who sold us the service of the rental car and boat ride. But Mr. Zhu seemed unconvinced. He insisted we give him the names and addresses of the dam migrants we wanted to visit. We didn't have any, so we begged, promising a good tip for each migrant he helped us find. He sighed and said he would contact his friend in Hechuan, where he used to trade fowls for restaurants.

"No guarantee, though. It's been ten years since my last trip," he said. "Let's keep our fingers crossed."

He found his friend in the first mahjong house he stopped by. It was Monday afternoon. The place was packed with male gamblers. They stared as we waited outside.

Mr. Zhu came out with Mr. Xiao, a thin man in his fifties.

"Come and have a cup of tea at my place," he said, smiling from ear to ear.

"Where are the migrants, Mr. Xiao?" I asked.

Mr. Xiao nodded and said nothing. Mr. Zhu gave me a warning look. I followed them in silence.

Mr. Xiao lived on the third floor of a concrete building. A young couple was eating in the kitchen. A gigantic TV blasted a funeral scene. Mr. Xiao's wife served us loquat, a fruit that cures coughing. Two little girls were playing on a fake leather couch.

Mr. Xiao took out his little phone book. "So you want to see the migrants? I'll call the mayor. He can come over and give us some information."

I tried to stop him, but he was already dialing. If the mayor came and saw my blue-eyed, blond-bearded American colleague, not only our interview would come to an end, but also we might end up for hours in his office explaining why we were there and who had sent us. The phone rang, but no one answered. Mr. Xiao put it down with disappointment. I sighed with relief.

"He's not in, I guess. Where can he go on such a hot afternoon?"

Playing mahjong, perhaps? I thought to myself.

Mr. Xiao pointed to the TV. "My son."

A young man in uniform appeared on the screen, smiling and waving cheerfully to the solemn music that sounded like a funeral procession.

"His son sacrificed his life rescuing his comrades in the 1998 big flood," whispered the driver in my ear. "This is the video the army made in his memory."

No wonder the sadness in Mr. Xiao's perpetual smile. President Jiang Zeming came on, shaking hands with the parents of the soldiers who died in the flood. Mr. Xiao and his wife were among the crowd.

"I'm terribly sorry," I stammered. "Your wife must have cried her eyes out."

He smiled and pointed to the stunningly beautiful girl dancing to the TV music on the couch. "We lost our son, but we got her. The Party let us have another child. We wanted a son, of course, but she'll do just fine. Her future is set. The Party will send her to a military college and groom her to be a commander. Both my wife and I have good pensions, and we can travel anywhere in China for a week every year, all paid for by the Party. My son is dead, but his spirit watches over us. Even our nephews and nieces have benefited from his martyrdom."

"Mr. Xiao is the town's rich and famous," says Mr. Zhu. "His words weigh more than the mayor's."

The TV stopped. Mr. Xiao pressed the remote and started the video again.

"How's the river now?" I asked.

"The dam has tamed it. The Party said no more floods or sacrifices. Would you like to see the migrants' housing now?"

The heart-wrenching music started again when we stood up to leave. Did Mr. Xiao keep the tape looping 24/7? He must. Our driver, Mr. Zhu, seemed to know the story.

We drove through the town, its main street paved with ancient blue slabs, including its sidewalks. It must have looked grand in the old days. But moss crawled over every stone, and the place looked like a ghost town, if not for a couple of old people sitting at the crumbling doors with bamboo fans in their hands.

"Old town," Mrs. Xiao said apologetically. "Our new town is much nicer, thanks to the migrant funding."

I sat up. "How so?"

"Well, each migrant is entitled to a piece of farm land. The migrants sent their representatives to different parts of the country and picked out the land they wanted. They just pointed to the place, and it would be theirs. We give them whatever they want because it means cash. No one farms the land anymore. It's a money-losing business. On a good year, we can barely break even. If there's a drought or flood, we can't get our seeds back after a year of sweat. It's better to let the fields grow weeds. Most young men and women go to the cities to work in factories. Those who stay behind kill time playing mahjong. The dam is a cash machine for us. Once the migrants pick the land they want, our mayor negotiates the price with the migration bureau. The Party has rules and prices on everything, but there's always room to negotiate. Then, the Party has money to build housing for the migrants. Who is going to contract the construction? We are, the local government and business people. Who is going to be hired to build the housing? We are, the local peasants. That's why we welcomed the migrants like fortune gods. When their scouts came to inspect our land, we showered them with red-carpet treatment, music, food, wine, and showed them our best land in the best location. Are people worried about losing the land? No, we're delighted. As I said, no one farms anymore except for stubborn old folks. Everybody has left to work in factories. Our fields are empty. Our town is empty. We need cash to boost it up. Here is the housing project."

We got out of the car. A three-story building with eight aluminum storefronts blinded our eyes in the afternoon sun.

"The first floor is for businesses, like groceries, bike repairs, car repairs, or home industries. The second and third for the living," Mr. Xiao said proudly.

Three floors for one family. Not bad at all.

"Can I go in and talk to somebody?" I asked.

"No one is here yet. They are coming in two weeks."

"Impossible! The news says they've been here for two years, and some of them were even elected into the town government." I shook the paper.

Mr. Xiao smiled. "You must have lived in America for too long. You've forgotten some of our officials like to exaggerate good news. The migrants are coming in two weeks, if everything goes well. We have another site for them. Want to see?"

From the car window, we looked at the cream and orange tiled building.

"They've got it good, lucky bastards," murmured the driver as he started the car.

Everyone nodded.

I noticed how close this building was built to the highway, no more than twenty feet away. Where would the kids play? Where would they raise their pigs, chickens, goats?

The second site was on the back road. It had the same impressive façade with one less story—six storefronts with aluminum gates and living quarters on the second floor. Across the dirt road, a rotting pool table lay upside down in front of a mud house. A girl peeked out from the door and vanished into the darkness when she saw my raised camera.

What kind of business could the migrants do here? To whom would they sell cigarettes, liquor, candy, and other goods? For whom would they repair cars and bikes?

I kept my mouth shut as everyone praised the new project.

One aluminum gate was wide open. I walked in, stepping over the concrete mixer, empty cans of paint, rolls of plastic, and other construction materials. The second floor had a big family room, a master bedroom facing the street, and a small room facing the rice paddies and cornfields. In the middle, a tiny windowless room reeking of urine. I groped for a light switch but couldn't find any. I squinted and saw a hole in the concrete floor. No water tank for flushing. Everything looked gray—the walls, the floor, the staircase. The migrants would arrive in two weeks.

"This is what they want," Mr. Xiao said behind me.

I jumped and turned to face him.

"The government gives money to the migrants to decorate the interiors for themselves. Everyone has a different taste. Some like hardwood floor, some prefer tiles. Some like wallpaper, whereas others would rather have the walls plastered and painted."

"They're loaded," Mr. Zhu said, as his face appeared on the landing.

We walked to the kitchen. Three peasants were sealing the deck with tar.

"We guarantee no leak or crack," said Mr. Xiao. "And we promise that the new arrivals could cook their first meal the day they move in." He pointed to a small coal stove in the corner and a stack of honeycombed briquettes along the wall. One worker blew his nose into his hand, flung the snot against the wall and wiped his fingers on his pants.

"Where's the chicken coop and pigsty?" I asked.

"They won't need it," he said.

"They will," I insisted.

He stared at me, shocked by the tone of my voice.

"Because I've been a farmer, because those migrants have been farmers for thousands of years. As long as there's land, they'll till and plant. As long as they plant, they'll need animals to grease the soil, their rice bowls, and their pockets. Animals are their cash machines and friends."

Everyone laughed, including the workers and my American teammate.

"Cash machine? Yes! Friends? No!" said the driver.

"Things change. People change," said Mr. Xiao. "Our town is a totally different place from five years ago. So am I. It's life. It's fate."

"But certain things never change," I cried out, pointing outside the window to the school children singing, trotting home along the thin field path.

"Everything changes. Nothing stays the same," said Mr. Xiao in a quiet voice.

I opened my mouth. I wanted to shout: stop looping your son's video then and let him rest in peace! Instead, I thanked him for showing us around the village.

9

Wanzhou Orchids

"Quick," said Mr. Wan, our new friend from Wanzhou, "shoot the girls."

I turned my camera, but the curtain had dropped, only a glimpse of a white dress and black hair, a whiff of sweat. Above the door were four plain characters in black—he ping wu ting—peace dance hall, and handwritten ads for hairdressers, massage girls, apartment rentals, and cures for genital warts. A man lingered outside the door.

I turned to the woman selling steamed bread and chicken gizzards on the street. Her child slept in a cart behind the stove, under the highway bridge.

A girl peeked through the curtain, hurling obscenities at us.

We climbed the narrow steps to flee.

On the bridge, we could see the whole Wanzhou city on the bank of the Yangtze. Located between Chongqing and Wuhan, the two cities that mark the beginning and end of the Three Gorges area, Wanzhou played an important role as "the middle port" for thousands of years, reigning over the Yangtze as the City of Heavenly Son. Built on ancient limestone cliffs, the city is now famous for girls, hot fondue, and bangbang army—porters with yokes and ropes to carry suitcases, products, sometimes passengers, from the top of the hill all the way down to the port and vice versa. Along the port, ships gather like clouds. On both sides of the street, peddlers sell fruits, herbs, vegetables, clothes, fish, pots, meats, and steaming lamb, dumplings, ribs, innards from food stands. . .

It's a city of dust, herbal stores, restaurants, and hair salons with "floating girls" eager to pleasure men.

From the bridge, Wanzhou looks like an ancient scroll hanging on a cliff.

At a distance, a yellow sign of 175 meters. By 2008, the river would rise and everything would go under.

Most of the old town already went under—including the Bridge of Eternal Peace. When it was blown up in 2003, people gathered here in white mourning clothes.

Part of their souls went down with the bridge.

A few feet off the bridge stood a building built in the 1980s. No light from the windows. No shadow flickered behind the shades. On a bamboo pole hung a skirt, a bra, and socks—abandoned by the owner. Bulldozers were digging away under its foundation, constructing a water park for fishing, boating, and barbecuing for the rich.

Across the bridge, the girl in white was talking furiously to a broad man, hands chopping the air like daggers. The man glanced at us and started walking in our direction.

"We're in trouble," murmured Mr. Wan. "Just keep your mouth shut."

We met Mr. Wan and his father-in-law, Mr. Zhang, through Professor Wang in Beijing. Since the dam started in the mid-1990s, Professor Wang had been spending his summers in the Three Gorges area, collecting memories from old people—songs, stories, myths. Mr. Zhang was one of his informers. He was a good storyteller indeed. We met in an empty teahouse. He chatted nonstop for two hours, pouring his entire life out to us.

His mother died giving birth. His father soon married a young girl, his third wife, who refused to take care of the baby. So Mr. Zhang grew up as an orphan, begging food from village to village. A few families tried to adopt him. Some were quite wealthy. But he always ran away. A free soul can't stand the restrictions, he said. He didn't go to school until he was twelve. In the 1960s, he went to the countryside to be a peasant and married a girl there, and soon, they had a daughter. Ten years later, he returned to his birth town and worked in a store selling rice, flour, and noodles. Just when his life was settling down, his wife divorced him, and his daughter couldn't find a job after she graduated from high school. Now, his house was going to be flooded, but the government wouldn't give him a penny. He had bought the property under his wife's name, and he had never changed the deed after she left. The government would compensate according to the paperwork only. So his wife would get paid for the house he bought with his sweat money.

"I wish I could be big-hearted and let go of my house to support the Three Gorges Dam," he sighed. "It's our country's need. But I still need a place for my old bones."

He showed us the photo of himself blowing out birthday candles with friends. "My sixty-fifth birthday," he smiled. "Also my last night in my old house. I'll take you there tomorrow. But there's not much to see," he warned, puffing his pipe. "The whole town is gone, nothing but broken tiles, bricks, and garbage. The only thing standing is my house, sort of. The roof is gone already. And Mr. Ran's, my lifelong friend. You'll meet him tomorrow. He's still living in the ruins. I was going to stick it out with my pal until we got paid, but my daughter and son-in-law made me move in with them. My grandson needs my company. They work thirteen to fifteen hours a day in restaurants, seven days a week. So we keep each other company, the old and young. I'm glad I'm still useful in my old age. I'm a lucky old man with a filial daughter and son-in-law," Mr. Zhang sighed.

His son-in-law nodded. He was on the phone arranging a hot-fondue party for us in the restaurant where his wife worked as a waitress. He had purple bags under his eyes, his leg covered with blisters. "From the boiling oil," he said. "I was filling up the bottles when I dozed off and dropped one on myself."

Mr. Wan whispered behind me, voice full of fear, "If the man wants to see your camera, let him. You didn't photograph the girls, right?"

Before I could assure him, he added, "Do whatever he asks. Don't argue with him." He hobbled away before the broad man came close.

"Howdy!"

I smiled at his giant jade rings, thick gold chain, his bumpy pumpkin face.

"From Beijing?"

"Minnesota, Meiguo," I pulled out my business card and handed it to him. The best thing to do was tell the truth. "This is Professor Evan. We teach at Macalester College."

"America, beautiful country like Wanzhou," he shouted as he looked up from the card. "Well, professors, let me show you the fun places we have here." He pointed to the brightly lit hilltop and started naming the places: the best dance hall in town open 24/7, the best massage salon with the best looking hairdressers, the best restaurant . . .

He had the same chopping gestures like the girl in white. Did they train in the same karate school?

My mind drifted to Xintian County, where Mr. Ran's house stood alone in the ruins. Would our visit tomorrow bring them trouble? Wherever we went, people noticed us—one a bearded, blue-eyed foreign devil and the other who looked Chinese but didn't move, talk, or smell like one. The government seemed extremely jumpy on the topic of the Three Gorges migrants. Whenever I called their offices for information, they immediately wanted to know where I was from. At first, I told them the truth, and they either hung up on me or told me to report myself to the Migration Office right away and explain why I wanted to know the whereabouts of the Three Gorges migrants. I found some articles on the subject by Chinese journalists online. When I called the authors, they all claimed they had nothing to do with the subject anymore and had forgotten everything they had written.

"So what are you doing here, Miss Professor?"

I put on a quick smile. "To see the beautiful river and Three Gorges, of course. And you? What do you do?"

He looked stunned by my question. Even a five-year-old kid would have known his profession: a pimp. He saw that my question, or ignorance, was genuine. Chuckling, he scratched his crew cut. "I'm a scientist."

I laughed. "Really? What kind?"

"Orchids. I study and collect them. There are thousands of varieties, just in China alone. The rare ones cost thousands of yuan, you know that? But money isn't important. It's their beauty, the delicate fragrance. I have over a hundred pots."

I nodded. I didn't believe for a second that this man could have studied his way into college and studied his way out with a degree in science. But I did believe, from the fire in his eyes, that he loved his orchids, perhaps even more than his money.

"I heard there're many wild orchids in deep mountains there. My dream is to hunt them in those beautiful forests. I'm working hard to make it happen."

I nodded, was about to wish him good luck when his cell dinged with a text. "Have a nice visit. I'll call you when I visit America," he said, as he put my card in his chest pocket and trotted down the bridge to his Peace Dance Hall. His girl across the bridge was leaning over the fence, her voluptuous body curving against the dark steel. She was one of the human orchids he had collected.

"Time to go," whispered Mr. Wan behind my ear.

"Did he come over just to talk about orchids?" I turned to him.

"The girl was telling him that you took many photos of the dance hall and were going to sell her images to porn websites."

I turned on my camera to show him what I had. There's one shot of Peace Dance Hall. No girl or pimp. Only a shady man passing by, head turned to the drawn curtain. Above the door, a fading red number—177 meters.

"Stinky bitch," commented Mr. Wan.

My heart, however, ached for the bitch and her pimp. In two years, the river would rise to the red mark. Everything would go down, including the orchids from the Peace Dance Hall—the ocean of desire.

10

The Last Nail in the Dam

From Yichang to Chongqing, giant white billboards dotted the riverbanks: 156 meters, 170 meters, 175 meters—the final reach of the rising river by 2008.

In Xintian village, the number 175 was carved and painted in red into a tall stone on a hill, overlooking the ancient village below. The entire village had been flattened, as if hit by an atomic bomb. Women and kids salvaged bricks in the ruins that used to be their homes. A bus came, stopped, then continued, oblivious that the village no longer existed. Along the demolished road, a stream flowed to join the Yangtze.

Mr. Ran's house still remained, the last "nail" that stood in the way of the biggest dam on Earth. The government had cut off his water, electricity, shattered his windows, taken down the doors, and threatened jail. But Mr. Ran stayed put in his house. He showed us the eviction notice from Wanzhou district, three days past the deadline. The coffer-dam would explode in two days, and the water would rush in. His daughter begged him to leave, but he refused. He was born, grew up, and raised his family in this house, just like his father, grandfather, and great-grandfather. The compensation couldn't buy the smallest apartment for his old wife and himself. He would have to take a loan. He hadn't been able to find work. Who would hire a sixty-five-year-old man when the streets are crowded with twenty-year-olds waiting for a job? He held tight to his one-year-old grandson in his arms, as he showed me his pig in the sty, his chickens scattered in the vegetable garden.

"They keep me fed and alive. The new apartment doesn't allow animals or gardens. What am I supposed to eat? Wind?"

Outside, someone put a chair on top of the brick pile for Professor Evan. He sipped tea on his throne and looked very pleased. The crowd gathered around him, laughing and watching with amusement.

The police arrived in shiny black Landcruisers. We tried to flee, but the broken road punctured the taxi's ethanol gas tank.

"Don't be afraid," said Mr. Ran, taking my hand into his burning palms when the police pulled us into the station.

"Don't be afraid," he said again, as we were dragged into separate rooms for interrogation. "We have nothing more to lose."

11

Maverick in Three Gorges

Holy crap, we're surrounded by Landcruisers, two front, two back, two on each side. Oh my God! I've got to run. These cops are worse than devils. How can I outrun them in this shitty car? Oh my gas tank, I think the bricks just punctured the propane gas tank. Shiiit!

It's all Maverick's fault. She's nothing but trouble. I smelled it the moment she came into the travel agency in Chongqing and asked for a car rental. She looks Chinese, speaks Chinese, but 100 percent not Chinese, 100 percent not woman! I should have known better. I was on my way out, exhausted from my trip. Then, I heard her say Wanzhou and migrants from the Three Gorges Dam, and my ears perked up. I had been thinking of going home, just to see what's going on after the dam construction, how many of my old friends still remain. But I couldn't take a week off because the summer has been crazy busy since everyone wants to see the dam. If I took her and her blond partner there, I could kill two birds with one stone. So I raised three fingers to the sales girl behind the counter and mouthed: three thousand. The girl said: "You got lucky, miss. Usually we take people there by boat. A car rental would have cost you five thousand yuan. But here's a driver who's willing to do it for three thousand. And he knows that area like home because he was born and grew up there." She cackled as if she were in heat. Bitch!

Maverick turned to me and said, "Deal."

I should have known better. Anyone who was so quick to pay three thousand yuan for a two hundred yuan ride meant trouble. But I hadn't slept for two days. I was distracted. Now I'm paying for it.

The cops are closing in. Eight of them now, shining silver and thick tires and sirens, surrounding us from all directions. I can't outrun them. Not on this broken road! The debris had just punctured a hole in my gas tank. How did they come so fast? I mean this dump is so far away from the city, nothing left except for the old man's house in the ruins, the last nail house in the small town that has been sleeping on the Yangtze River for thousands of years now finally making way for the biggest dam on Earth. I mean, what does the old man want? His house is just pathetic, no windows, no doors, no electricity, no water—everything cut off to force him to leave, and he should. The buffer dam will be blasted in two days, and the water will rush in, sinking this whole dump under 176 meters of water. The red mark is way up there on the hill. The old man said he would sink together with his ancestors' house? For what? A tree dies from uprooting. A man thrives from moving around. Look at me. I was born and grew up in Fengdu, the City of the Dead, just a few miles away. I scooted out of the town as soon as they announced they were moving the whole city across the river to a higher slope. Most people cried their eyes out; yet, I volunteered to move first, got some cash award, and became a driver in Chongqing. And I'm doing fine, though my heart skipped a few beats when we passed the old place now under the water. The new city looks hideous, not at all like my old home Fengdu. So what! Nothing stays the same. Things change constantly. Tough! True, the old man is too old to start all over. No one will hire him for any kind of work. And he'll have no land to grow his own food. He and his old wife will depend on his daughter and his son-in-law. I can tell he's not happy about it. I don't blame him. His daughter looks like my ex-wife—a bitch, not easy to live with. What would I have done if I were him, old and homeless? I might as well sink with the house, like him.

And this maverick who looks like a Chinese but doesn't behave like one. What is she doing on the floor of my back seat? Ah, memory cards from her camera! Not a bad hiding place. It's full of holes there. And that blond American has left so many bottles there, Coke, orange juice, and beer. He looks clean and intelligent, supposed to be a professor and a lawyer. What a pig! Laughs at everything she says, everything he sees, everything he eats. How can one be so happy sitting in his own pigsty? I tried to clean it up, but it's pointless. What is she doing with him anyway? What's to see or do here? The old towns are nothing but ruins, and the new places are hideous. Why doesn't she take the luxury boat flowing down the river along our beautiful Three Gorges, like all the foreign tourists? Why does she travel on the treacherous roads looking for the wretched people displaced by the dam? What's the point of taking pictures of their wrinkled faces and listening to their sad stories? They're all the same: loss of their old homes, loss of their old land, loss of the money promised by the government, loss of jobs, hopes, future, blah, blah, blah. Well, I'm one of the two million displaced people. I've lost all of those. How come I don't cry like them? What's the use of crying anyway? The sky never drops pancakes just because you whine like a baby. No. The big fish eat the small fish, the small fish eat shrimp, the shrimp eat whatever they can catch—it's the law of the jungle.

My wife and I moved from our village to Hechuan, into a godforsaken place. After a few months of hell, we sold the house for half of what it's worth and started a new life in Chongqing. We opened a small restaurant. My wife is a lousy cook, but she's pretty and merry, so we got some faithful customers. Three months after, she ran away with a man who owns a chain of karaoke bars in town. I lost everything in three months. Did I cry? Only a little. I really loved her, you know. We grew up together like brother and sister. I hope she has a better life with that karaoke pimp. The other night, I sneaked into the bar where she sings. I barely recognized her. She's so skinny and light that a wisp of wind could blow her away. Her heavy makeup couldn't cover her wrinkles. My heart ached. I left before she could see me. I didn't want to cry or make her cry. I'm thirty-five years old, alone in a big city with my beat-up car, working long hours to save money to find a woman who is willing to give me a son. Not in the city. Too expensive to buy a home there. Ten thousand yuan a square meter? My savings can buy a bathroom at most. That's why I'm using this trip to check out my hometown, where a good woman and apartment may cost less.

Oh my God, the cops are jumping out of their cars. They look like they would eat us up alive. I hope that crazy woman has hidden all her camera's memory cards. What? Why the hell is she taking pictures now? Oh, the landscape. Good. The cops are no fools. No one would believe that she has such an expensive Canon but has no pictures in her card. Lucky she doesn't have a notebook. She just takes pictures and listens. Strange for a writer. But good for me. If the cops seize the conversations she has had with those whiners, we could all go to jail. The buffer dam is going down in two days. The cops are going crazy making sure foreigners talk to nobody.

We almost got caught at Fengdu, the new town. I was feeling bad because we couldn't find a single migrant since I took them on the trip. When I took the job in the Chongqing office, I had patted my chest and said we'd find them everywhere. You'd think it's true, right? Two million of them. Where else could they go? Well, for the first three days, we couldn't find a single migrant.

The woman called a dozen offices set up for the dam migrants, but they hung up on her or ordered her to report herself to the office right away when she told them she was a professor from America. I felt so bad that I was contemplating if I should tell that I was a migrant myself. Not that I wanted to have her big nose poking into my life. I'm not terribly proud of who I am now. Once I open my mouth, there's no stopping. This woman knows how to get to the heart of things.

Well, I got lucky. The bellboy in the hotel is a migrant. I think I know his parents, kind of. His father is a doctor from the old town. He treated my wife once. A nice man. They got an apartment in the new town. The boy took us to see it. It's nice and big but empty. The father can't find a job here. So he's working in Fujian, in south China, and his wife somewhere in Yiwu, east China, far away from her husband and son. The boy lives alone in the cold apartment, working at night in the hotel to support himself while preparing to take college entrance exams. He wants to become a navy officer. Nice boy, handsome and tall. He misses his parents, I can tell. Every boy needs a mother and father. Who cooks for him? The kitchen is cold. A box of take-out leftovers on the floor. The American professor was thirsty. No hot water in the thermos. So we went downstairs to get water bottles.

The ground floor was a small grocery that sells water and chips. No business. Of course not. Who would come to a back street in a ghostly new town to buy chips or water? Only this maverick would. Those losers were playing mahjong at the dinner table when we got in. What else could they be doing anyway? The place was dead: no jobs, no land, no future. All the migrants were cramped in the new buildings like pigeons in cages waiting to die. That's why I scooted out of there as fast as I could. They all turned to stare at us—the blue-eyed devil. As I said, no one visits this dead place, let alone a foreigner. We got three bottles of water and were on our way out when the maverick opened her big mouth: Do you know any Three Gorges Dam migrants? And boom, we were surrounded by an angry mob. Suddenly, everyone was a migrant, the storeowner and his wife, the mahjong players, the man on the motorcycle with his son, the old woman chewing nuts on the steps—somehow, they knew my clients were from America. Well, it's not that hard to figure it out since we got a blue-eyed devil towering over everyone else, right?

They all shouted into our ears: Where's our money, where's our money? Well, how would I know? I ask the same question myself every day. I see all the filthy rich people running around in their fancy cars and fancy clothes between fancy restaurants and hotels with their fancy mistresses and whores—and I ask: Where is my share of this crazy wealth?

The hotel boy turned pale and pulled Maverick's sleeve: "Let's go, Auntie, please let's go quickly. The cops will come soon. Yesterday, they arrested lots of people here, including an eighty-year-old grandma."

You'd think this would scare her, right? No! The crazy maverick pushed the boy toward me and told me to take him and the foreigner to my car. She would wait for an old man to bring her his petition against the government. And I saw him stumbling to us along the muddy street, shouting as he waved a roll of paper: "I want you to bring this to America. I want the whole world to know what we're going through for this dam!"

I was feeling dizzy, thinking oh let's get out of this mad place, when I heard the siren, far away, but coming at a fast speed. I grabbed the boy and the maverick. Run, I said, run. She pushed the foreigner toward the car, shouted some gibberish and the devil ran like a son of a rabbit. The maverick rushed to the old man and took his paper before she dived into the cab. As we were leaving, the cops arrived. The mob surrounded them to allow us an escape. That was close. Really close.

I hope she hid the old man's petition. That would guarantee jail if the cops seized it. I think she photographed it in my car yesterday and got rid of the paper. Good. The less evidence, the earlier we can get out. Oh crap, the cops are hooking my car to theirs. Where are they taking us? The police station, where else? Oh man, oh man, for three thousand yuan, I put myself in this shit hole. How am I going to get out? I better warn the maverick that we are just tourists, and we got in here by mistake. Some young man played pranks on us, telling us this is a great scenic place. Ah, she's tearing up papers. Good for her. She's crazy but smart. She grew up in China. Well, she should know how to deal with those cops.

Oh no, what's wrong with the foreign devil? His face flashed colors like a chameleon: redder than blood in one second, paler than paper in another. And he's shaking as if he were having a seizure. My God, they're rounding up all the villagers, the old man and his nasty daughter and her son. They followed us from the town center to visit the old man's house, standing alone in debris like a rusty old nail. Now, I understand why they call it "nail house." How cheerful they were a few minutes ago, gawking at the blue-eyed devil on a pile of debris laughing like a piglet and drinking tea, as the maverick talked to the old man and took tons of pictures of his old house, his old pig, the old river running quietly behind—it has been a good show for everyone until now, rounded up and shoved into the Landcruisers.

Now, we're back to the town center and into the police station. The iron gate is closing slowly. Who betrayed us? We don't know a soul here. We came here because the maverick got the old man's name from a professor in Beijing, who has visited here a few times. How she knew the professor is beyond me. Well, she teaches stories in an American college. They must have connected through the Internet. Ah, that fat man at the gate is looking at us with a smirk. I saw him in the crowd when we got here in the morning. The villagers immediately surrounded us of course, because of the blond devil. And I saw the man lurking around like a rat. He must have ratted on us. Just wait until I get out. I'll find my old buddies. We'll blindfold him, gag him, and beat the rat into pulp.

The maverick looks stone-faced. Where's her emotion? She cries every time she hears a story from the losers and gives them money. I guess she makes good money as a college professor. Driving me mad. What is she doing here anyway? She has a car, a house, and two sons in America. Why can't she just enjoy her good life over there? Why does she have to come back and stir up troubles? Our lives are hard as it is. Now this shit! How am I going to get out of this?

The cops are lining us up in the yard; the locals in one line, we in another. My God, I'm just a cab driver. Nothing to do with the foreign devils. The blond man looks so mad. He's screaming at the cop and grabbing his ID from his chest. Please don't be so stupid. Cops nowadays don't give shit about who you are, blue eyed or red haired. They will smash your camera and beat you up before they talk to you. How pale the maverick turns. She looks scared for the first time. Good. She's grabbing the foreigner's hand and telling him to shut up. And he did. How did she do that? I can never stop yelling once I start. It's like a volcano erupting from inside. One of the reasons my wife left me. I hope she found someone with a milder temper. Won't be easy. Everyone seems to have a volcano inside.

You would think people must be happier these days. Compared to the past, we have more stuff: TVs, cars, better food and clothing, bigger apartments. Are we happier? I don't think so. Compared to the old man, I'm much better off. Compared to the cop, I'm pathetic. Compared to the rich in Chongqing, I might as well hang myself. Oh, I miss my old town, the quiet life I had with my wife. We didn't have cars or phones. The whole village had one radio. But we were happy.

Maverick said something to the blond, and he pulled out his cell phone. Calling his American connection? Smart! Making sure that the American authority knows where he is. Ha, now they'll think twice before they throw us into a jail. The old man is shaking. He doesn't look scared. Wouldn't be standing on the riverbank like a nail if he's a scared cat. They were taking him and his family into Room 1. Oh God, they are taking me to Room 2, Maverick and Blondie to Room 3. So they'll question us separately. Why is the old man running to us? Oh no, he's grabbing my hand and her hand, squeezing. The old man is strong. Don't be afraid, he said. Don't let the pigs bully us. Funny it comes from him. The old man is about to sink into the river with his house and everything, and he's telling us not to be afraid. Guess when you have nothing to lose, you have nothing to fear. Well, what do I have? This car? A piece of junk. Home? Gone six years ago. My twenty thousand yuan in savings? Nothing will be left after I fix my broken tank. So I might as well man up and give the cops a piece of my mind. Ouch!

The cop must have military training. His fist hurts like a motherfucker. What? I'm innocent. I know nothing about that crazy woman and the foreign devil. I just drove them here for sightseeing. The travel agency assigned them to me. No, I didn't take them to visit migrants. What for? They come to us. They're everywhere, like ants. Hotels, restaurants, dance halls, hair salons—I'm a migrant myself. They could have interviewed me if they were interested. But they're not. They never asked me any questions. And I said nothing. I think they're crazy hippies. Trying to be different from other tourists, you know? Everyone else takes the boat down the river, so they take the road. There's no law that says they can't, right? Otherwise, you guys would have put up roadblocks. Ouch! What are you hitting me for? I'm not being fresh. I'm sincere. All I want is to make some money, like every Chinese. Those fools, they think they're so smart and know antiques. So I stopped at every stand that sells fake stuff along the river. And they bought them as if they found treasures. Treasure my ass. Oh, how we laughed watching them spend thousands on the junk. I should get a medal for contributing to the socialist economy. Why are you punching me again? How much percentage did I get? None! I'm telling the truth. Okay, okay, I did get a few slips when I took them to the dealers' homes but only if they spent over a thousand yuan. I got three hundred out of all the deals. I swear to God that's all. The street vendors gave me nothing. Just a pack of cigarettes here and there. It's all part of the socialist economy, right? I'm just doing my job as a good citizen. My gas tank broke. Who's going to pay for it?

What? Five hundred yuan fine? What crime did I commit? What? Three weeks not working? How am I going to eat? The west wind? Okay, okay, I'll shut my big mouth. I don't want to rot here.

Oh, mother! What have I done to deserve this? My car is broken. No work for three weeks. And I have to write a five-page confession. Shiiiiit! I'd rather pay money than write crap in this dungeon. Why is the old man so quiet? He was screaming like a fiend just a minute ago. Did they let him go? Probably writing the five-page confession like me. Who's laughing next door? The foreign devil? Fuck! Why does he get to be treated as a guest? Look, the pig is bringing a cup of tea to him. What? A bowl of beef noodles! It smells so good. I can't believe it. Just because he's blond? Oh great! He's singing a Russian song, and the cop is singing along. What the heck is going on? Must be Maverick's doing. She's a witch. She opens people's mouths as if she had a key in her hand. How many times did I almost lose my control and spill my story to her? Ha! This means we could get out. Yippee! But where can I go once I'm out? No car, no money, no wife. Maverick better compensate me for all the suffering she's caused. Perhaps she can take me to America. I can drive a taxi there. She'd been calling the hotel boy like mad, said she would adopt him and get him into a college in America. Ha, if she could find him. He has vanished since we left town. Probably rotting somewhere in jail. Well, she can adopt me. I'm in need of help as much as the boy. She mentioned her next stop would be Lhasa. Well, I had better pray for her safe return so that she could take me to America. I may be a bit too old to be her son. But who cares? As the saying goes: whoever has milk is my mother.

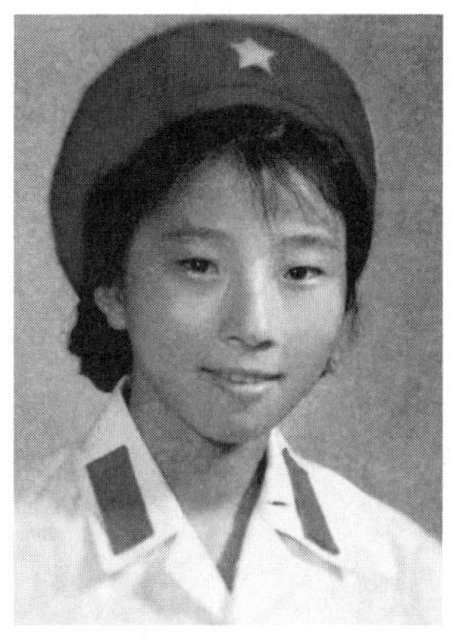

Dressed as a People's Liberation Army soldier at fourteen, before leaving home to become a peasant in a village for my college dream

Resting on the way to Everest

Grand Canal of China

Wushan, Three Gorges

New Wushan after the dam

Wuxi villager in the ruins of his ancestral home

Shigu village, upper Yangtze

Whistling Sand, Dunhuang,
western China

Monk

Flowing Sand Mountain, western China

A migrant and his grandson in the ruins of his ancestral home, the day before the dam flood

Choctaw Island, lower Mississippi River

End of the Bird's Foot, Venice, Louisiana

Louisiana bald cypress, Atchafalaya Swamp

Paddling down the Mississippi with Quapaw

River flags bridging the gulf at Venice, Louisiana

River flags at Yamdrok Lake, source of the Yangtze

River flags over Everest

Pilgrimage to Lhasa

Climbing Everest with river flags

From the roof of the world, wind is releasing wishes of peace from the river flags made by people along the Mississippi, Yangtze, Ganges, Amazon, Po, and other rivers

12

The Road to Joy

I'm happy, very happy. I own my house, four stories, built it myself. Its value shoots up every day. Yichang exploded as a commercial hub since the Three Gorges Dam began its construction. Now that the dam is complete, the tourists come like bugs to a fire. They keep me very busy. I own this car, a brand new Santana, and I make a thousand yuan every day driving tourists around. On the riverbank overlooking the Three Gorges Dam, my wife runs our restaurant. She's a charmer and a fantastic cook. Her clients always come back for her smile and food. We have over a million yuan in the bank, for our son, who graduated from college and now works in a pharmacy. He makes about a thousand yuan a month, less than what I can make in a day, but he brings us honor as the first college graduate in our Chen family, which you can't buy with money.

I came from the countryside fourteen years ago. Why did I leave my village? To work in a restaurant and pay off my debt. Ten thousand yuan, equivalent to a million nowadays. I got into this debt for my three-year-old son, the second child born illegally, and we had to hide him all the time. He was home alone a lot when my wife and I worked in the fields. One day, he must have been bored and cold. He found some pine twigs and started a fire in the yard. That day, he was wearing the synthetic wool sweater and pants my wife knitted for him. When the fire got him, it spread like swarming locusts. Whoosh, and his whole body burnt, head to toes. By the time we got home and unlocked the gate, we thought he was dead, lying in the ashes all curled up. We rushed him to the hospital. Third-degree burns over 92 percent of his body, and the hospital wouldn't take him unless we paid five thousand yuan up front. I pawned my house to get the money and borrowed another five thousand to keep him alive for three months. He didn't make it. My wife cried every day, wouldn't eat or sleep, just sat at the window like a zombie. The pigs and chickens were hungry, and I was hungry. But she just ignored us. Our debtors gathered at our door wanting their money back, threatening to tear our house down and sell the wood. Finally, I told them I was going to the city to make money. Just give me a year, maximum, and if I couldn't pay it back by then, they could do whatever they wanted to my house and me.

So I sent my wife to her parents' village and carried all my chickens and ducks and pigs to my cousin as my investment for his restaurant. My cousin had just opened a small eatery on the bank of the Yangtze in Yichang City. Pretty risky business in the early 1990s because no one knew for sure if the government wanted us to be rich for real or if they just had a three-day policy fever. You know how the political wind changes, faster than a teenager's mood. But I had no choice. I worked as a cook and waiter and dishwasher. I had never cooked or washed dishes in my whole life, but I learned fast. My food became well known in the district, and our restaurant expanded. I paid back all my debt within a year as I promised. The next year, I saved ten thousand yuan.

My original plan was to go home after I paid off the debt, but two years of working in the city changed me. I could no longer go back to the fields and work my ass off for nothing. So I brought my family to the city, sent my wife to the best doctor, and our son to the best school in town. I didn't care how much it cost. After my second child's death, nothing but my family matters. What good would the money do for me unless we're together and happy? When my wife got better, we opened this restaurant together and money came in like a daily tide. Then, my son graduated from middle school, the first one in our family, and got into college, also the first in our family. The tuition cost me a fortune, but so what? How many peasants' sons could go to college? That was the year I got a car and started the car service business. I worked longer hours, running between driving and managing the restaurant. But I was happy as a clam.

Am I content? Well, China has many filthy rich men nowadays, billions of yuan in the banks all over the world. Compared to them, my million yuan savings is pathetic. But I believe I'm happier than most of the rich, frighteningly so, when I think about my past and how my second son died and when I see two million locals lost their homes and scattered all over the country because of the dam. I feel lucky and guilty at the same time. What have I done to deserve a good living while they lost everything? Those peasants have roots here for thousands of years, you know. Their only wish is to live and get buried in their old homes, even if it means it's under the water. At night, I pray to my ancestors, thanking them for protecting me and giving me all this good fortune.

One must have gratitude; otherwise, one will never feel joy. Now I live in the city, in a four-story house with my wife, my son, and brother-in-law's family. Our life is harmonious. My wife and I never have fights. She's gentle and beautiful, works like a mule, and smiles like a lamb. Hard to find such a good woman these days. Not that we have time to quarrel anyway. We both work more than twelve hours a day, seven days a week. Our only wish is that our son gets married soon. Every week, he brings a new girl home, each more beautiful than the previous, and we just can't keep up with who is who. Even he himself can't remember their names. Is he ever going to settle down with one nice girl and give us some grandchildren? We still have the land in the old home, where my second son was buried. It's rented out to my neighbor for growing vegetables and rice, a thousand yuan a year. We'd like to build a nice house there, and as soon as we have grandchildren, we'll retire from the city and raise the kids where there are still trees and clean water and birds in the sky. And we'll never leave them alone at home, ever.

13

Morning Cloud, Evening Rain

A dream is not just a dream
A butterfly not just a butterfly
In the clouds, a pining soul
A flower between fate's teeth

At dawn, our cruise ship passed the roaring Qutang Gorge and entered Wushan on the Yangtze. The deck was finally empty after an all-night party of drinking and gambling. I sneaked past the sleeping guard to do yoga on the area reserved for first-class passengers. When I looked up from a back bend, she appeared before me like an apparition, her slender waist and full hips shimmering through a silk gown, her painted toes curving through golden slippers, bleached blond curls hugging her breasts.

Her beauty took my breath away, though I am supposed to detest her—a woman dressed to give pleasures to anyone who could pay. Yet, she pulled me like the moon. The melancholy between her eyebrows made my heart ache.

Below the deck, the tour guide was knocking on the first-class cabins, her shrill voice cutting through the metal floor. "Get up. We're reaching Wushan Goddess Peak. Your tour means nothing unless you see the goddess." When no one stirred, she shouted, "I've done my job. Don't regret it later. Don't ask for a refund."

I smiled as I listened to the commotion downstairs. She knew how to move people. Money is the engine that drives China forward.

Thick clouds hung on the mountains, shrouding the river, the boat, and the girl in white silk. How did she get here? Since I boarded the three-star boat yesterday afternoon, I had walked through the first-, second-, and third-class cabins, hoping to find passengers who lived along the Three Gorges, or used to, before the dam ousted them. I should have known better: Why would any locals squander money touring their homeland?

The girl couldn't have boarded the ship with us. I'd have spotted her right away.

Light peeked out of the clouds, casting her shadow on the river. Even her shadow was beautiful and forlorn. It pointed north to a steep mountaintop, where mist hugs the shoulders of a slender rock. Was that the Wushan Goddess the guide has been bragging about, the crown jewel of our three-day tour? Everything else pales after her, the guide said to my blue-eyed colleague. The enthusiasm in her gleaming eyes surprised me. As a shrewd businesswoman, what's her interest in a rock that doesn't have much commercial value except that it provides her a job?

We disliked each other the minute we met. I hated her heavy makeup and elaborate hairdo, her tight T-shirt and jeans that show every inch of her robust curves, her shrill voice, and the purple bags under the bulging eyes, revealing her oversexed lifestyle. Likewise, she seemed to detest everything about me: my blunt questions, my casual traveler's clothes, my fluent English, and my American colleague. The minute we boarded, she announced in her broken English that it was her duty to give her personal attention to the only foreigner on board. Evan couldn't understand first, asked me what the lady had just said about him, then laughed when I translated her words into comprehensible English. She glared at me with her watery eyes, pulled Evan to her side, then pointed at me as she said: "This woman no Chinese. No trust for her."

What a bitch!

"There she is, everyone, our goddess, our Chinese Venus!" the guide shrieked through a megaphone. The deck was now packed with tourists. Evan stood next to her, craning his neck to locate the peak. She took his hand and pointed it to the north. "There, the slender rock that looks like a girl facing cloud, beautiful?"

There seemed to be someone in the folds of mountains
With eyes that hold laughter and pearls of smile.

She started singing "Shangui" from Qu Yuan's *Nine Songs*, a ritual performance for gods and kings from two thousand years ago. Shangui is a goddess roaming the Three Gorges, gathering herbs as she waits for her lover—God of Wind and Rain.

She surprised me again with her knowledge and singing voice.

The girl in white seemed afloat, her legs, waist, and hair circled by rings of mist, a perfect illustration of Shangui, the pining goddess of Wushan who rode tigers and leopards and made herbal potions to call back her lover.

"My dear friends," shouted our guide through her megaphone, "our Wushan Goddess appears everywhere in Chinese myth, history, folktales, temples, mountains, dreams, poetry. She's the twenty-third daughter of the Sun God and the Western Queen. She's *yu fu*—fish that can resurrect and change into a snake, then a beautiful woman. She's linzhi—the magic mushroom that helps lovers meet in dreams. She is Shangui—Qu Yuan's mountain goddess, and Tushan Goddess who married Da Yu and helped him dredge a waterway to clear the Big Flood. She's *nu shi*—priestess who guards temples and invites gods to the Earth with her songs, who prays for harvest and prosperity with her sex, who cures the sick and blesses the dead with her dreams. She is the goddess of virginity, sex, birth, medicine, harvest, earth, life. And above all, she is the goddess of beauty, love, and lust."

The crowd became quiet. Everyone was listening for a change.

"That's right, goddess of lust, my dear friends," she nodded at Evan, as if he could understand her Chinese. "In ancient China, lust symbolized fertility; therefore, it was beautiful and moral. The more lovers a woman had, the higher her rank and the more respected she became. They lived in temples and came out during the festivals to initiate youth into adulthood with music, dance, herb, sex."

Before I started the journey, one of my friends had told me about the sex industry in China. "The whole country has become a giant brothel," she lamented. "Wherever you turn, you'll see girls selling their bodies: hotels, bars, restaurants, massage salons, barbershops. The tour service has also joined in. Many tourists have government or company money, which means they can spend big and free. *Da kuan da kuan, da bu guo gong kuan*—no matter how rich you are, you can't compete with government funds. When they book a tour, the first thing they want is a beautiful college student for their guide. She must be young and smart, with a good figure and fair skin . . ."

"And watch out for Sichuan girls," she warned. "Those spicy, bewitching girls will eat you alive."

Sichuan is known for beautiful girls with bright eyes, fair skin, and well-toned legs. Most of the beauties, however, came from Three Gorges, the land of clouds and rain. They say it is the morning mist and dusk drizzle that moisten women's skin and eyes. And the sweet water from the most spectacular mountains on Earth nourish the herbs that give women magic powers—making them hot, sweet, beautiful, vigorous, mysterious, and soul snatching.

Our guide snatched Evan's soul five minutes after we boarded the ship. She gave him a free pass to the deck, the best spot to view the river and gorges. I asked for one, arguing that I deserved the same privilege since I had also paid for a first-class cabin; she just laughed and took Evan to the deck where a party had begun with beer, music, and girls.

When Evan came down to use the bathroom, I confronted him in the hallway. We were supposed to find the dam migrants and interview them, and his job was to videotape our conversations.

"Relax, will you?" His voice was slippery from beer. "How do you know I'm not working? How do you know she may not turn out to be a migrant we could interview?"

"She may turn out to be a whore."

"You're jealous because she likes me," he said and kept walking.

"She likes your wallet, Evan."

"So what? Finally, I got someone who is willing to talk to me. Remember, mingling is part of our research."

I muttered under my breath. "Not with a prostitute."

He turned to me. "Since when did you become my social worker? She's a big girl, free to choose whatever she wants to do as long as nobody puts a gun to her head. It's good money, perhaps her only way to earn a decent income."

"It's evil money, too."

"You're judging. Besides, how do you know she doesn't enjoy it?"

"Oh, you must be having great fun judging China with your double-standard American human rights crap," I mocked. I knew I shouldn't. Evan volunteered as a human rights lawyer to help immigrants seeking asylum. He didn't have to. He just wanted to help. He meant well. I knew how much time and effort he put into this, having helped him with a Chinese case for two years. But his attitude about prostitution just rubbed me the wrong way.

His face tightened. "Do you know how many times, since we entered China, I've been pulled aside and told that you're not really a woman, definitely not a Chinese woman?"

"Yeah, that bitch. Her words count that much to you?"

"Other men and women said that, too. They called you *kuang*, maverick. No wonder your husband ditched you. You're too self-righteous, Ping. It's hard to be around you 24/7."

I banged my cabin door closed.

"Dear tourists," the megaphone blasted again, "who knows the love story between the goddess and the kings of Chu? And the poet who immortalized her?" Her sharp eyes swept across the crowd and fell on me. My heart thumped. Was she going to throw me off the first-class deck? But she looked away. Perhaps I, too, have become invisible, like the girl in white? No one seemed to have noticed her at all, including the eagle-eyed guide and my amorous colleague.

"Anyone?" the guide asked again. I almost raised my hand but thought better of it. Why push my luck further? Besides, the story belonged to the guide. She was, after all, part of the Wushan legend.

"Our goddess was immortalized by Song Yu, a royal poet, over two thousand years ago. When the King of Chu saw the cloud on the mountaintop rising and falling in the form of a lovely girl, he asked Song Yu what it was, and the poet revealed the following story:

"'Your majesty, this cloud is called "Morning Cloud." Long ago, when your father visited here, a beautiful woman appeared in his dream while he was taking a nap and offered herself to him. When he woke up, the only thing he could remember was the dream and a promise that he could find her again on the sun terrace of Wushan, where she lived as the morning mist and evening rain. For days, your father gazed at the mountains and saw the clouds and rains exactly as the goddess described. He named the peak as "twilight cloud" and built this Twilight Cloud Temple where we're staying now.'

"The young king asked the poet if he could meet the goddess too. So the poet wrote an ode to summon Wushan's spirits: its terrifying storms, melancholy cries from long-armed gibbons in the forests, and gods in forests. That night, the goddess came to his dream. She lit the room like the rising sun and softened it like the moonlight. Her skin was smooth and warm like jade, her face blooming like a flower. She was about to make love with the king, then changed her mind. At the threshold, she gave him a tender look that made the young king weep until dawn arrived. In the morning, he asked the poet to write another ode in memory of the goddess. Thus, the loveliest goddess was born. Her beauty has no match on Earth. Whoever sees her will be haunted for the rest of his life, for his longing will never be fulfilled, and his love will only leave him empty shelled.

"Alas, both kings of Chu lost their minds over the goddess. She had a slender figure, so the old king favored his women with a thin waist, causing many of his concubines to starve themselves to death. He exiled his minister Qu Yuan, who wanted him to fight back the king of Qin instead of chasing women, then ventured into his enemy's territory to seek his dream goddess, only to die there as a hostage. His son fared no better. Following the path of his late father, he trusted those who provided him with flattery and pleasures, allowing his country to fall further apart under Qin's attacks.

"In 223 BC, Qin annexed Chu. In 221 BC, China was united under the rule of the first emperor Qin, who burned books and buried alive intellectuals, astrologists, wizards, priests, and along with them music, dance, sorcery, astrology, medicine, ritual, and dreams, the fruit from the misty kingdom of Chu.

"Scholars believe the goddess toppled Chu, the most sophisticated of the three kingdoms during the Warring States. China would have been a different civilization if not for her."

The whole ship was now wrapped in clouds. It started to drizzle, but nobody moved. Even Evan, who was obsessed with his umbrella, stayed put. He seemed to have understood the story, though I hadn't translated a word for him. I raised my camera. The guide's wet face glowed with a melancholy beauty. Behind her, the girl in white gauze hung by the edge of the crowd, her feet dissolving into the mist, and the goddess peak half hidden in white clouds.

"Dear tourists," the guide's voice resumed her cheerful tone, "because of the love story, Wushan clouds and rains became the synonym for love, sex, fantasy, and unfulfilled desire. Thousands of poets have written poems about the goddess and Wushan—Mount Wu. It connects Sichuan and Hubei Provinces, Daba mountain range, and through its belly flows the Yangtze. The mountain runs like its name—巫—two humans floating between the sky and earth, two female shamans sitting between men and gods. They are the origin of Chinese medicine, astrology, astronomy, religion. They initiate men into the world of the invisible and connect them with the spirits and gods. They make them see, hear, touch, and feel."

I almost clapped. Amazing. A few hours ago, I'd despised her as a prostitute. Now I wanted to applaud her for making the best feminist manifesto! She had touched every passenger's heart, including mine.

Our ship was cruising through the impossibly narrow gorge, so narrow that I could see the deep holes in the cliff above the water, a path hanging like a thin rope. It looked ancient and crumbled, some of it submerged in the river. Could it be the famous *guzhandao*—the ancient road from two thousand years ago?

"Dear friends, we are leaving the Wushan Goddess and the last stretch of *guzhandao*—ancient trade path. If our goddess is the yin, then this road represents the yang of the Three Gorges. Even with our modern technology and equipment, it is extremely difficult to open a path along the cliffs. Can you imagine how our ancestors used their bare hands to drill over ten thousand holes and paved a road on the cliff? It's a miracle, a symbol of the wisdom and strength and courage, just like the goddess is the symbol of beauty and sex. For two thousand years, we've been walking on that path to fight enemies, carry food, salt, and other goods and pray to our goddess. Please take a good look at both, and say goodbye because our ship is leaving the Wu Gorge. In two days, the dam will be complete, and the river will rise to 175 meters, and the entire path will be buried in the water forever. Our goddess will be left alone on the peak, cut off from this world and the Wushan people. Thousands of us have left our land for this dam. We sacrificed our old homes for the sake of the big family. They say we're given gold and silver for our sacrifice, but let me tell you something, my dear friends, gold nest or silver nest, it's not the same as our old, mud nest. Scattered in strange places, we're homesick, homesick."

She was choking with emotion. I looked at Evan, hoping he'd whip out his video camera to capture this. We'd been traveling a whole week to find dam migrants for interviews, and here's our opportunity, and all Evan could do was to gaze doe-eyed at the guide. I raised my camera, but only white drops of rain appeared on my lens. I gestured wildly at Evan, but he ignored me. Was he losing his mind like the king of Chu? I started wondering if I should grab the video camera from him and start shooting myself when the crowd stampeded toward the counter piled with shiny souvenirs. The guide was holding up a gold-gilded book and shiny red brown mushroom.

"Dear friends, this mushroom, linzhi, is the magic herb that grows from the goddess's chest, the best love potion on earth. A girl takes it, and she becomes an alluring beauty; a man eats it, and all his fantasies will come true."

She tucked it in her bra, stem first. The mushroom appeared blossoming out of her chest. I saw Evan pushing his way toward her. He wanted to be the first to buy the magic herb. She raised the book above her head.

"This book is a collection of coins from the Warring State period that gave birth to our goddess, from the ancient graves about to go under the water. It is a limited edition of two thousand copies and since there'll be no more graves to dig after the water rises to 175 meters, your coin collection will increase in value a hundred-fold. Besides, 15 percent of the sale will go to the Wushan migrants. So I thank you, my dearest friends, for your compassion and support."

She moved behind the counter, where a long line had already formed. People thrust big pads of cash into her hands. By the time Evan managed to push himself to the counter, all the linzhi mushrooms were gone, including the one between her breasts. He grabbed a coin book, his first purchase in China. The guide gave him a smile as she took his money, eyes still wet from her speech. Suddenly, I realized how much she resembles the misty girl in white gauze. I looked back to the tip of the boat. My goddess had vanished, a cloud drifting away from the deck, up toward the peak.

A crowd gathered below to get off the boat. Our tour group split at Wushan Port. One group would sail into the Little Three Gorges, known for its jade bamboo on the cliffs, wild monkeys begging for corn, and locals singing love songs from their flower boats. The rest of us would continue toward Yichang to see the biggest dam on Earth. I heard a commotion among the first-class passengers and those from the hold. Everyone wanted to get off first and grab a good seat on the smaller boat. The guide hugged Evan and wished him good luck for the rest of his trip. To my surprise, she turned and hugged me tightly.

"Sister, it's really good to know you."

I lost my words. Her breasts felt warm and bouncy on my chest. "Thanks, thanks for your story," I stammered.

"It's yours, too," she said and then vanished into the cloud.

She left something in my hands. In my right palm, a red pass to the deck where I could see the river and mountains without obstruction. In my left, a giant linzhi shone with the color of red earth, glistening with her moist spirit.

"Can we trade?" Evan shoved his coin book to my face.

I held the mushroom to my heart. "No, it's my ticket home."

14

Petition

Forty percent of the budget for the dam went to the displacement. Theoretically, each migrant should have received a substantial sum, enough to purchase a new home and start a new life in a new place. By the time it trickled through the gates of bureaucracy, only a few thousand yuan remained for each individual, enough to buy a door, a few windows.

In the city of New Fengdu, I encountered the first angry migrant mob, after many days of searching along the river. I had entered the grocery store to buy a bottle of water and asked if they knew any dam migrants nearby. Immediately, we were surrounded. The crowd got bigger and louder, each trying to tell us their stories: cheated out of compensation by corrupt local leaders, cheated out of buildings with good locations for small businesses, cheated out of their fertile farmlands, cheated out of hope.

Wang Yu, the hotel boy who took us to see his new home, pulled my sleeve and whispered: "We must leave NOW. The cops arrested a dozen people here yesterday, including an eighty-year-old woman."

He was crying with fear. I told him to get into the car with Professor Evan, whose blue eyes and blond hair would complicate the situation if the police caught us. I had to wait for an old man to come back with his petition. I promised him I would not leave until he returned. He kept looking back at me as he ran, just to make sure I was not going anywhere.

I waited. The siren, faint first, was getting louder fast. The old man reappeared between the buildings, running. I waved. He hastened his steps. I could hear him wheezing, then his hot acrid breath on my face as he thrust a stack of paper into my hands. "My government in Beijing would not hear my story. Please bring this to America."

The siren chased us as we pulled away from the crowd. Wang Yu looked ashen. "It's over, it's over, I'm ruined," he murmured.

I stuffed the old man's petition into my bra. Our taxi driver made a few sharp turns in the alleys until we no longer saw the flashing lights behind us.

We took Wang Yu back to his hotel, since cops had surrounded his apartment building. We had met at the hotel where he worked as a bellboy. When he heard we had a hard time finding the dam migrants, he offered to take us to see his new home. His parents had gone their separate ways to find jobs when the dam demolished their old home, leaving Wang Yu, their only son, alone in the desolate new apartment, preparing for his college entrance exams while working as a bellboy in the hotel. He hoped to get into Dalian Naval Academy, established in 1949, when Mao liberated China with his Red Army.

I had tried to call him every day while we were in China. I would like to bring him to St. Paul as a foreign exchange student. He could finish his high school at Highland High in St. Paul then go to college. But his hotel manager told me he no longer worked there. His cell phone was canceled. A stranger was now living in his apartment.

I had a morbid feeling that the cops had gotten him. If it were true, his dream for the naval academy would have shattered, and I was directly responsible. Remorse flooded my heart.

I had asked Evan to keep the old man's petition in the secret compartment of his suitcase and sent its photocopy to his email address. If the police came after us again, he had a better chance to get out with his American passport. He would have a better chance of bringing the petition back to America.

Back in St. Paul, I opened the old man's petition. It was dog-eared, stained by sweat and tears. The title seemed to be inscribed with rusty-colored blood.

World, Please Hear Our Pleas!

All Roads to Lhasa

15

The Tiger Leaping Gorge

Welcome to Hutiaoxia, the Tiger Leaping Gorge. My name is Nima Zeren. Yes, I'm a Tibetan, your guide for the crown jewel of the Golden Sand River, the upper Yangtze, higher and more beautiful than Three Gorges, less populated, more pristine.

According to the local legend, a tiger leapt across the river to flee from a hunter, and the gorge has had the name since then. It's the narrowest point—eighty feet wide—of the entire river. The Golden Sand is one of the four major tributaries of the Yangtze. It flows through the northwest of Yunnan Province then continues its way into the Three Gorges. The geographical effect from the Qinghai-Tibet Plateau has created vertical differentiations in water and heat in the deep-cut river valleys, providing one of the world's most biologically diverse temperate ecosystems. It is home to many rare plants and animals. The Yangtze sturgeons swam from the sea to spawn here for millions of years. No earthquakes or even the Ice Age could stop them, until the Three Gorges Dam. The Yunnan golden monkey thrived here too; now, it's one of the most endangered primates on Earth. The mountains and rivers are home to at least 1,700 plant species, including many herbs used in our traditional Tibetan medicine.

See those patches of terraced corn and yam fields, scattered on steep slopes, under the tiny stone villages? They belong to the families that migrated here from the Three Gorges during famines or floods. Life is not easy here. Water is hard to get. You're smiling, professor. You don't believe me. Yes, the river has tons of water. Just listen to its roar ripping through the wind! And look at the giant boulders the water has carried here! Bigger than buildings. Do you know how long it takes to get down there and come back? A whole day! And that's for the mountain goats like us. For you, it'll take much longer. So our water has to come from distant waterfalls through a steel pipe around the mountain path. Lots of work to keep the pipe flowing, repairing leaks, preventing stealing . . . Sometimes bloody fights among villages during droughts.

Water keeps our population low, and the mountains clean.

So enjoy this terrifying beauty, still pristine, still untamed, but not for long. In 2003, the government invested 400 billion yuan and started building a dam in Xiluodu Gorge of the lower Golden Sand River. It would have been even bigger than the Three Gorges Dam, raising the water to six hundred meters high, flooding nine counties in Sichuan and Yunnan, submerging more land than the Three Gorges Dam. The construction started without much fanfare because the government wanted to avoid the media trouble, a hard lesson from the Three Gorges Dam. But Mr. Zhang, a hydraulic engineer from Beijing, heard the news. Mr. Zhang was born and grew up in one of the mountain villages here, where his parents and his uncles' families still live. He began to petition the government to stop the project. His endless pleas were like meatballs thrown into the dog's mouth: nothing ever returned. So he went back to his hometown and took the villagers to visit the flooded Three Gorges. They witnessed how the displaced people were stranded in their apartments, landless and jobless, their meager compensation vaporized like water. They witnessed young girls loitering in hotels, ports, and barbershops for clients, young men waiting on street corners with their yokes to carry goods for passersby for a few yuan, old men and women picking garbage or begging . . . Mr. Zhang collected thousands of names on his petition to the central government. Still no response. It was like a mud ox swimming in the sea with no hope of ever returning. Then he had a "heart attack" in his apartment, at the age of forty-four. He was strong like a horse, with no history of any health issue. Rumor spread quickly that he was murdered for his petition activity. Through media and the Internet, it spread faster than a flash flood. Soon after the New Year, 2005, Beijing halted the construction. Over twelve thousand workers went back home, even though the site had already been leveled and prepped for the construction and ten thousand people moved out of their homes. The reason: violation of environmental protection! Everyone believed Mr. Zhang's sacrifice made the miracle happen. Villagers set up altars and burn incense in his memory. He's become a martyr, a semi–river god.

Now the government has come up with a different plan: to build twelve elevated dams, starting from Xiluodu and ending here, the Tiger Leaping

Gorge, to bring water up to the same level where the abandoned dam would have brought it, but with much less flooded land. They've already started the prepping at all sites, the nearest one only a few miles away from here, at the Two-family Village. When it's complete, everything will change: the valley, the mountains, birds, fish, air . . .

I don't know where I will go then. I moved here to escape the city. After I got my economics degree from Sichuan University, I worked for a health food company, selling organic tonic boosters made from factory and restaurant waste oil. Every day, I felt nausea as I lied to the customers. When my father passed away from liver cancer, I went home and saw the half-consumed green-gold tonic my mother had bought for my father. I grabbed it and asked my mother how much my father consumed of this product.

"Five and a half," she said tearfully. "I wish I had known it earlier. I wish you had told me about it earlier.

"My father might be still alive," I shouted, tearing the packets into pieces. I called my boss and told him he could go drown himself in the muck of oil and lies. Mother cried. She and my father had pulled out their pensions to send me to college, and now this. How was she going to support herself at this age, with her husband dead, her son unemployed? I tried to find something in the city, for my mom's sake, but my boss had put me on the black list. And I didn't want to work another single day for those monsters. So when my uncle offered me a job as a tour guide and manager for his hostel, I came. My uncle started this tour business five years ago, Professor Zhang's Hostel, famous among the hikers all over the world. It's listed in the *Lonely Planet*. I help him with his business and make extra money as a guide. I get by. I don't care about becoming rich anymore. I would rather keep my heart clean. I have a lovely wife from the nearby village. We have a beautiful daughter. What more can I ask for?

But things will change when the dams are complete, when the water rises and my Golden Sand goes down. They say the dams will create clean power for cities and industry. Bullshit! The nearest factories and cities are a hundred miles away, blocked by high mountains. So where would the hydraulic power go? Oh, did I tell you these new dams would make power much bigger than the Three Gorges Dam? Aha, your mouth is wide open! When the river is raised to six hundred meters high through the twelve dams, the enormous power will be used to drill tunnels through the mountains and bring water to the west and north for agriculture and industry along the Yellow River. This is the biggest project in Chinese history, bigger than the Great Wall, Grand Canal, and

Three Gorges Dam. It'll divert water from the Tibetan Plateau to a very thirsty part of China—the west and north. The water will turn vast deserts into rich farmland, revive the dead agriculture and industry down the Yellow River, and transform them into China's Silicon Valley.

The whole world is watching. Tibet is Asia's water tower. Its snowcaps and glaciers feed its major rivers that flow into India, Burma, Laos, Vietnam, and China. If Chinese take all the liquid gold, all the rivers will dry up. All the countries will be screwed, including China. India has threatened to use nuke bombs. Other countries have brought complaints to the UN. But do you know what's the biggest danger? Climate change! The diverted water will dry up the wetland. Tibet Plateau will become the biggest and highest desert on earth.

16

Lhasa Square

Miss, miss, I beg you please don't take photos of those soldiers. They will smash my window and take away my license. Of course, they'll smash your camera. Perhaps you don't care. But I have to make a living. No, you can't shoot those people, either. They're cops in Adidas. Trust me. I've seen a lot of them since the uprising. Spies everywhere. In fact, everyone is a spy in this town. You can't trust anyone, not even yourself.

You're not from China. How do I know? I just know. You look Chinese but don't act like us. Are you from America? Isn't that country going downhill? Squandered all their wealth in Iraq and Afghanistan? I heard China owns all their debt now. Ha ha, who would have known ten years ago? Ten years ago, every Chinese wanted to go to America, including myself. But now every American wants to come to China to make a fortune.

Me? I'm from Qinghai-Tibet Plateau. Nope, not one of those nomads. I don't visit temples or fight on the streets. I work. I don't get money from the government. Oh, you don't know? The nomads get monthly stipends. How do I know? From my license training class. Do I want to be a Tibetan? Nope! There's no free lunch in this world. With the government money, the nomads can no longer roam with animals. If they want to visit relatives, they have to get permissions from a gazillion party leaders. What fun is left to live like that, confined to a plot like a cow, a yak, a sheep? I heard they're starving. Pastures have to be rotated every year or the grass won't grow. I know because I used to herd cattle. Well, I hope their monthly stipends will keep them alive. But are they grateful to the Communist Party? NO! They burn stores, smash windows, and want Tibet back, after what the government gave them: new roads, new railway, new buildings, new rules. Government lies? Tell me a government that doesn't lie! So why do I still believe them? I don't! These are just words they made us chant until they're engrained in our brains. They keep me safe. You never know who's taking a ride. Could be a spy. You could be a spy, too. Be careful. The men in Adidas are plainclothes. Don't point your camera at them. They're ruthless. They don't give a crap if you're American or Chinese or Tibetan. They will do whatever they want with you. Thank you for the business. Watch your wallet. Lhasa is not what it used to be. I never had to worry about my things or lock my doors. Now, everyone has become a thief since the railroad came.

17

Old Home

I'm from Shandong Province, Zhaozhuang, a coal city. Oh, you know that place? Your father worked there for three years? And your old home is from Shandong? What, your surname is also Wang? I can't believe it. We're *laoxiang*—folks from the same home. I feel so lucky. How's business? Not so good. Tourists are all going to Shanghai Expo. Everyone in Lhasa, except for the super rich and powerful, is suffering, hotels, restaurants, and of course, us taxi drivers. No, I don't own this cab. I rented it with a friend. We take turns driving, day shift, night shift, both have good and bad sides. We pay the owner a thousand yuan a day. If I want to make two hundred yuan a day, I'll have to make a thousand: five hundred for my share of the rental, three hundred for gas and maintenance. Lhasa is not a big city. Each ride costs ten yuan. So to make a thousand yuan a day, I have to pick up a hundred clients. There are so many cabs these days. Peasants swarm here every day from Sichuan, Qinghai, Shanxi, Henan, Ningxia, and other provinces, all hoping to get rich fast.

Is it possible to get rich fast here? Well, if you have special skills for high-paying jobs or capital to start your own business, then yes, it's very possible. But only a few people have that luck. Most people are like me: no skills, no connections, no money, only our youth and hope, and our willingness to work sixteen hours a day.

Or if you have the right connections. I mean the RIGHT connections. Everyone comes here through some kind of connection. My brother is an army officer here. He helped me get here and connected me to other Shandong taxi drivers. But that's it. He said I don't have skills for other jobs, and he doesn't have money to set me up for a shop or restaurant. So once a month, he takes me to a restaurant and we chat and eat and then say goodbye. Besides, he stays in Lhasa only half of the year doing his duty in the army then goes home to his wife and children in Chengdu or to some resorts by the ocean, designed for Tibet army forces to relax and restore their health. They get paid a lot for taking vacations. I guess their work here must be hard, though I can't really tell what they do exactly apart from patrolling the city and beating up the locals and some dumb tourists. Why didn't I join the army? I didn't finish high school. Besides, soldiers don't get such benefits. Only the officers. To become an officer, you need a college degree. To get a college degree, you need money.

My brother got lucky. My family could afford his tuition because our land was taken for mining the year he got into college. We were given a choice: half a million yuan cash or a job in the mine until retirement. My parents had passed their working age at that time, and my brother, who had just been admitted into a military college, declared he would rather die than become a *mei hei zi*—a black coal miner. I was only six years old, too young to work. So they took the cash, divided it into three, one for my brother's tuition, one for my future college, and one to open a restaurant in the city. The restaurant business went pretty good until my mother got sick with stomach cancer and she could no longer work as a chef. My father tried to cook himself, but he was just terrible and lost almost all the clients. So he had to hire a chef. All the profit went to the chef and my mother's medical bills. I was getting good grades at school. My teacher told me I could get into college, even a better one than my brother. I thought that would be my destination: college in a big city, perhaps Beijing.

Then one day, the city declared bankruptcy. The mine was depleted. Worse, the city was no longer safe because the ground underneath was hollow from the mining and could collapse any day. The whole city had to be relocated. Each family got ten thousand yuan for the move, enough to buy one square meter of a decent apartment. The city said that was all the money they had. But Zhaozhuang was supposed to be one of the richest cities in China. Where did all the money go? All stolen by those officials, who came in and out of our city at a fast speed, each got fat quickly from the coal money then left before they got caught. Coal is money, and there was a lot of it under our city. Whoever could get his hand on it got rich super fast. And who had the access to the black gold? You got it: the officials. The government caught a few and put bullets in their heads to scare the rest, but no use. If you don't accept bribery, you can't keep your position. So everyone steals. But the little people like us? We had to scramble for ourselves and get by from whatever trickled through their sausage fingers. When the city was gone, the fat cats scattered.

The only money left for my family was my college tuition.

So one night, I sat my parents down and said I was not going to college. They started weeping, saying I'm sorry, son, so sorry. They knew this was our only choice if we wanted to get out of the sinking city. You ask why my brother didn't help? He should and wanted to, as an oldest son who benefited the most from the family. But he's married with two kids, and he's henpecked. He said he would use his pocket money to buy me a plane ticket to Lhasa. So I moved my parents to a neighbor city, which was just discovered to be rich in coal. We got a cheap apartment at the edge of the city, crowded with other refugees from Zhaozhuang, and set up a small dumpling eatery in that neighborhood to keep them busy and alive. Then, I flew to Lhasa. That was five years ago.

I'm going home. I like Lhasa and the locals here, the nicest people on Earth: kind and generous. But I don't belong here. The land is harsh. The Tibetans have lived here for thousands of years, and their organs have adapted to the climate. Not us Chinese. Many of us have enlarged hearts and hardened lungs from the high altitude. I'm okay for now, but I can't guarantee the future. Besides, too many people here for too few jobs, and things are expensive. Everything has to be transported by planes or trains or trucks. It's hard to save in the city. My parents are getting old. They need me. And, I hope you won't tease me. I just got engaged. My parents want me to get married. This is the picture of her. Ah yes, she is beautiful. I still can't believe my luck. Why would such a pretty, smart girl want me, a lowly taxi driver? But she said it's hard to find a good man these days. She heard what I had done for my parents. She knows she can trust me; some things you can't buy with money.

So tomorrow I'm going home. Our encounter is a good omen. Tomorrow, I'll start a new life. My fiancée's father has found me a job in the mine. I'll go to an online college at night. I guess my karma is turning. A good woman is hard to find these days. When you find one, hang onto her like you hang onto a diamond.

18

The Grand Canal of China

No, I'm not from Sichuan or Henan or Shandong. I'm from Ningxia Province. No, I'm not a Tibetan or a Muslim or a Mongolian. Just because I have dark skin and a big nose doesn't mean I am not a Han. You have a big nose yourself. Does it mean you are Tibetan or Huihui Muslim? Yeah, I'm a Han Chinese, 100 percent. I can trace my ancestors all the way back to the Sui dynasty. When Yang Guang became the emperor, he appointed my ancestor to expand the old canal from Hangzhou to Luoyang, the capital of the Sui dynasty.

Your eyes popped. You don't believe me. How could you? But my ancestor did build the Grand Canal of China, 1,500 years ago, connecting the Yangtze, Yellow, and other rivers. It flows from north to south, through Beijing, Tianjin, Hebei, Shandong, Jiangsu, and Zhejiang, and empties into the Qiantang River and East China Sea. It's still the world's oldest and longest man-made river, and the largest irrigation and transportation system. I know you don't believe me. Yeah, sometimes I don't even believe it myself. But I can show you my family genealogy book at home. My ancestor designed the Great Canal for the emperor Yang Di of the Sui, and he totally regretted it. Why? Because the emperor was a tyrant and pleasure seeker. He built the canal so he could bring rare fauna and flora from the south for his new palace at the capital and launch wars. In 605, Emperor Yang Di levied a million peasants to start digging, and it took almost six years to complete the project. By the end of 610, this undertaking had involved more than 150 million man-days of work. The completion of the "Daoji Ditch" from Luoyang to the Huai River alone took more than five months, using a total of over a million man-days. In some places, even women were forced to work. Over three hundred thousand men and women died of starvation, fatigue, and illness, and many were simply beaten to death. The canal is about five thousand *li*, and each *li* is paved with fifty lives. More people died digging the canal than building the Great Wall.

As soon as the canal was built, my ancestor asked for the permission to retire to his homeland in Hangzhou. He sensed the anger among the people and the imminent toppling of the dynasty, and he wanted to keep his family safe. The canal originated in the mouth of the Qiantang River, where the king of the Wu dug the river to start the war on the kingdom of Qi, 500 BC. My ancestor built that river for the king, and it became the Grand Canal of China a thousand years later.

The emperor granted his request, on the condition that my ancestor accompany him from Luoyang to Jiangdu, now the city of Yangzhou, along the new canal. They set off right away because the emperor wanted to catch the blooming season of the rare qiong flower. The only place it would bloom is Jiangdu.

On the day of their departure, Emperor Yang Di and his wife boarded their dragon boats, four stories with palatial suites and a hundred luxury rooms, followed by thousands of ships carrying maids, servants, civil and military officials, nobilities, Taoist priests, and Buddhist monks. In their wake were several thousand more boats with guards and weapons aboard. Sailing bow to stern, these boats stretched a hundred and more kilometers. On the banks were eighty thousand boat trackers and two escorting cavalry troops. At night, the vessels lit up, and the sound of gongs and drums thumped through heaven and earth. Along the way, the emperor demanded the choicest and most exquisite foods, the most beautiful maidens. He determined the merits of his officials by the tribute they paid. As a result, officials along the canal resorted to ruthless extortion. At the end of the extravagance, the emperor returned to the eastern capital Luoyang. My ancestor continued his journey to the south along the canal and settled in his ancestral land of Shaoxing. Living in seclusion, he declined the emperor's invitations of three more "inspection tours" along the canal. When he heard that the emperor was strangled to death in the hands of the rebellious soldiers in Jiangdu, hence the collapse of the short-lived Sui dynasty, he wrote in his family book: "No man of the Kang family should work on canals or dams or anything related with water. Just stick to the land and live a peaceful life."

But water runs in our blood. It's our destiny, as all rivers run to the sea. No ancestral warning can stop it. Our family book shows that in every generation there has been a Kang man involved with water. They finessed the canal system and kept it running in perfect condition. The canal ended the Sui dynasty but brought prosperity to the Tang dynasty. When the Tang ended and the Mongolians took over, the Mongol emperor appointed my ancestor to expand the canal all the way to Beijing, the new capital of the Yuan dynasty. This is the canal we see today. The Mongols didn't last long in China, but the Ming and Qing dynasties really benefited from the canal, which created three of the most powerful cities in the world during their eras: Hangzhou, Xian, and Beijing, plus thousands of smaller but busy cities and towns along the canal.

Everyone knows the Great Wall of China. Only a few know the Grand Canal and what it means to the making of China. The Great Wall stands as a fence, a symbol of separation and enclosure. The Great Canal, however, links all the rivers of China together, an artery that brings culture, commerce, and wealth from north to south and vice versa, a true unification of China.

Don't think I blast my stories to every tourist I pick up. I don't. I tell you because you're not a tourist. No tourist would go visit a dam sixty miles out of Lhasa. What for? There's nothing there. No temple, no shop, no trees or grass, no humans. Just a river, rocks, and yaks. I tell you the story because you're interested in water. I smelled it the moment you got in my car. River runs in your blood too.

How did my family end up in Ningxia? Good question. Apart from having rivers run in our blood, we also have big mouths. Many of my ancestors were exiled or killed for advising the emperors to learn the lesson from the emperor Yang Di's disgrace: no extravagance, no new palaces or tombs, no heavy taxes on peasants. New constructions of canals and dams should have the sole purpose for irrigation and controlling droughts and floods. During the Qing dynasty, my great-great-great-grandfather got his majesty so mad that he ordered a thousand-cut punishment for his water minister—a slow, painful death. He was saved at the last minute by one of his old friends, also a minister. He suggested to the emperor that my ancestor was the last heir to the Kang family, and some day, he might be useful. So why not just exile him to Ningxia instead and have him fix the big bend area of the upper Yellow River, which had been causing many floods for hundreds of years? So my ancestor went straight from the execution ground into his exile, shackled and on foot, his family followed in a cart. They traveled two months to Hetao, the upper Yellow River, and settled down there. And we've been there since then.

Why did I come to Lhasa? You see, my ancestor tamed the ferocious Yellow River and transformed the place into a "Jiangnan on the Plateau." The rice and wheat from that region tasted so good that it became the emperor's special meals. The grassland raised the best horses for the royal armies, and the lambs produced the best wool and tastiest meat. Hetao, the big bend of the Yellow River, became our home, more beautiful and richer than our old home in Jiangnan, south of the Yangtze River. For hundreds of years, it was the most magnificent place on Earth, bounded by the Yin Mountains in the north, the Great Ming Wall in the south, the Ala Mountains in the west, and the Luliang Mountains in the east. My hometown is also called Yingchuan Plain, the silver valley. Why? Because the Yellow River used to flow through it like a white silk ribbon around a dancing girl's waist. Not anymore. Our Mother River's milk is polluted and dried up. My hometown has become a desert. My sheep and cattle all starved to death. We have no water to cook, feed animals, or wash ourselves. I felt so ashamed. Me, the descendent of the river experts, yet my son shares a shirt with me, and my wife and daughter smell funny when they bleed monthly because there is no water to wash themselves. I am not a man. I should just die.

A friend visited me and said there was work in Lhasa, restaurants, construction sites, taxis. The city was booming, and there was money everywhere as long as I was willing to work. I sold my last cow and bought three months' worth of potatoes and water for my family. "Just hang on until I send money back home within three months. If I make it there, I'll bring you over. If not, then you just get out of here and try to live on your own." We didn't sleep that night, just prayed and asked our ancestors to forgive us for abandoning their graves. The next morning, I walked twenty miles to the highway and hopped on a truck that was going to Lanzhou, where I sneaked into the train to Xining, dodging the cops because I didn't have money for a ticket. I got caught and thrown out before I reached the capital of Qinghai. Luckily, I got rides from a group of truckers that transported gasoline from Qinghai to Lhasa. I earned my ride by telling them stories, singing songs, and cooking for them. Oh, they loved my entertainment. The drive between Xining and Lhasa through the high deserts and snow mountains was arduous. The air was thin, the weather was cold, and roads were treacherous. Many of the drivers had purple lips and puffy faces from enlarged hearts due to the high altitude and lack of oxygen. But they needed money. Like me, they're peasants who lost their land to developers or deserts. Some have to pay medical bills for their family members who got cancer. The long road was full of them, carrying fuel, metal, wood, coal, food, clothes into Tibet, and taking herbs, wool, minerals, and other stuff out of Tibet. The job used to be done by Muslims on horses and yaks, but now there are so many people in Tibet, adventurers and dreamers, and the soldiers, the trucks and planes cannot bring enough food for them. That's why they built the railroad.

My new friends taught me how to drive a truck during the ride. When we got to Lhasa, they even helped me get a license so that I could drive with them and keep telling them stories. I did that for two years. The pay was good. I sent money home the first month and brought them over to Lhasa a year later. We rented a room from a Tibetan in the old section of the Bakhor. My wife set up a little stand on the street selling treasures from our hometown: Gouji berries and *fa cai*—the black hair fungus. People like it because of the sounds of the name: *fa cai*—get rich. Something to keep her busy and happy. For people like us, if we sit at home doing nothing all day, we'll get sick and die. Besides, she makes enough to cover the rent and some of her own pocket money. My salaries go to my son's and daughter's tuitions. They're good students, especially my daughter, number one in her class and in her entire school. Her teachers told us: if anyone can go to Beijing or Qinghua University, it'll be her. It's in our genes. My ancestors were all great scholars and scientists. Water is in our genes too. I know it'll cost a fortune to send them to college. But if she gets in, she'll be the first girl in our Kang family. I'll work myself to death to make it happen. My whole family will work ourselves to death to make it happen. Even my son said he's willing to give up college if she gets into Qinghua, and he will look for a job to support her. I said, "Son, if you can get in college, I'll beg from door to door to get the money."

That's why I started driving the cab. I took out every penny I had saved from trucking, all my wife's pocket money, everything from my kids' piggy banks, and bought a quarter of this cab with my friends. The new railroad brought millions of tourists to Lhasa, I mean millions, foreigners and Chinese. Tibet suddenly became the hottest dish, and everyone wants a bite. They swarm in like locusts. Some get sick and die, some get rich and stay, some look for troubles and get sent back home—it's all good. I was doing well in the first few years. But the train also brings thousands of peasants to Lhasa. And their only goal is to make money. And they have no skill other than driving a cab, if they are not hired to work on construction or service business.

Then the streets became flooded with cabs, the government raised the license fees, and the gas shot up like crazy. I don't get it. How can gas cost more when we have the train? I'm thinking of selling my share of the cab, but everyone else is thinking of the same idea. I am sinking again, like when I was back at home watching my house swallowed by sand, inch by inch, and I could do nothing. I don't know if I could send my son to college anymore, not even sure if I could send my daughter. I try to look cheerful during the day. Don't want to worry my family. They've suffered enough already. But at night, I cry and pray to the gods to pull us out of the rut.

I'm sorry to bother you with my troubles. Here's the place you want to see, the Zhikong Dam, built the year after I came to Lhasa, making hydraulic power for Lhasa, Shannan, and Naqu districts. You can't go in there. Soldiers guard it, surveillance 24/7. Crazy. Who'd dare to go in there to break anything? Ah, the water level behind the dam is low. How do I know? Just by looking at the flow. Lhasa River is getting smaller every year, as I told you earlier. The receding glaciers, the desertification of the grassland—I'm getting worried. The central government is planning to build many super dams, much bigger than the Three Gorges, on the major rivers in Tibet, almost four-thousand-meter-tall dams that would hold the water of about four Yellow Rivers. Tunnels will be drilled through the Himalayas so that the water can flow to the source of the Yellow River, to the deserts of Xinjiang, and to Qinghai and Yunnan. This will be the biggest water diversion project on Earth, bigger than the Great Wall, the dams in Holland, even bigger than the Grand Canal my ancestor built. And the cost? Trillions of yuan. If they really do it, my hometown will come alive again.

Am I happy about the project? No!

Tibet is changing so fast. All the rivers are shrinking. Lhasa River, Yaluzangbu River, Lancang River, Nu River, and Golden Sand River. When I was driving the truck between Xining and Lhasa, I passed by Sanjiangyuan, the three-river source. It's the origin of the Yangtze, Lancang, and Nu Rivers. It used to be the highest and largest wetland; now, it's becoming a desert. When the source dries up, what'll happen to the rivers in Asia? And the dams that hold so much water it's like creating five or six Lake Superiors on the plateau. How will it affect the climate? No one will know, just like nobody predicted the massive landslides and earthquakes after the Three Gorges Dam. The project is making India and other Asian countries nervous. I heard India threatened to use atomic bombs to stop the damming.

The railroad brings much stuff to Tibet every day, making life easier for sure. But at what cost? Look at the dust in the city from the construction and cars and trucks. Dust clouds the sky every day. Only afternoon showers clear it for an hour or two. Even the birds have stopped coming here. They used to cover the river in winter, black-necked cranes, whooping cranes, ducks, and many other kinds. Nobody believed it when I told the tourists that Tibet has warm winters and cool summers, and rain almost every day, and definitely the best water on Earth, clean and clear from the glaciers and sky. Now, look at the mountaintops around us, blasted for minerals: copper, gold, silver, zinc, crude oil, the largest deposits on Earth.

Hurry and take your pictures. The soldiers have already seen us. They have telescopes, powerful ones. And we're the only car far and near. Nobody comes here, as I told you. Shoot quickly and we go. I don't want to get caught and get a fine. Can't afford it anymore. Besides, they will crush the camera and give us a good beating before questions. You can't reason with soldiers with big guns. This dam is nothing compared to what they're planning to build—the ultimate "west-water diversion" project that will save China from the water crisis, as my kids chant every day.

You must know China's water-diversion super project—the three sections in the east, middle, and the west? The east line is complete, using the Great Canal to bring the Yangtze River to the north. Since it's so polluted, it can't be used even for agriculture. So nobody wants it. The middle line is almost complete, which will bring clean water from Danjiangkou Reservoir to Beijing, our capital that is sinking and dying from thirst. Thousands of miles of pipes are being built underground. Why an underground canal? To prevent evaporation, pollution, and stealing. It costs billions of yuan; yet, nobody seems to notice that the rivers feeding the reservoir are shrinking. When the reservoir dries up, the middle line will die.

Well, I think the government knows. That's why they put all the hope on the west line: the sky-river canal that diverts all the water in Tibet to the Yellow River and the western and northern part of China. My children are very excited, especially my daughter. She's a fanatical supporter of the water-diversion project. So is my son. But they're newborn calves who don't know the danger of tigers. They see only the temporary benefits of bringing water from Tibet to quench a very thirsty China, not the aftereffect of the diversion. I can't shake off the foreboding feeling of the emperor Yang Di, his downfall after the Great Canal. China is a superpower, but so were the emperors of the Sui, Tang, Ming, and Qing dynasties. They come and go, like the moon and tides. Yet, if Tibet becomes a desert because of the water diversion and global warming, the world will be in trouble. So perhaps I should listen to my ancestors' advice: no involvement in water projects. It may be the heaven's will that I can't afford to send my daughter to college. But I know she will go no matter what, even if she has to support herself by working in karaoke bars as a singing girl; I see the will in her eyes. I won't be able to stop her. So I stop worrying. If it's her destiny to shine, even for a brief moment, then let her be.

Let's go. Someone is coming at us. You can't see them. But my sixth sense can. Hop in. Hurry. Do you want to hear the story how Jiangdu got its name? The city used to be called Guang Ling—the grave for Emperor Yang Guang, the tyrant who built the Grand Canal. So the emperor changed it to Jiangdu, the river capital, hoping to avoid his death. But the name couldn't save him from his destiny: rebels strangled him and buried him in Jiangdu. If you ever have a chance to visit the city, you should visit his grave. Few people know it. You can admire the *qionghua* on his tomb, the heavenly jade flower that enchanted the emperor. He depleted the nation to build the Great Canal for a glimpse of its fleeting beauty.

19

Kelisu Diner

I wake up with a pounding pain at my temples. Altitude sickness? But I should have been acclimated by now, after three weeks in Lhasa. I take out my acupuncture kit and tap needles into my temples, neck, chest, and ankles to stop the pulsing ache. I swallow a double dose of the altitude sickness pills, stretch, meditate, pray, but the pounding won't go away. Perhaps some pumpkin rice porridge would help? A bowl of hot and sweet porridge would for sure give me some strength to fight the pain.

I get up and ring the bell at the front desk. The hotel manager staggers out to open the door padlocked from inside. I ask her where I could find pumpkin porridge for breakfast. She smiles sleepily, says we're in the Muslim and Tibetan quarter, and nothing would be open this early, and they wouldn't have the porridge I want anyway. But if I walk a few alleys this and that way, I should be able to find the street with Chinese restaurants, which might have it. She wishes me good luck, locks the gate behind me.

After needling through narrow lanes reeking of urine and shadows of Adidas plainclothes cops, I find myself in a square mobbed with men in black jackets, black pants, black beards, holding black scales. The only color is the yellow straw on their heads and the pink plastic bags in their hands. Nobody talks or displays commodities; yet, I know they're trading. The market hums with their heavy breathing. I squeeze through the crowd, shouting, "Excuse me, excuse me," just to break this terrifying silence that's not really a silence and to give myself some courage to walk through this black ocean of men. Nobody seems to hear or see me. Their eyes are locked on their partners', their hands reaching into each other's plastic bags, rubbing and weighing the contents inside, heads shaking or nodding as they "talk" deals. Far away over the ocean of straw hats, a man takes something out of his pink plastic bag and weighs it on a scale. I can't tell what it is, but by the delicate manner in which those rough-looking men handle their goods, it must be precious. And every man on this silent market seems to deal the same commodity.

I have my Canon with me, but I dare not raise it. This crowd holds a mysterious power over me, more so than those soldiers with machine guns and grenades who stop me several times a day, checking my camera and telling me to erase the content. I had fun playing hide-and-seek with the cops and soldiers. Not with this crowd, though. My "street smarts" won't work here. I can shout, push, and kick, but I'm a ghost, my presence carrying no voice, no weight or substance. I start sweating profusely. The morning sun stabs my eyes with its daggers. I'm dissolving like a vampire.

I stumble through the crowd and turn into an alley. Everything is closed except for one little store with a red sign in Arabic and Chinese: Heritage Chongcao Herb. I walk into the store with two small tables against each side of the wall and, in between, a giant refrigerator. Each table has four small folding chairs and two chopstick holders. It looks more like a diner than an herb store.

A woman clad in a black headdress comes out. "Hello, some breakfast?"

I point to the sign. "Chongcao herb for breakfast?"

She smiles, a dimple on her slightly puffy cheek, and I want to kick myself for being such a smart-ass.

"Oh, that. It was a chongcao store a month ago. I just rented this place and haven't had a chance to take it down yet. Besides, I need to come up with a name to replace it. Please take a seat."

"Do you have pumpkin porridge?"

I want to kick myself again. Of course she doesn't have it.

She smiles. "No, but I have noodles and buns and dumplings. Would you like to sit down and have some tea?"

Her smile is soothing like her voice. I sit down with my back to the street, which I dislike under normal circumstances. But I would dislike even more sitting with my back to the hostess. "I'll try a bun and a bowl of hot and sour noodles, just sour, no hot please."

"Just sour?"

"Just sour. Hot pepper gives me diarrhea."

She nods, pours me a cup of tea, then opens a giant steamer next to the refrigerator. "Potato filling or beef with garlic chives?" she asks through the steam.

"Beef."

She takes out a fluffy white bun and places it in front of me then pulls out a giant bloody chunk of meat from the freezer. It's a whole hind leg of a cow, almost as tall as the owner, hoof and hair still attached at the end.

"What's that for?" I point to the leg, slightly alarmed. Is she going to put it into my soup?

"For your soup." She walks into her kitchen, cradling the meat in her arms as if she were holding a baby, a man-sized baby.

I bite into the bun. It's juicy and tasty. There are lots of chives, for sure, mixed with shredded carrots. I can't find any meat. Is she really going to dump the leg into my soup? I'm getting worried.

"I thought it was a beef bun," I say through the window that opens into the kitchen. I can only see her back and the cleaver's up and down as she chops the frozen meat.

She pokes her face through the window, face flushing with beads of sweat. "I know," she smiles apologetically. "The meat price shot up like crazy, and I can't raise the bun price, or nobody would buy it. So I just put less ground meat and a bit more meat sauce in it. I'll chop more beef for your soup."

"It's okay, really. I don't like too much meat anyway. The bun is delicious, by the way. Can I have another, please?"

She gives me the second bun and fills up my tea before returning to her kitchen. The diner is tiny, and the kitchen, separate from the dining area with a window and thin wall, is even smaller. She moves gracefully in her confined space as she chops meat, makes buns, puts them in the steamer, and cooks my noodles all at once. It's 7:00 a.m. She looks like she has been working since 3:00.

"What's your name?"

She stops chopping, picks up the cow leg, and carries it back to the refrigerator then fills up my cup with hot water.

"You know, you are the first customer who asked. Nobody calls my name anymore."

I laugh. "How do they call you then? Can't just shout 'Hey, you' all the time. What does your husband call you?"

"Hey, you!"

We laugh together, then a brief silence before she goes back to chopping.

"Does he help you in the morning?" I ask, as I watch two construction workers rushing toward the diner, carrying their tin lunch boxes.

"Oh, he's busy at the market." She drops some beef slices in the wok and sautés them. The sizzling drowns her voice.

What market? I want to ask then realize it must be the silent one I just walked through.

"What are they selling there?" I ask, but the workers have burst in.

"Hey, you, *laobanniang*, sixteen buns, half potatoes and half chives, right away, and lots of hot sauce, quickly, quickly. We're late for work."

Laobanniang—female boss—that's what her clients call her. I bite into my second bun while watching her pour tea, bring out two dishes of red chili sauce, and pile two giant plates with buns. Her pale face is now red with sweat, and I wonder if she would ever remove her headscarf to cool off under any circumstance. Would she let me help? What's her husband doing at that market? He should help his wife chop and sauté or at least bring food to the customers . . .

The workers gobble down half of their buns and pack the rest in their lunch boxes. The older man pulls out a twenty-yuan bill and slams it down on the table.

"Change, laobanniang."

She rushes over with two coins. "Thank you, big uncle. Please come back tomorrow."

"We will if you put a little more meat in the buns, laobanniang. Still, how did you make your buns as juicy as these?" He leers and brushes his hand across her chest. "Are these your secret ingredients?"

She dodges. "Please walk slowly, big uncle." Her smile vanishes as soon as they step out of the diner. After placing the bill in her pouch, she starts cleaning the table. She moves slowly, as if that business transaction depleted her. So her buns cost one yuan each, less than the sum of a nickel and dime. If I drop the coins on the floor, my sons wouldn't even bother to pick them up. Yet, she has to get up before dawn to knead and raise the dough, to chop the vegetables, to roll out the skin, to make the buns one by one by hundreds, to steam them, and hopefully sell them all. How many thousands of buns must she sell to make some profit?

"Can I have another bun?"

I can't call her boss. It sounds almost like mocking. She works like a slave.

"The noodle soup is almost ready."

"Oh, but your buns taste so good."

She smiles, a genuine one because she knows I mean it. She opens the steamer and picks out the puffiest bun. "So glad you like it. I use my mother's recipe."

"What is it?"

Her eyes twinkle. "That's a secret. It's what keeps my business going. You see this location—deep in the alley, at the end of the market. Tourists won't find it very often, only those chongcao dealers who get hungry, or those who heard of my buns by word of mouth. If my rivals steal my recipe, I would be out of business within a week."

I nod. So that's what her husband is doing: trading chongcao, the worm that's eaten alive by fungus and turned into a root through the winter in the soil. Chinese people believe this fungus-filled worm can enhance their lung capacity and virility. The price reached sixty thousand yuan a kilogram around the 2008 Beijing Olympics. The herb is found in Sichuan, Yunnan, and the Qinghai-Tibet Plateau, but chongcao from Tibet scores the highest for its size and quality. Every early spring, the highland is packed with the Tibetans who own the land or by those who pay the highest bid to get a permit to search for the herb. They form a tight line and get down on their knees to comb through every blade of grass, and behind them are the Muslim traders who buy the herb on the spot. They are there because the worms become more scarce each year, and their presence at the site will guarantee that they get the precious herb, and most importantly the genuine one. Because of the price and scarcity, fake chongcao has flooded the market. Dr. Chi, my herb teacher at the academy, warned that I must not, under any circumstance, buy anything in Tibet, especially stones and herbs, and among the herbs, especially chongcao. "99.99 percent of the goods are fake," he said.

"Is your husband the first-, second-, or thirdhand dealer?" I ask the shadow in the kitchen.

I learned a little about chongcao from Mr. Ma, a fellow passenger I met on the train from Xining to Lhasa. Mr. Ma was a heavy smoker. So we chatted between the carriages where smoking was allowed. Tall and handsome, he moved like a wild horse.

"I've been a firsthand dealer of chongcao for ten years," he said proudly, "roaming and fighting like the American cowboys. Firsthand dealers must be young and strong and not afraid of fighting or dying. We travel deep into the Qiangtang Highland, above five thousand meters, where the air is thin and the best chongcao grows. We follow the nomads and collect the herbs they dig: hongjingtian, tianma, but chongcao is the most prized. We pay twenty to forty yuan each, depending on the size and condition of the plant. We sell the fresh ones right away to the local collectors for eighty yuan to two hundred each. The rest are dried and guarded with the greatest care until we reach Lhasa or Xining, where the herb could be sold for a tripled price to the storeowners—the secondhand dealers, who have street-front stores with lots of cash. They are the fat cats who control the chongcao market. The thirdhand dealers are individuals who hang out on street corners, markets, restaurants, selling to tourists and other thirdhand dealers. Their goods are scraps, small, broken, and glued together and often fake. I know you want to know why they would sell the fakes among themselves."

Mr. Ma threw his cigarette butt into the bucket that collected water from the hot water tap and lit another one.

"Something for them to do, I guess. Only the weak, sick, old, or the young in training do the thirdhand dealing business. Occasionally, they catch some suckers from Shanghai, Beijing, or America. Ha! I go there sometimes, just to hang out, greet old friends. It relaxes me. It takes a lot to be on the frontier. Every May, we rent a truck with a group of men. The roads are crowded with the nomads and their caravans. Often, the whole families come to hunt chongcao. Some nomads bring their cattle. We follow them, as if they were yaks and sheep. But sometimes when I'm too cold to sleep at night, I have this funny feeling that perhaps we are all nothing but sheep, shepherded by the frivolous desire of the invisible rich. But of course I can't tell anyone about this, or they would think I'm insane. The trip lasts about three months, until the herb becomes too old to have any value, and everyone's nerves are so tight that they're ready to kill whoever comes across their path. When we come home, our wives and children can't recognize us, skeletons in long beards. Sometimes, not all of us come home alive. But we see things that most people would never see in their entire life. The land is so high you can almost touch the sky. The air is so clean that you can breathe free, really free. And there are beasts everywhere: donkeys, gazelles, horses, yaks, all wild and beautiful, not like the tamed ones at home."

He sucked his smoke to the end of the butt, and exhaled, his chest heaving. "I can't wait to get home and get on the road again. Everything is ready, the truck, the men, the tents, and food." He looked at me through his ring of smoke. "You're welcome to come along if you think you can handle it. I know you can't stay that long, but you can always hop on the train if you want to go home."

I was dumbfounded by such a gift. What had I done to earn such trust?

"You're wondering why I'm offering this," he said slowly. "The truth is, I would like to make a connection in America for my daughter. She's a junior at Lhasa High School, a straight A student. I'm wondering if she might have a chance to go to college in America. You're a professor. Perhaps you can point her way there? She's fourteen, very beautiful and smart, almost too old and too educated to marry. No girl in my clan even goes to high school. Even if a man from my clan wants her, she won't be happy. I know her, a wild horse like me. She's the pearl in my palm. I want her happy, at any cost." Tears started pooling in his eyes. He turned to wipe his face. "Think about it and let me know. My truck leaves the day after we arrive in Lhasa. Here's my cell phone number. Call me if you decide to go."

I promised that I would be in touch no matter what and would do my best to help his daughter with her college application.

Lao Han met me at the train station. We hugged and joked like brother and sister. He had been my host in Tibet all these years and treated me like family. He seemed to remain the same: passionate, boisterous, and overflowing with life force. This year, he had put on weight around his belly. I patted and squeezed the pot. "Life in Lhasa is too good, Lao Han?"

He guffawed, but it sounded like sobbing.

I told him about Mr. Ma's offer on his chongcao hunt.

"Absolutely not, Ping! You'll never come back alive. The plateau will tear you up like a blade of grass, and those men, do you know what they carry with them on the trip? Rifles, guns, grenades. Why? Hundreds of thousands of people want chongcao, which has become scarce. Each year, the grassland is red with blood. If you go with Mr. Ma, I may never see you again."

"My husband's health doesn't allow him to travel as a firsthand dealer." The restaurant owner's voice is faintly apologetic and bitter. She places a bowl of soup in front of me. "Your hot and sour noodles. No hot in it." She fills up my teacup for the fourth time. The tea is now as bland as water. "Besides, we don't have that kind of money to rent a truck or own a store front."

"You have this store," I gesture at the place then feel bad when I see her face. "Sorry. It's a bad joke. How much do you pay for rent?"

"Too much. The owner wanted three thousand yuan a month. We argued that it's a bad location for business. At least five of them have gone south before us. He argued that it may not be the best location for chongcao business but may still work as a diner, especially considering I'd be the only one here. The store next door sells the traditional bread only. If only a third of the chongcao dealers from the market come to eat here, I would be rich quickly.

If we don't want it, there are plenty of other Muslims in town. We begged and haggled, and finally, my son-in-law came over and settled with him for two thousand."

I shiver as I try to calculate how many thousands of buns she has to sell to earn the rent. I take a sip of the soup, but I've lost my appetite. I feel a lump in my throat. Her husband should be here helping her.

"How much can your husband bring home from that market?"

She's silent for a while. "We're new here. Just moved from Linzhi a month and a half ago. It takes a while to establish business, any business."

"Linzhi? That's a rain forest area, rich and beautiful, I heard. Why did you leave?"

"Linzhi isn't our home. We bought a grocery store from a relative. But business was terrible. Not enough Muslims there."

"Where's your home?"

"Oh, we're from a small village in Qinghai Province, Maduo, the source of the Yellow River. Ever heard of it?"

Yes indeed. Maduo is known for its grassland. For years, it was the richest county in the whole country.

"Why did you leave Maduo?

She gives me a sad look. "Home is a desert now. No water. The trees are cut. The river dried. Animals died. Fields cracked. Nothing grows. Sand and rats eat up everything. Even our house. We left after my son was born. I told my husband that our son should have an education, perhaps go to college. So we went to Lanzhou, then Xining, then Tibet. We've been wandering for three years, like nomads, except we have no sheep or yaks, just ourselves. I do hope we can settle down here in Lhasa. My daughter lives here, and her husband's family is well-connected."

"Can she help you in the morning?"

"She has her own chores to do. Besides, she's still recovering from a miscarriage," she said slowly, looking at the dough and a giant tub of chive filling. "She may come later to help out. She's a good girl."

"How many children do you have?"

"Two, my daughter and my son. I lost quite a few in between."

"What about your husband? He probably can make more selling buns than selling worms."

She walks into the kitchen then looks at me through the metal window that seems part of her black lace headdress.

"It's not about how much he can make over there. He needs to be in his world. It makes him feel at home. It gives him hope."

What about you? I want to ask but know better and remain silent. Who gives you hope? Who makes you feel at home?

Six workers come in for buns. The place is getting too crowded. I stand up and gesture for my bill. "Thirteen yuan, please," she says, looking at my untouched beef soup sadly. I tell her I love the soup but had too many of her delicious buns. And I'll for sure come back for more, perhaps for lunch. I leave quickly. She chases after me with the change. I wave my hand, but she puts it in my palm.

"Just come back to see us," she says and runs back to her store.

I stand in the alley. To my left is the market. I can feel the heavy vibrations of the silent dealings. To my right is an empty alley. I walk into it. The sun is high up in the sky, but the alley stays in deep shadow. A few women with black headscarves open the front metal doors, revealing their merchandise: shoes, bags, belts, socks, shirts, pants, skirts, pots, brooms, dustpans. They all look puffy and tired.

"Where does this road lead?" I ask a woman with patches of powder on her face.

"Jokhang Monastery," she says, turning away to hang a black shirt with an Adidas logo on the right chest. It's priced twenty-five yuan. A fake that looks real. I can have an Adidas shirt for four dollars.

The alley actually leads me to my favorite teahouse, Makye Ame. It's said that the great poet, the sixth Dalai Lama, frequented the place in search of a beautiful girl, whom he believed to be the Goddess Tara. I come here every day because of the location—the center of Barkhor Street, the center of Lhasa, and the third floor, where I can see the entire market.

I order a thermos of yak butter tea and pick a place where I can see the crowd moving clockwise. Everything remains the same, the throbbing crowd, the waiters, the music, and the smells. The only differences are the patrolling soldiers in camouflage and secret police in black uniforms or Adidas under the Coca-Cola umbrellas. Their number seems to exceed the throngs of the pilgrims and tourists. I pull my camera away from the street. Two soldiers on the rooftop next to me are looking in my direction through their telescopes, their machine guns glistening like knives in the sun. No need to bring trouble to the restaurant. I point my camera at the mountains far away. The snow and glaciers are gone. The peaks look bare and vulnerable. The tea comes. I pour a cup for myself. It looks weak and doesn't have the thick, strong flavor that comes only from yak milk. Lao Han told me that real yak butter could be found only in monasteries or in nomads' tents nowadays.

I take out my notebook and write down the date: May 10, Makye Ame. I want to write about the diner, but my mind is a junkyard full of scraps. The three buns sit heavily in my stomach. The owner's face floats in front of me. I want to help her, but how? I don't even know her name.

I get up. The waiter rushes over. "No lunch here today?"

"I promised someone to have lunch at her place."

"Not thirsty?" He picks up the full pot.

"It was delicious, but I've got to go somewhere."

I join the clockwise flow. With so many police and soldiers, even the peddlers from the stands on the Barkhor seem much more subdued. They used to surround me and thrust their stones, knives, swords, and scarves into my face, shouting "cheap, cheap, buy, buy." Now, they just sit behind their goods, watching through the curtains of pearl necklaces that hang over their stands. Some of the owners seem to have given up. They gather together and play cards. Or perhaps they're fake business owners who don't have to sell? Lao Han warned me to be careful with my words on the streets, especially on Barkhor. Half the business owners are actually spies.

I walk through the market packed with prostrating Tibetans, sitting tourists, guards in full armor. The sun blinds my eyes. Troupes of soldiers in yellow and green camouflage thread through the market like pythons. Camouflage is the fashion of the year. Soldiers, gardeners, cleaners, teenagers, even kids, are wearing it.

I approach a stand that sells prayer flags and incense. The owner is shouting his bet to his card partners. I ask how much the flags cost. He barks out a price then goes back to his gambling. A woman with a Sichuan accent sells me five prayer flags and two bags of peace knots. I have promised my Buddhist friends in the Twin Cities that I would bring back something from the monasteries in Tibet. I asked Lao Han what I should bring back as gifts. He said nothing is cheap here anymore. A decent tangka costs at least one hundred thousand yuan. He laughed when he heard me gasp. Yeah, a masterpiece starts at a million. So that was out. Jewelry? Everything is fake. You can't believe anything they say except for one truth: nothing is real, said Lao Han.

"Perhaps some prayer flags for your American Buddhist friends?" he suggested, when he saw my disappointment. "And get them blessed in Jokhang

Temple? There is a lama there under the Buddha's feet. Just donate something, and he will bless your presents."

I find the ticket window and pay eighty-five yuan for the entrance fee. The monastery must do extremely well, since it receives thousands of visitors every day. I follow the crowd into the dark temple. In the main hall, rows of lamas in red robes chant in unison, each with a bowl of yak butter tea and bills of twenty-, five-, and one-yuan notes piled in their laps. Money floats everywhere: in donation boxes, under Buddha's feet, in every crack and corner . . . The whole Jokhang Temple, like all other temples in Lhasa, seems to float in a sea of yuan. Does Buddha want all of this? I gaze up at the gilded statue studded with gems. The line to Buddha is endless. Everyone waits to touch his foot for good luck. The poor want to be rich. The rich want to be richer.

Two lamas behind the desk take in the donations and write down the donors' names. A new lama comes over to help as the line gets longer and thicker. People before me and behind me, mostly Hans, wave wads of one-hundred-yuan notes. I planned to donate fifteen yuan, the change I got from buying the ticket. Now I wonder if it might be too little. But Lao Han said it doesn't matter how much I give, as long as my motivation is pure. I just want to bring some blessed items to my Buddhist friends in Minnesota. Is it pure enough? Perhaps I should bring something to the diner owner. Perhaps a peace knot? Would she accept it? Would it be offensive to her? She's Muslim, after all. The lamas chant in a low voice, intermingled with a high-pitched singing. A young lama, no more than twelve years old, is singing at the top of his lungs, swaying and laughing at the same time, money spilling out of his lap.

I finally get to the lama and hand him a one-hundred-yuan bill. This is all I can give. China is getting expensive, and so is Tibet. The ticket alone from Minneapolis to Shanghai was $2,700, and the hotel would have cost me two thousand yuan a night if Lao Han had not helped me get a discounted rate. The lama takes the money and waves me to the Buddha without looking up. I'm about to ask if he would write down the names of my friends as blessing when I see the amount of money recorded in the book: five thousand yuan: Mr. Wang Kai; ten thousand yuan: Mrs. Li Feng; one million yuan: anonymous . . .

Only the rich get their names written in the book. Capitalism has reached Tibet.

I walk over and brush my prayer flags and peace knots against the Buddha's foot. May Buddha bring peace and happiness to my friends and some luck to the Muslim woman at the diner. May she get some help making buns. May she sell all her buns every day. Around me, people kiss the Buddha's feet and pray, the shine from their diamond rings, earrings, and jade bracelets mingling with the Buddha's jewelry. How much richer do they want to be? The smoke from the lamps and incense chokes me. I walk out into the sun.

It's 11:00, too early to go back to the diner. A taxi stops next to me. The driver doesn't say a word or look at me, just sits behind his wheel smoking. I get in and open the window as wide as possible. Every taxi driver in Lhasa chain-smokes. We sit until he tosses his butt out of the window.

"Where?"

I look at the red thread in his braid coiling around his head. A Kangba Tibetan. I look down. No Kangba knife around his waist. This is something new. Kangba men never leave home without their knives, which are decorated with precious stones and silver. Lao Han told me that knives had been banned since the 2008 uprising.

"Do you know a temple that doesn't require money to enter?"

He smiles and lights a new cigarette. "There's no such a place in Lhasa anymore. But I can take you to the temple that has the lowest fee."

"Let's go then."

The streets are packed with people: soldiers, tourists, and pilgrims. The air is thick with the exhaust from taxis, army vehicles, and trucks loaded with construction materials.

"How's business?"

"Okay. Tourists went to Shanghai Expo this year."

"How long have you been a taxi driver?"

"Two years."

"You like it?"

"No. But I don't have a choice. Someone from Beijing bought my land, in fact bought the whole mountain where my village used to be. They wanted the minerals underneath, copper, gold, and other stuff. They came and blasted the mountains. Dust everywhere, water poisoned, yaks died from the water. We protested and got arrested. They were backed by the government and Australian mining companies. What can you do but leave? They paid me some money. And I used it to buy this car. I don't have skills other than riding horses and herding. But we have to eat. And I want my son to get some education. Perhaps he could have his own business like those Sichuan people." He pointed to the stores and restaurants along the street.

"Why didn't you open a business yourself?"

He laughs. "I don't know how to read or write Chinese. How can I compete with them? They have their tightly knit networks, those Sichuan people, the biggest population in the city, then people from Shaanxi, Shanxi, Hunan, Shandong . . . They swarmed here with one goal: make money. And they have a few thousand years of experience in their blood. They laugh at us, say we nomads only know things by piles, like yak dung piles, black tea piles, salt piles . . . It's true that until recent years, we had been trading goods by sheep or yak. The Muslims were our middlemen. They brought us salt, sugar, tea, and clothes in piles and traded for our animals. We didn't know much about money, cash or checks, let alone credit. You Chinese have money running in your blood, and ours has only yak, horse, sky, and Buddha."

We're out of the city center now. No tall government or commercial buildings on either side of the street. Only shabby small businesses that sell Sichuan food, bike parts, and used cell phones. He stops next to a bus stop, in front of a small market.

"Here it is."

The market sells dried junipers, incense, bottles of white spirit, and turnips. All the buyers and sellers are Tibetans. I smile at the goods arranged and sold in piles. No tourists. No patrolling soldiers. Only one guard in a black uniform squats at the gate chatting with a turnip seller. I look into the smoky yard and see a small monastery. It has a gilded rooftop, dimmed by years of smoke and dust, and the beams need lots of repair. Still, it's busy, its visitors all Tibetans with incense and bottles of liquor. What's that for? Buddha likes yak butter, not alcohol.

"What temple is this?"

"Zhaji. You owe me ten yuan."

I hand him the bill, thank him, and get out. A bus stops by and unloads a crowd of women with children. I follow them, past the guard who's still chatting with the young woman, past the closed window that has a sign: Ticket—15 Yuan. I look back to make sure that nobody is chasing after me. Amazing. This is the first free temple I've visited this year.

I join in the long line at the door. It leads to a small sanctuary on the left. I look in, but the crowd and a gigantic trough block my view. Two monks take the bottles from pilgrims' hands, and pour the liquid into the trough. They work fast, never stopping to look up or wipe the sweat from their faces, but they still can't keep up. Another monk runs over to help. The temple reeks of alcohol.

What's going on here? Monks are not allowed to touch alcohol, let alone drink troughs of it. Is it for lighting lamps? I look around and see the lamps fueled by butter, not the sixty-five-proof white spirits. Two rows of monks chant on mats, some eating balls of barley flour mixed with tea.

Interesting! I raise my camera and look around for "no photo" signs. Nope. The only sign I see, and immediately I find it everywhere else, is the warning of pickpocketing. Strange. The visitors here seem poor. And the money in their hands are one- or fifty-jiao bills, one-tenth or -fiftieth of a yuan, occasionally one- or five-yuan bills. No one has the pink one-hundred-yuan bills like those in Jokhang Monastery. I look again to make sure there's no guard. I take one shot of the liquor-pouring monks, then the chanting monks. Nobody seems to care.

I ask a young woman what the liquor is for.

"For Goddess Zhaji. She helps women get pregnant, stops their husbands from beating and cheating on them, and helps their children get into college."

"What about them? What do they want?" I point at the men.

"She's also a goddess of fortune. She helps them get rich."

"Is that why she drinks so much?"

She laughs. "There is a story behind it. I'll tell you later. She's good at helping people, especially if she likes the bottle she's given."

I laugh and remember the Muslim woman from the diner.

"Could you hold the spot for me, please? I need to get something. Will be back in a minute."

She nods approvingly, knowing what I'm trying to get. I run outside. In the atrium, two monks are selling bottles at a stand. Two brands, one four yuan and the other eight yuan. They look exactly the same, both clear, both with a red label. The only difference is the price.

"This one, please," I point to the eight-yuan bottle. Hopefully, the goddess can tell the difference.

I run back. The woman is handing her bottle to the monk at the trough. I get there just in time. The other monk takes mine and pours it all into the pool of white spirit, where the cheap and expensive liquors mix together.

I follow the crowd into the little sanctuary and see Goddess Zhaji. She looks entirely different from all the deities I've seen. A mop of black hair tangles around her shoulders and chest, a red tongue sticks out of her mouth, and her wrathful eyes are wide open. She looks more like a drunken ghost than a goddess. The woman I talked to is kissing Zhaji's foot and touching it with her white hada while praying rapidly in Tibetan. Around me, everyone is doing the same. I take out my bag of presents that contains the peace knot and prayer flags and brush them against her feet, press my hands in front of my chest, and pray for the Muslim woman and her business, for my children to grow up healthy and happy and get into college that may lead them to good jobs, for the oil spill in the gulf to stop soon, for my friends, and my own peace of mind. When I'm done, I feel dizzy, as if I was drunk from breathing the ethanol air. I look up. The goddess looks less angry. Perhaps she likes my bottle?

The young woman is gone. I go into the main hall to look for her. I want to hear Zhaji's drinking story, but she has vanished. I look up at the deity, a regular one just like all the Buddha statues I have seen, tall, big, gilded, covered with precious stones and money, but he doesn't send shivers down my spine like Zhaji. I take a shot of the monks seated in front of the Buddha, wondering why I didn't photograph Goddess Zhaji, when suddenly someone grabs my arms, almost lifting me off ground as he pushes me to the door. When he puts me down outside the temple, I turn and see a stout monk in his forties, his tan bare arm thicker than my thigh, his eyes bulging and angry like Goddess Zhaji. Before I can say a word, he points at my camera and shouts in Tibetan. I can't understand a word, but I know he's mad.

"There's no sign here that says I can't photograph," I say.

He glares at me, legs apart in the warrior's stance.

"I can pay." I take out my wallet, trying to remember how much a monastery would usually charge to take photos. Twenty-five yuan? Thirty yuan?

"Out!" he shouts in English, pointing to the gate, his face redder than that of the guardian deity overlooking the threshold of the monastery. In fact, he resembles the ferocious guardian deity on the wall behind him.

Did I hear him speak English? Perhaps I heard it wrong? His anger, however, earns my respect for him. Finally, someone I can't buy with money! I bow and apologize in English.

"I'm truly sorry. Please forgive my ill manners."

His face softens. "Where from?"

"America." So he speaks English.

He nods, a tiny spark in his eyes. "New York?"

"I used to live there, twelve years. Now I live in St. Paul, Minnesota, ten years." I speak very slowly, using my fingers to illustrate the numbers, but he still looks puzzled, and his eyes wander away to the monks folding sutras in yellow silk at a table nearby. I whip out my BlackBerry and type my address in St. Paul into the Google map.

"Look, here's where I live, on the Mississippi, the biggest river in America. My house is across this bend, Fort Snelling, where two rivers meet, the Mississippi and Minnesota." I am confident that he will understand as I trace the rivers, streets, and my house with my finger. For the first time, I'm grateful to my BlackBerry Storm. All the troubles I had with my phone become worthwhile. Other monks gather around us, smiling and laughing.

He looks into my BlackBerry and murmurs, "Mississippi, Minnesota," saying each syllable slowly as if he were chewing the sounds. Suddenly, he points to a little dot under the bend. "Indians?"

I'm shocked. His finger is right on Pike Island, a small island created by the silt from the Mississippi and Minnesota. This place used to be, still is, sacred to the Sioux Indians and many other tribes, regarded as the origin of the world. In 1805, the U.S. government wanted to build a fort in this area to protect the fur trade and bought one hundred thousand acres around the area. They agreed to pay $200,000 for the land, yet only paid $2,000 when Fort Snelling was built. The Indians starved from the loss of their hunting and gathering land and from the government's failure to send them food or other provisions according to the treaties. In 1862, they rebelled, led by Little Crow. The Indians lost and sixteen hundred men, women, and children were held as prisoners on Pike Island. Through the winter, hundreds of them became sick and froze to death. The rest were exiled to Crow Creek in South Dakota, where many more died from the worst drought in Dakota history. After the war, the Sioux people were banned from living in Minnesota.

How can I explain it all to him in English or any other language?

I touch the island with my fingertip. "It's a place full of dreams, tears, and blood," I say, first in Chinese, then in English.

He listens with eyes closed, his lips trembling as if he were praying. I know I don't need to say more. He gets it all, the sorrow of that place, of any place. Pain may not be well expressed in words, but it can definitely be felt across space, time, and culture between the bodies that know the taste of sorrow.

He looks at me now, his moist eyes as clear as the blue sky. "Thank you for sharing the story."

I bow. "Would you tell me the story of Zhaji? Why does she like to drink?"

He laughs out loud, and I start laughing too, though I have no idea why I'm laughing. It just feels good.

"Zhaji is from China," he finally says, wiping tears with his sleeved arm. "She ran away from home with her lover, who sold her to a brothel when he lost a card game. She wanted to go home, but her parents had disowned her. She drank herself into a stupor and drowned. Her homeless soul wandered along the Yangtze. A lama took pity on her and brought her to Tibet and built a sanctuary in Lhasa. She has become a deity for women since then, a pretty good one, depends on her mood and how much she drinks. After all these years, she still prefers white spirit to yak butter. By the way, would you like some tea?"

"Yes! I love yak butter tea."

He looks pleased and gestures to a young monk to pour me a cup. It looks real, yellow cream floating on the top like honey.

It tastes real, too, salty and pungent and rich. The dull pain in my head goes away.

"Thank you for the tea."

"Thank you! You're the first Chinese I know who likes our tea."

Two monks push the full trough out of the temple. Another two monks bring out the buckets full of empty bottles. The four of them start refilling the bottles with the alcohol in the trough.

"Recycling?" I point to the scene.

My monk friend smiles and sips the tea.

"Why two prices?" I point to the liquor stand.

"Same difference," he says slowly. Seeing the confusion on my face, he adds, "Chinese, Tibetans, Indians, Americans—same difference. Joy, pain, kindness, cruelty, life, death—same difference. Four yuan or eight yuan, you give what you want, what you can. Money is not a bridge to the heart of the goddess. It's the intention that counts in the end. Same difference."

We sit in silence, drinking tea. No more words come to us. No need. Thick smoke wraps the temple like clouds. Bells and chanting float from the dark interior of the temple. Warning posters about thieves cover each column and window. The monks take the refilled bottles to the stand, which are quickly grabbed by the waiting worshipers. Four yuan or eight yuan, same difference. I don't have a blessed scarf for my Muslim friend. I only have my thoughts and wishes. Same difference.

I finish my tea and bow. "Thank you so much, master."

He bows back. "Have a safe trip."

I walk into the sun. My eyes don't sting as usual. The yak butter tea gives me strength to endure the strong light and high altitude. My phone beeps. Lao Han texts me, inviting me to a tea party in a five-star restaurant at 4:00 p.m. I know there will be food, the expensive kind. But I have promised to eat lunch at the Chongcao Diner. I look for a taxi. There is none. Outside the gate is the bus stop. I have no idea where it goes. Should I just take it? People say all the roads in Lhasa lead to Patola Palace and Barkhor Market.

"Just cross the street and you can get a taxi from the Minzu Hotel. It's a five-star hotel, with good services," says the guard, looking up from his chat with the turnip woman. She hasn't sold a single pile of her turnips, and yet, she looks as content as a clam in her rags. I feel a pang of envy. One can read ten thousand books and still can't reach that level of enlightenment.

The taxi takes me to the chongcao square. "No, not here." I say. "Can we go to the diner from a back alley?"

"I can't go further. You have to walk," he says and speeds off quickly after he takes my money. I look. No more men in black suits and straw hats. The square is abuzz with the noises from selling vegetables, meat, shoes, socks, pots and pans, noodles. Watching people eating makes me hungry. I dodge patrolling armies and children running around through the stands as their mothers bargain with the sellers. I smell the sweetness of melons, apples, pears, watermelons, tomatoes . . . the fruits that used to be brought in by planes but are now grown by Sichuan people in the greenhouses rented from Tibetans. Most of the peddlers are Muslims. The atmosphere is so cheerful, even the soldiers seem less threatening.

In the diner, a young girl is persuading a child to eat beef from a bowl of noodles. It looks like the bowl I left behind that morning. She looks up and smiles.

"Welcome. Please sit down, and I'll bring you tea. What would you like for lunch?"

She smiles exactly like the owner. Both have fair, smooth complexions. But she can't be her daughter, married for three years. The girl looks fourteen. The boy looks a bit small for a four-year-old, but he must be her son. Who is this young girl then? His babysitter? Where is the owner?

"Welcome back." She walks out from the kitchen, eyes sparkling. "Did you have a good morning looking around? You must be hungry now. What would you like?"

I order spicy dumplings, the most expensive item on the menu, and two buns. "No chili pepper, please."

The girl giggles, covering her mouth with her hand. She has white teeth, slightly crooked, but they make her even lovelier. The smiling mother slaps her head gently and scolds her. The girl sticks out her tongue and brings me a cup of tea.

"Your daughter is beautiful," I say to the owner. "I didn't know you have two girls."

"I have only one daughter. Still like a child, though married for three years. When is she going to grow up?" She pats her daughter's cheek affectionately and enters the kitchen.

My chin drops. Everything about the girl—the blushing cheeks with baby fat, the down hair around her lips, slim wrists and hips, and shy smile—indicates she's just a girl, no more than thirteen. She can't possibly be a woman married for three years, or have had a miscarriage.

"How old are you? What school do you attend? What grade? Your favorite teacher?"

She giggles, and her face becomes shadowy as I shoot one question after another.

"I'm sixteen. I quit school when I married."

"What's your favorite subject?"

She looks up, eyes moist. "I like to read and write."

I perk up. "Stories, poems?"

"Stories. I like to read and write stories."

"Do you still . . . ?"

She shakes her head. "No school for the married. Home is busy. Have to cook for my husband and his whole family, parents, brothers, and sisters. I didn't really know how. I do know how to cook for a few people but not for so many. They are nice to me and don't complain much. But I can tell that my cooking isn't up to their standard. When I have time, I go help out in my husband's store. He sells flour, rice, dried noodles in Lhasa. If I still have time, I come here to help my mom."

"Do you miss school?"

She shakes her head again then nods. "I was a good student. My teacher wanted me to finish middle school, perhaps go to college. But what did she know? No girls in our village finish middle school, let alone college. If we don't get married by age fifteen, people start talking and looking at us weird as if something is wrong with us. By eighteen, if we're still single and live with our parents, we become official spinsters and have little chance to marry, and the whole family will be shamed."

"How old are you, really?" I stare at her hard, hoping to find the truth. The more I look, the younger she seems.

"Sixteen." She looks at me in the eyes.

"Isn't it illegal to marry before you turn eighteen?"

She rubs her thumb and forefinger together. "Chinese say money can make ghosts mill flour. For two hundred yuan, we can change our birthdays. So, officially, I am twenty-one." She laughs. I laugh with her, but my heart aches when I see her childish face crunching like a little old lady.

"How did you meet your husband?"

She blushes. "I married my cousin. I was betrothed to him when I was six."

"You love him?"

She giggles, covering her mouth with her hand again. "We get along. He's three months older, so we're almost like brother and sister. I grew up alone as a child. My mother lost a few babies before she had my little brother. When he was one, my family moved to Lhasa. So it's nice to have someone to talk with and play with. Just wish I had more time with my husband. He's so busy in his store, working seven days a week except for holidays."

Her brother tugs her sleeve and points to the grocery store across the street. She holds his hands firmly. "No, no candy unless you finish the soup," she says. The boy blinks his eyes and cries. The mother comes out with my dumplings. She places them in front of me and picks up the boy.

"Baby, baby, don't cry. Eat the soup, and we'll get you some candy."

She looks up apologetically. "All he wants is potato chips and cookies and candies. I know it's not good for him, but we got him so late and he's sick a lot. So we spoil him."

The boy tugs his mother's scarf and points at my dumplings.

"No, baby, no, you have the beef and noodles. Eat this," his sister says.

I pour half of my dumplings into an empty bowl. "Please, I can't finish this anyway. Let him help me."

"Thank you. But this is too much." The mother goes back to the kitchen as if ashamed. The girl picks up a dumpling with her chopsticks, blows on it, then feeds it to her brother. He takes a bite, frowns, then spits it out. His sister scolds him. The boy cries, pointing to the store, his sallow face wrinkled. He is thin and small for a four-year-old and really crabby.

"Is this chongcao?" I point to the plastic cup that holds three wormlike plants.

She looks up at me. "Yes. My father brought it home during lunchtime."

I pick one up. It looks exactly like a worm, head, wrinkled body with legs under the belly, and tail, but it's hardened like a root, with a dried sprout through its mouth. Mr. Ma told me that chongcao's full name is *dongchong xiacao*: a worm in winter and a plant in summer, or Chinese caterpillar fungus. In the fall, bat-shaped moths lay eggs on the highland grass. Larvae hatch, grow fat, and some of them get infected by fungus, which absorbs nutrients from the larvae to replicate itself. In pain, the larvae crawl into the soil, always heads up, and die slowly in the winter, becoming young chongcao. In May, June, and July, fungus bursts out of each larva's mouth and blossoms into a tiny purple flower. If it's picked on the first day of flowering, the herb will be the most potent. By the third day, the plant is nothing but worthless weed, losing all its medicinal potency. Mr. Ma also said this worm plant, if real, benefits every organ in the body, kidney, lung, liver . . . It heals bloody sputum, night sweats, coughs, impotence, pains in the back and legs, the hepatocirrhosis from hepatitis B. If one takes this often, he will stay healthy, strong, and peaceful and live to be 120 years old.

I lift the herb to the sun. The worm plant looks perfect and real indeed. It's so tiny and light. It takes tens of thousands of them to make a kilogram. Mr. Ma said often a hunter would search a whole day without finding a thing. Every year, the vast grassland is turned over several times by the chongcao hunters. The fragile vegetation will never grow back once it's destroyed. That's why the herb becomes more scarce and expensive. The digging is turning the grassland into a desert.

"It's real. No glue, no plaster, no dye," says the owner's daughter. "My father brought it home super excited. It's rare to find such a treasure at the market these days. He's so happy that he went to the bathhouse to celebrate."

I remember the signs for a bathhouse in the alleys. So that's where the man of the household hangs around, first the market, then the bathhouse. Does he ever help his wife?

"Would you like to buy it?" The mother comes out of the kitchen, wiping her hands on her apron. "I'll give you a good price."

I shake my head. I'll never have peace of mind if I take this herb while knowing I'm contributing to the destruction of Tibet's grassland. Her smile stiffens, and she looks worried. Does she also have to sell chongcao on top of selling her buns? Will she be yelled at if she can't sell it? I gaze at her pale, puffy complexion, a sign of lung and heart deficiency. Her crying son is now tugging at her sleeve, pulling her in the direction of the candy. His scrawny face indicates that every organ in his tiny body is malnourished and deficient. Both of them can benefit from this magic herb.

"You and your son should eat this," I say, holding out the worm toward her.

"No, no, no!" she gasps, shaking her head violently. "We can't afford it; we don't deserve it."

"You deserve this a thousand times more than anyone else in Lhasa," I shout, stepping forward to grab her hand and press the herb into her calloused palm. "Make a bowl of soup for yourself with this, for God's sake, and eat it before your husband comes home. Here, I'm buying this," I pull out four one-hundred-yuan bills and thrust them into her other hand, "only on the condition that you take this for yourself, now."

"You're hurting me," she says, tears flowing down her cheeks. She puts the money back into my hand and flees into the kitchen with the tiny worm plant and closes the door behind her.

The boy pounds on the door, wailing. "Mom, I want candy, I want candy."

I stand there. What have I just done? The last thing I want is to hurt her.

The daughter touches me gently. "Please, sit down and eat your dumplings. They're getting cold." She picks up the boy, whispers something in his ear, and he smiles, waving his hand. "Now, I want to go now."

I stand up and pull out a twenty-yuan bill. "Is this enough for the lunch?"

She looks at my untouched food. "You don't like our dumplings?"

I sit down again and spoon one into my mouth, then another. "The best dumplings I've ever had. Did you help your mom make these?"

She nods, glancing at the closed door. "We made them last night. We used the flour from my husband's store, the best kind. It's more expensive than the flour from the Chinese stores, but it's 100 percent pure, nothing else."

I open my eyes wide. "You mean there's fake flour too?"

"There are all kinds of stuff in the flour and everything else. You've heard the fake baby milk powder story, right? The same with flour. It's much easier to mix it with other things, like potato, yam, ash, sand, in the powdered form. Who could tell the difference? My husband's store is probably the last one that won't do that trick. So we can't compete with the Chinese stores who sell their goods at a much lower price. I don't know how long he can keep doing this."

"Don't people know?"

"They do. But when they see the price difference, they always go for the cheaper, even though they know well that our store sells the best rice and flour and noodles."

"What about Muslims? Surely they buy things from your store, right?"

She sighs, a deep furrow between her arched eyebrows. "It's all about money these days. Only money, nothing else."

"Hey, what do you do for fun with your husband?" I want to lighten the air. She's too young to shoulder so much weight. In America, she would be going to school and celebrating her Sweet Sixteen with her friends.

"Fun?" she looks at me as if I were an alien. "We pray."

"Don't you travel together, like take a vacation? Don't you want to visit Shanghai Expo?"

She laughs as she picks up her brother and walks out of the diner. "Perhaps in my next life. I would like to go to college like you, Auntie, and perhaps visit America and the rest of the world, if I pray hard enough, and do as many good deeds as possible this life."

"What's your name?"

She hesitates a moment. Before she steps over the threshold, she says in a low voice, "Jiang Aixue."

Aixue—love school. "Beautiful name. I'll keep my fingers crossed for you, Aixue. May your wish come true next life, perhaps even this life."

She smiles, a deep dimple in her left cheek, revealing her white, crooked teeth. My heart aches at her loveliness. "Aixue, please . . . " I stop, not knowing what to say next. I want to do something for her, but what can I really do? This is her world, tightly knit and closed in. No girl has ever broken away from her clan, as she said. I remember Mr. Ma's wish to send his daughter to college. I will do everything I can to help her.

Aixue stands on the threshold waiting for my words. I finally ask: "What's your mother's name?"

She looks at me as if I were crazy, as if it had never occurred to her that her mother, too, has a name. We look at each other until she whispers, "Kelisu."

I nod. What a nice name, just as lovely as her daughter's! Why does she keep her own Muslim name and give her daughter a Chinese one? Does she want her daughter to fulfill her unfulfilled dream? I watch Aixue walk across the street carrying her brother on her back. She looks like a middle school girl; yet, her steps are firm and determined. She knows where she's going.

She looks back to wave goodbye, her bright eyes glistening with tears. I raise my camera to stop my own eyes from tearing. "Remember how lucky you are, Ping," I say to myself as I click. "Just remember how damn lucky!"

My phone dings. Lao Han reminds me of the tea party with his friends. I take out a peace knot from the bag blessed in Jokhang Monastery and place it on the twenty-yuan bill. It looks small and insignificant on the paper money. I remember the monk's words: It's not the size or how much; it's the intention of good will.

I stand up and talk to the closed kitchen. "Kelisu, I'm sorry if I offended you. I didn't mean to. I just want to give you my best wishes for a happy life and flourishing business. I'll keep my fingers crossed every day for you, your daughter and son, and your business. This red knot is blessed. Hope it'll bring you peace and safety. I'm going home tomorrow. I hope I'll come back and eat your buns again."

The diner is quiet. The only sound is the hum of the refrigerator. The only movement is the steam rising from the gigantic bamboo steamer. I put the teacup on the money and leave. Once outside, I look back. Kelisu is looking out from the small metal window, her face a dark silhouette against the light.

I'm horribly late for the tea party. Lao Han welcomes me with his bear hugs and laughter then introduces me to his friends: a skinny aristocrat who owns a Tibetan herb company, a handsome Kangba Tibetan incense merchant who speaks fluent English, a big-headed Anduo Tibetan who got rich smuggling gold and other precious metal but now runs a chain of five-star hotels in Lhasa. They drink, sing, and grope courtesan girls. Lao Han bellows a Tibetan drinking song with gusto. I sip tea, smiling at Lhasa's rich and famous. Lao Han thrives in China's economic boom, judging from his lifestyle. Yet, I hear sorrow in his booming voice. I love his poetry and art that burst with passion and compassion. How does he deal with the chasm between the rich and poor? My mind drifts to Kelisu and her face from the diner's window. Would she be able to sell all her buns? The aristocrat raises his whisky at me. I raise my tea. We click. He tells me about his purebred Tibetan mastiff, the king of the plateau, each costing him half a million yuan, and he has four, still trying to get two more so that he can breed them for friends.

I excuse myself before the party is over. I have to pack for my train to Shanghai early in the morning. A cab glides over and takes me back to the Muslim square, for the third time that day.

The square is empty when I get there, but suddenly, black-hatted men in black suits come from all directions. They gather briefly then stream into a dark alley and disappear. I look up. Under the gold dome flutter the Tibetan prayer flags. The black mass recedes from the market like a tide, and the square becomes quiet and empty again, then a long, melodious voice from the mosque, the calling of Azan, followed by the prayers from the invisible men. My knees wobble as I listen to the collective singing. Two people walk into the square, one woman and one girl. The woman looks very tired as she holds onto the girl's shoulder. Both are covered in black, except for the girl's pink headscarf. Jiang Aixue, I almost shout but check myself. They walk to the center of the market and stop next to an abandoned sewing machine. Eyes fixed on the mosque, mother and daughter listen to the sound of praying, oblivious to me walking toward them, oblivious to any distractions from other worlds. As I get closer, I saw the little peace knot, my gift for Kelisu, on Aixue. She has peeled back her daughter's scarf and pinned it to her black hair.

In the sunset, the red peace knot lights up the girl's temple like a torch.

Bridging Yangtze and Mississippi—Kinship of Rivers

Summer 2010, I attended the *Ten Thousand Waves* premiere in Shanghai, a film I wrote for the drowned cockle pickers at Morecambe Bay, directed by British filmmaker Isaac Julien. After the premiere, I took the train to Tibet, to install an art project I collaborated on with a Minneapolis artist. It was a small banner of six artists' work on fabric, including mine. I brought two banners—one for Shanghai, one for Tibet—thus spanning the entire Yangtze, symbolically. I asked a fisherman to bring the work to an island at the end of the Yangtze. He refused, said the monster faces in the flags were ugly and unlucky. I had to bribe him with a thousand yuan to accomplish the mission. When I brought the second banner to Tibet, I was worried. What if the Tibetans hated this? The air was thin at five thousand meters above sea level. I struggled to tie the banner with millions of Tibetan prayer flags. I stepped back. Our flags blended in seamlessly. Fluttering in the sea of prayers, the monster faces no longer looked ugly. In fact, they became beautiful.

I felt weightless. I saw myself making flags with thousands of people along the Yangtze and Mississippi, each flag a bridge to bring the world together through prayers.

Kinship of Rivers was born, a project that would link the Yangtze, Mississippi, and all other rivers as sisters through poetry, art, music, food, prayer flags.

This would also fulfill my vow I had made during my first trip to Lhasa.

In May 2012, I started the journey down the Mississippi with Immanuel, from its source at Lake Itasca to the Gulf of Mexico, a river of 2,530 miles (4,070 kilometers) through Minnesota, Wisconsin, Iowa, Illinois, Missouri, Kentucky, Tennessee, Arkansas, Mississippi, and Louisiana. I brought a thousand river flags made along the upper Mississippi, the St. Croix, the Missouri, the Minnesota, and many other rivers.

My plan was to hang the flags on riverbanks, bridges, islands, and confluences—as I traveled along the Great River Road that runs parallel along the Mississippi, from Lake Itasca to Venice, a small fishing village at the end of the road, the end of the river.

From there, the Mississippi spreads into the Gulf of Mexico like a bird's foot.

And I would follow that bird into the sea, with our prayer flags. They would travel back to Everest in 2013 and 2016, the source of the Yangtze and other major rivers of Asia. From there, they would spread peace, joy, and harmony to the whole world.

IV

The Great River Road

20

Gypsies at the Cahokia Mound

Our first stop is the Cahokia Mound, St. Louis. I want to camp there on the first night, to pay homage and get blessings for the journey. That means we must drive straight from St. Paul to St. Louis and reach Horseshoe Lake, a state park at the foot of the mound, before sunset. Five hundred thirty-four miles in one day.

Immanuel drives. We met at an art gallery a year ago, his oil paintings displayed next to my photographs. We started dating, and soon, he moved in with me.

Aiden and I split three years ago. It was inevitable, as Aiden said. We are different species. Would have parted much earlier if not for the kids.

I make phone calls to set up events along the road. I want to visit Andrei Codrescu in New Orleans, the Romanian American poet and NPR commentator, but he just sold his place and is living in an Arkansas forest. Stay with Dave Brinks, he suggests. Ah, right, Dave Brinks, the poet who runs the Gold Mine Saloon, a bar that hosts great poetry readings every Thursday night in New Orleans. He brought me to his place the year before Katrina, put me up on the second floor, right above the bar. I dial Dave's number.

"Hey, Ping, when are you arriving at New Orleans? I've been following Kinship of Rivers for over a year. What a project!" Dave picks up on the second ring. We haven't spoken for ten years, but he sounds exactly the same, breathlessly excited. "I'm preparing a turtle feast for you, Ping. Of course you can stay with us. You must. River flag event? Of course, Thursday night, the entire saloon is yours. Oh, I have a giant dragon made a decade ago for my wife's birthday. It's the year of the dragon again, right? The black water dragon? Perfect. Time to bring her out. We'll celebrate the black water dragon with music, turtle, flags, and poetry. You're going to paddle and camp on Choctaw Island? My grandparents are Choctaws, buried on the island. Thank you for installing the flags there in their memory. You want to go to Venice and the gulf? My uncle is a fisherman there. He has a big boat. I'll hook you up with him."

I put down my phone, turn to Immanuel, and we high-five. What an auspicious start! Now that we have arrangements for New Orleans and Venice, the farthest destinations, the rest of the journey should be easy.

At 6:00 p.m., we arrive at Horseshoe Lake State Park, east of St. Louis, at the foot of the Cahokia Mound. We drive around the campsite. It's small, with the lake on one side and soybean fields on the other. A dozen RVs and tents in the wooded area. Around the bend, by a lone metal trailer, a man is chopping wood. I go over and ask him how to register for a campsite. He looks up, and his green eyes beam on me for a split second then dart away. "Go to the office and put eight dollars in an envelope then choose a place you like," he says, his face changing from old to young, young to old, his eyes from green to blue then to hazel. His accent also shifts like his eye colors.

I pick the spot next to his trailer.

As we set up our tent, he comes over to say hi. His name is Brent, a circus performer from Europe. He's going to perform in St. Louis for a month, starting next week. Could he make some coffee or espresso for us? I don't drink coffee. Immanuel just quit. I suggest we share some tea and take out a little tea box, a gift from Yu Jian, the Chinese poet from Yunnan. I have saved this tea for a special moment. Brent runs in to his trailer and brings out a can of Chinese tea from Taiwan, insists I take two bags, and I insist he take two scoops from my tea box. We chat about how expensive tea is these days. In China, a pound of good tea costs from $200 to $1,000 nowadays, with no guarantee if it's real. Brent nods and comments that fake products plague China, from cow milk to medicine to clothes. We chat until Immanuel reminds us that we need to visit Cahokia Mound before the park closes.

I bring my rice cake and tobacco. My Native American friend Allison told me to offer them to the place and the spirits there, asking their permission to enter and leave. I asked her if I could place some wishes there. Of course, she said, and you should. So I bring them along, one for my mother's recovery from her blindness, one for my sons' better grades and health, one for Allison's job interviews, and finally for our river trip.

The Cahokia Mound is located a few miles west of Collinsville, Illinois, and a few miles east of St. Louis, Missouri, where the Missouri and Mississippi meet. It is the largest burial mound on Earth, containing the remains of the most sophisticated prehistoric native civilization north of Mexico, a city built and inhabited between AD 700 to 1400. At its peak, the city covered nearly six square miles and had ten to twenty thousand inhabitants. More than one hundred minor mounds have been found there.

When we arrive, the sunset is lighting the mound in shimmering gold. I offer the gifts and wait. A gentle breeze, and the sycamore tree in the fields sways, as if giving us permission to enter the park. It reminds me of the Blood Run, the burial mound Allison took me to visit two years ago in Good Earth Park, near Sioux Falls. Every mound seems to have a tree like this: sinewy and old, standing alone to guard and guide the visitors into another world. I bow and enter.

The mound feels surrounded by an invisible fence. Once inside, time and space flow in all directions, folding back and forth like an origami. This is not a maze because a maze has only one direction and three dimensions. This place has more, many more. The air feels cooler, cleaner, and moister. I inhale, lifting my spine, then exhale, dropping my shoulders, relaxing my face, abdomen. I walk, my feet light as if I were flying in a dream. Is this the world inhabited by spirit people, as Allison told me at Blood Run?

But Cahokia Mound feels different.

At the foot of the hill, I pause. Children run up and down the steps, laughing. They run as if they were in a dream, like me. Perhaps they also feel the power of the place? The mound is made of 40 million cubic feet of soil, carried over by baskets. With every step, I can feel the vibrations of the mound builders' footsteps, children, elders, women, men, each with a basket of earth in their hands, on their heads, backs . . . Their footsteps echo with the footsteps of thousands of Chinese peasants carrying gigantic stones up the steep hills of Mount Swallow, building the Great Wall of China.

The Chinese emperors built the Great Wall, with chains, whips, swords, to keep out the Mongols and other invaders. Under the wall, thousands of bones, still pining to go home after two millennia.

The natives built Cahokia Mound to honor their ancestral spirits and keep peace among the living. The pamphlet says nobody knows how or why or when or where the Cahokia tribe vanished. Perhaps depletion of resources or climate change or war. Nothing just vanishes. It's hidden somewhere, waiting to be unburied. I can feel their dreams. In fact, those mound builders have scattered to the south, known as Peoria, people who "come carrying a pack on his back." The federal government signed many treaties with them then broke them all. They're still wandering along the river, carrying their ancestors and cultures on their backs, waiting to come home.

Immanuel reaches the top, raising his arms to the sky then bending over, as if he were prostrating.

From the flat platform, I can see the Arch of St. Louis and the Mississippi. I walk, clockwise, like the Tibetans walking the Jokhang Temple and all sacred sites. The top also reveals the mound's structure: the ceremonial site, the council site, the living quarters, the fields that stretch all the way to the horizon, to the river. Another breeze. Did the Cahokia leaders feel the same breeze when they chose this spot to build their civilization? A Chinese feng shui master would have chosen this spot too: water, prairie, mound—a site where dragon and phoenix dance in harmony. No wonder the Cahokia people flourished on this land.

Now, a highway runs through its belly, cutting it in half. Students and their professors from all over the world are gutting the mound in the name of anthropology.

A bird appears on the northeast corner, small with intensely blue wings, the kind of blue you only see in dreams. I raise my camera but it flies to another branch, then another. The spirit of the mound is telling me something. I put down the camera and offer some tobacco to the bird, then the four corners, finally the center. I know dreams will come to me tonight.

When we return to the camp, Brent is still outside puttering around. I take out the fried rice from the cooler. We sit on the picnic table and eat our dinner from the plastic container with one spoon. Before our departure, I prepared sesame noodles for lunch, which we devoured while driving, and fried rice for dinner because I wasn't sure if we would get to the campsite on time and I didn't want to cook in the dark. It's delicious. Brent comes over, and we chat more. I ask him if he had his dinner yet.

"Oh yes, with my family," he points to the trailer, "pasta with tomato sauce."

They seem awfully quiet in the small trailer.

Brent reads my mind. "Oh, we are very disciplined people. My master goes to bed early so we can get up to train. Anything I can do for you before I go?"

I ask him if it would bother him if we make a fire. Not at all, he says, and goes inside. In a few minutes, he comes out with an electric saw to cut up wood and then piles logs by the pit. "For your fire," he shouts, "and enjoy your night." He vanishes into the trailer.

"Wow," I whisper to Immanuel, "can you imagine a Minnesota camper doing this? This must be the southern culture."

"St. Louis may count as the south," says Immanuel. "But Brent has a British accent."

"Ah, yes, you're right!" I slap my forehead.

We make a fire. I take off my clothes and wash myself at the tap water, sighing with pleasure. Soon, he takes off his clothes too and joins in. When we go back to the fire smelling clean and feeling cool, Immanuel says, "That was a good idea, Ping."

"As usual," I say, and we laugh.

We run into the tent and fall asleep right away.

Cattle, large herds of cattle, wild, hairy, and unruly. I'm taking them to Dakota, Nebraska, Colorado. Along the route, I fight endless battles. I wake up, fall asleep. The same cattle come back. The same battles. Red flood through cities, people on fire.

I wake up with an intense pain on my hip. A raised welt across my buttocks.

Immanuel lights his portable gas stove, a big smile on his face. He makes tea, and we offer a cup to Brent. He comes over slowly, looking like he stayed up all night. Has he already done his training? There's no sign of sweat or any stirring inside the trailer. Immanuel brings the omelet he just cooked on the stove. It looks burned and dry. I shake my head. Immanuel devours it in a few gulps.

"Where's your dog?" I point to the warning sign on his trailer window.

Brent smiles. "I apologize. There's no dog or person inside. I'm the entire family here. I wasn't sure who you were yesterday. Now I know, after I saw your dreams."

I look into his green wolf eyes that accompanied me and the cattle through the prairie and mountains all night long. So those beasts are not cattle but buffaloes that have been roaming on this land for thousands of years, in body and spirit. I slept on their land, and we met through our dreams.

Brent holds my gaze, admitting me into his clan. We are gypsies. Roaming runs in our blood.

21

Alton Ghosts

"There are even more eagles perched on trees along the banks," says the fisherman next to us. "We call it the last locks and dam, even though there are a few more after this, but this is the last significant dam on the Mississippi," he pauses then adds, "It marks the upper and lower Mississippi, the closing and opening of fishing season. Every year, millions of tons of commodities pass through here."

We are standing on the Melvin Price Locks and Dam, Locks and Dam No. 26, south of the Clark Bridge near Alton, Illinois. It looks gigantic with nine gates swarmed with bald eagles. Their cries travel back and forth across the shores. Below the dam, the river runs fast and furious, earth-colored waves rolling toward the south, carrying nutrients and energy from the upper Mississippi.

"Now I understand why the river is called Big Muddy," I murmur.

I discovered the dam by accident, a few months ago, during our four-day scouting trip from St. Paul to St. Louis. We visited the print shop Firecracker. Its owner, Eric Woods, told us we should visit the confluence point in Alton, where one could step into two rivers at once. We did that, placing one foot in the Mississippi, the other in the Missouri, straddling the two greatest rivers in North America, with wind howling against our faces and hands. It is one of the hottest spots for wedding ceremonies. Then we got lost, driving back and forth on the highway to get back to the Great River Road. And suddenly, the Melvin Price Locks and Dam sign appeared in the snow-covered fields.

"Let's go in and take a look," I said.

"Why? It looks locked and fenced," Immanuel said.

"Just drop me off at the gate, please."

He did. The gate was open. I walked into the National Great River Museum, through the exhibition hall, onto the dam. Immanuel followed.

From the dam lookout, I felt the mighty force of the Mississippi. How did it get so expansive, wider than Lake Peppin, and much more powerful? I remembered my paddle with my writing class through the narrow, winding stream of Lake Itasca. "Is this the mighty Mississippi?" asked Sarah, a freshman from NYC, her voice full of doubt. She wore a pretty sundress to our three-day paddle trip, her cream-colored skin flaming red from the prairie sun and mosquitoes.

"The river is young at the source," I said. "It has to be small. Imagine a baby born the size of a twenty-year-old? It would have ripped the mother apart, right?"

"Wait until you get to St. Louis," Don said, a senior science major from St. Louis. "You'll know why it's called the Big Muddy."

And he was right. Running on two legs, one from Lake Itasca, the other from the Rocky Mountains in Montana, the Mississippi and Missouri join at St. Louis and Alton. From here on, the river receives many more tributaries, each adding new blood to the river, until it reaches the gulf as the largest river in North America, and the fourth in the world.

I wished Sarah could see the river from the dam. The canoe trip in Itasca burned her skin but boosted her confidence. She survived three days of paddling in a sundress. After that, she claimed she could survive anything.

"This is the perfect spot to hold a Kinship of Rivers event, with all the flags fluttering in the wind over the Big Muddy," I said, dreaming aloud.

Immanuel scoffed.

I walked back to the dim museum, asked the front desk if I could meet the director. "What for?" she asked, her blue eyes narrowing with suspicion. I started talking about the river project. Before I could finish, she said, "Oh my God, hold it, I'll find Erica for you," and she ran in like a bunny.

Erica came out reluctantly. "What can I do for you?" she said with patience, her body blocking the door that opened to a long hallway lined with office rooms. I knew I had about three minutes to pitch my story before she turned and went back to her work. I opened my mouth and let the words run. Suddenly, she grabbed my arm and yanked me into the hallway.

"Show me the flags," she said. "What's the website address?"

She practically dragged me into her office and started typing on her computer: www.kinshipofrivers.org.

"River flags, right?" She clicked. "Oh, my God, this is perfect!"

I knew I hit the jackpot right there, and my dream to host a flag installation and workshop on the dam would come true.

"Can you be here May 19? We'll have 'Sleep under the Stars,'" an event for family camping on the dam. Would you bring the river flags? Can the families make some to bring to the Yangtze River?"

My heart skipped a few beats before I could answer. "Definitely! I'll bring all the flags to install at your site and bring the art materials for new flags."

I danced out of the museum like a dragonfly.

At 3:30 p.m., we drive to the Locks and Dam No. 26, the Great River Museum at East Alton. We get lost again, circling around the closed constructions for half an hour. My GPS has crashed, pointing at everywhere and nowhere, and I'm practically jumping in my seat, shouting, "We can't be late, we can't be late," and Immanuel shouts back about my bad sense of direction. Suddenly, we are in downtown Alton. We have no idea how we got here, as if someone lifted our car and dropped us in the middle of the street. We shut up and gawk. The city is quiet: not a single soul walking, not a single shop open. We pass a black building with an image of a birdlike creature covered in golden scales, and a gigantic sign on a colorful banner: seafood, steak, drinks.

"Let's have lunch here, when we come out of the water tomorrow." I point to the building. It looks empty inside, but the sign says OPEN in big red letters.

"What for?" Immanuel shouts, shivering.

Very strange. He usually jumps on any opportunity to eat out. And why is he shivering? A few minutes ago, he was complaining how hot it is in St. Louis, wondering how we would endure the inferno as we go deeper into the South.

"It's spooky here, I guess," I mutter. "I just want to talk to the locals and find out why it feels so quiet here."

"I don't want to eat here, and I don't want to come back to this town, ever!" he wails.

I look in the rearview mirror. The birdlike creature glares from the wall behind us. It has a man face, tiger whiskers, deer horns, its entire body armored with green, red, and black scales. Its tail coils around the body, over the head, and between the legs. I look into his red eyes through the rearview mirror. A shiver runs up my spine.

"What's that?" I point to the creature in the mirror.

"What?" Immanuel sounds alarmed. "What are you talking about?"

I peek at the mirror. Nothing but an empty road. I turn to look. The sun is setting low. No bird in the sky.

"Nothing. Let's get out of here."

Immanuel presses on the gas.

When we finally find our destination, families already have set up their tents along the riverbank. Outside the museum pavilion, a woman in uniform hovers around a grill so big that it can easily fit a whole pig inside. It has a mountain of charcoal on it, but won't light no matter how much liquid gas she squeezes into it. She keeps shouting at the man to get his lazy ass off the bench and help her out, but he lies still with a faint smile on his face. Around her are boxes of hamburger meat, hot dogs, veggie-dogs, burger rolls, buns, paper plates, a group of young women in uniform milling around. A government event? For a second, I thought I might have come to the wrong place, then the woman waves at us with her lighter. It's Erica, the education director from the National Great River Museum. She looks completely different in her uniform. I would not have recognized her if not for her shiny eyes and bright smile. Why is she wearing a uniform? Of course, the locks and dams, all within the system of the Army Corps of Engineers, hence, the federal agents.

Erica welcomes us, tongs and lighter in her hands, beads of sweat around her lips. She introduces us to her coworkers, then her aunt and her husband, Matt. He sits up on the bench and grunts.

"So, from St. Louis, eh?"

"We drove from St. Louis." I detect a sarcastic tone in his voice. The two cities across the river could be rivals. And Alton is definitely not a match to St. Louis. "We live in St. Paul. We drove ten hours yesterday and camped near Cahokia last night."

Matt jumps off the bench.

"St. Paul, I grew up there!" His eyes sparkle. "Which part of St. Paul?"

"I teach at Macalester and live in Highland Park."

His eyes narrow, and his muscles tighten with anticipation. "Perhaps things have changed these days. But do you know Highland Junior and High Schools?"

"My older son is a ninth grader, and my younger son a seventh grader there."

"I can't believe it, can't believe it! Her sons are going to the same school I graduated from," he shouts, turning to his wife. "Why didn't you tell me they're from St. Paul, silly?" Before she answers, he grabs the lighter from her hand and lights the grill with one click. Boom! It explodes with all the liquid Erica had poured in. We jump away from the fire, laughing.

Erica utters a big sigh of relief and turns to the food piles. "It takes a Minnesotan to get a Minnesotan off his butt," she mutters with a smile, tearing open the plastic wrapping of burger meat.

The sun is setting fast. Immanuel and I take out our boxes from the car and wrap the stone pavilion with river flags. The pavilion is big. We tie two or three banners together to hang from one post to the other. When we finish, the wind starts blowing, sending our flags high up into the sky, like a thousand kites. Children and parents stop playing and gaze at the fluttering flags. Even the women in uniforms stop chatting and look up. They feel something, even though they don't know the source of it: the wishes, imagination, and visions from a thousand people along the upper Mississippi, St. Croix, and Minnesota that are being released into Illinois's sunset. The fire subsides, and the charcoal looks ready for grilling. Erica is still unwrapping the meat and bun packages by herself. Her husband has vanished somewhere, and her assistants are chatting among themselves. Her aunt lights a smaller grill. Children start gathering around the table waiting for dinner. I walk over and open the packages. Erica flashes a smile at me, her face drenched in sweat.

"I can start grilling, if you wish?" I ask.

She looks at the children and the dimming skyline and nods. I bring a tray of burger meat to the fire. It's so hot I have to hold my breath.

"Do we have a spatula?"

Erica looks up and around. "Oh shit. My husband forgot everything, again. I can't believe it." She grabs a flimsy white flipper from the cardboard box and tosses it at me. "This is all we have."

I look at the plastic thing. It's good to flip pancakes or eggs but would melt in the fire. Nope. I'm not going to eat plastic.

I throw a patty onto the grill. It flies like a Frisbee, lands in the center, and starts sizzling away.

"Good aim," cheers Erica's husband. I didn't see him coming.

"You forgot the tools again," shouts Erica, her blue eyes bulging.

"Yes, we did," he says cheerfully. "Now, we can play."

He grabs a pack of patties and throws them on the grill one by one. I continue with mine. The crowd cheers and laughs with us. For a second, I thought I was back in NYC in my sixteenth-floor apartment. I was giving a dumpling party. Ai Weiwei came with other Chinese artists, musicians, poets . . . In the middle of making and eating dumplings, Ai Weiwei started tossing dumpling skin out of the window like flying saucers then looked down to see angry faces cussing up from the street. You can't do that, I shouted, but he just thrust a stack into my hand, and before I knew it, I started flinging the dumpling skins out the window, giggling like a five-year-old.

Soon, we cover the grill with a hundred burgers. The grease drips into the charcoal, and a huge fire shoots up. The patties are turning black.

"They're burning. Shut the cover, quick," someone shouts.

"Not me," says Erica.

I look at the gigantic cover. It's beyond my reach. The grill is burning like an inferno, orange fire licking at the handle with greed. I step back.

"Watch me," shouts Erica's husband. He has a pair of mitts made of cardboard in his hands, takes a few steps back, charges, jumps, grabs the cover, and slams it down.

Everyone applauds.

"Show off," says Erica, smiling big at her husband for the first time as she mixes her potato salad in a huge bowl.

Soon, the fragrance of grilled meat permeates the air. The pavilion is crowded with children and parents.

"The patties are ready," I tell Erica.

She looks at her husband, who looks at me, then at the crowd around him, grabs the cardboard mitts, and lifts up the cover.

The patties look perfectly grilled. If they are not taken out immediately, the flame will come up and ruin the meat. We all look at Erica's husband again.

"Someone else's turn," he says, shaking his head.

"But you forgot the tools," Erica says.

He has already slipped away like a fish in tall seaweeds.

I tie up my hair and dip the plastic pancake flipper in ice water. If I'm quick, the plastic won't melt. I run at the grill, aiming at a patty with my weapon. Swoosh! I scoop it up and toss it to the aluminum tray I hold at my waist.

People cheer.

I ask someone to hold the tray near the grill, and I attack the patties one by one with the plastic spatula, cooling it off in ice water. My speed and precision improve as I dance with the fire. I'm sweating torrents, but soon, all the patties are off the grill. They look and smell perfect. Even my own appetite is aroused. Perhaps I'll try one, I tell myself, when Immanuel is not watching. Not only does he refuse to eat anything conventionally produced, he also demanded I do the same after he moved in with me.

I throw in new patties, plus hot dogs this time, and then shut the cover again.

Erica sets the table with burgers, buns, potato salad, pickles, and coleslaw. People have lined up with their plates. Erica's aunt serves them one by one. The whole pavilion becomes quiet, only the sound of the lip smacking and finger licking. At the far end of the pavilion, I see Immanuel wolfing down a burger, his plate piled with coleslaw, potato salad, and chips.

Wow! He must be hungry.

Erica beams. She wipes sweat from her forehead then goes on pouring flour and cherry, apple, and peach fillings into the three cast-iron pans on the small grill.

"Cakes for desserts," she tells me. "My grandma's recipe. You'll love it."

"Where did you get these cast irons? They are beautiful."

"I inherited them from my grandma, and she from her grandma. Very old stuff."

"How long will it take to make the cakes?"

"Not long. About thirty minutes." She closes the lids, then scoops out some charcoal from the small grill and pours them on the lids.

I put my hand over the grill. Lukewarm. The fire is already dead.

"Can I start the flag workshop now, Erica?"

She looks up. The kids are getting restless after their meal. She looks down at the dead charcoal. "Hmmm, I was planning to have your workshop after the cakes. Let me get more charcoal to get the fire going. Then I'll let you know."

She runs into her office building. I look at her assistants, young, robust women who haven't stopped chatting since I arrived. Why didn't she send them to get the charcoal?

"It's hard to find people working as hard as Erica nowadays," I say to her aunt who is scooping the ripped packages into the garbage bag.

"Yes, indeed. Erica grew up with her grandma, who emigrated from Ireland during a famine. She taught her well. That's why she's different from most people. She stayed with me when she came to college in Illinois. She created this family camp program on the dam. It's a lot of work, and she has begged me and her husband to volunteer every year because there's no way she can pull it off by herself. Her assistants are good girls, but they're young, you know what I mean? She really doesn't have to do this. It's not in her job description, but she can't stop doing it. When she was a girl, she couldn't sit still, always doing something or circling around as if searching for her lost necklace."

I nod. "I know. I could never sit still as a girl. Still can't. My kids laugh at me all the time."

Erica comes back with charcoal and pours it into the small grill. She wipes her face with her apron.

"Perhaps you should start the workshop now. I'll find my husband and have him get the fire going."

I walk into the crowd. People stop eating and look up at me, some doubtful, most curious, a sea of blond hair, pink faces, blue eyes. Well, I'm in the heartland of America, the deep belly of the North American continent. Suddenly, the monster bird appears from the river, its gold, green, and red scales glinting in the sunset. I blink. Only the flags are fluttering in the wind with a steady rhythm, like flapping wings. Am I hallucinating? I close my eyes for a second then open them. A familiar face is smiling at me, her eyes and mouth curving like three new moons on her round face, her black hair wrapped in a sky-blue handkerchief. An Asian woman in the audience. Then, I see an Indian woman sitting next to her.

I take a deep breath and start talking. I tell the crowd that I was born and grew up in Shanghai, the mouth of the Yangtze, and now live and work on the bank of the Mississippi, near Fort Snelling, the confluence of the Minnesota and Mississippi. The two great rivers run through my mind and body every day, and I started the Kinship of Rivers project a year ago to connect the Mississippi with the Yangtze through the river flags, which gather people's vision and love for rivers. With a group of artists, musicians, and poets, I've paddled and traveled along the Mississippi, Minnesota, St. Croix, and Missouri Rivers, bringing the Yangtze stories to the people in America, who then write and paint their stories on the river flags. Over the course of a year, we have visited hundreds of schools, colleges, senior centers, galleries, and museums, teaching poetry, art, and making river flags. The flags around the pavilion are gifts of the rivers from two continents. The new flags from Alton will join the old flags and travel down the Mississippi until we reach the Gulf of Mexico, then travel the entire Yangtze from Shanghai to Everest. There we'll hang the flags and let the wind spread our wishes from the roof of the world.

People listen with attention. I know my words have sunk in, and they're ready. I point to the table piled with art materials: fabric that I cut, dyed, and ironed on wax paper, fabric crayons, paints, markers, seals, print-making inks, and the local grasses and plants I gathered to print on the fabric.

"Go for it, and have fun," I tell the crowd.

Children grab brushes and paints, crayons, markers and kneel on the ground to paint. I start making prints on the fabric. Grasses are my favorite—thin, long leaves flowing with such grace on cloth. I also love oaks of all kinds—their ancient spirits always shine through the fabric.

I watch the children sprawl on the concrete floor, painting away, using the most daring color combinations. They're the best artists, before they learn the binding rules and fear for failure.

The Korean woman comes over with her flag. "Cheon He," she says.

I recognize her accent immediately. "When did you come to America?"

"Twenty years ago. Too long."

"I came twenty-three years ago. Did you come here for school?"

She nods. "I thought I would return in a few years, but the Mississippi got me."

"Same here. I pledged to my professors and friends that I would go home as soon as I got my degree. Instead, I moved to St. Paul, into a loft overlooking the Mississippi."

We laugh, our eyes to the brown river under the dam.

"My river, I should say my parents' river in Korea, is also called Muddy River," she whispers, after a long silence. "It flows into the river that borders with China."

"The Yalu River?"

"We call it Amnock."

"Are you from North Korea?"

"My parents were born on the bank of the Amnock. From their house, they could see people crossing the bridge with baskets of fresh produce for the daily trade. In winter, they walked across the ice. Then the war broke, and they fled to the south. I was born on the bank of Imjin River that flows from the north, flowing along the DMZ. My parents built their house on the south side of the river. Every sunrise and sunset, they sit on the cliff, still and silent, facing the Amnock, where their home and ancestors rest. Seventy-five meters below, the Imjin purrs, trying to get their attention. But they only pray to go back home and burn incense at their ancestors' graves before they die. Their wish is to walk across the Yalu River one more time. For me, I only see and dream of the Imjin, wild, untamable, full of surprises. Every night, I dream of climbing the cliff, jumping into the blue ribbon, into the lion's roar."

"Mom, I'm done. What should I do with it?"

I look at the girl holding a flag. Her beauty takes away my breath: curly brown hair tied in the back, creamy skin tanned evenly with a golden hue, full lips, green eyes sparkling like cat's eyes, like Brent's, the wandering gypsy. She looks exactly the way Cheon He's daughter is supposed to look, even though their facial features have no resemblance. It's the fire that lights their souls from within, the fire in every Korean warrior.

"Sabrina, please say hi."

She flashes a smile and waves, then hands me the flag. I raise it to the light. Against the olive cloth, a golden river tumbles out of the mouth of a blue lock and dam. The water is so bright it turns her green eyes into glowing amber, burning like William Blake's tiger eyes.

"Powerful," I say.

"I'm going fishing, Mom. See you." She dashes down into the river.

"Wild and untamable." Cheon He smiles, shaking her head.

"She's your daughter. She's your Imjin."

Cheon He laughs, heavy and wet with sorrow from the people who have been away from home for too long. I join in. Then, silence again.

"My river," she finally says, opening her cloth mounted on waxed paper.

Three green, orange, and blue mountains stand against light blue fabric, majestic and heavy like her laughter, yet also fluid as they flow through the windy clouds. Upon a second look, I see the river, an emerald green that holds the mountains in place. Heavy and fluid at the same time.

"The Baekdu Mountain range," she says. Seeing my puzzled face, she says again, "Chang bai shan."

I can't believe my ears. Chang bai shan, the forever-white mountain range that borders China and Korea, source of the Yalu/Amnock River. I thought the Imjin is her river. I look up. Two drops of tears are rolling down her cheeks, one slightly muddy and thicker, the other clear and thin, and between her eyebrows, a crease cutting deep into her flesh, forming a 川—Cheon, the river. Suddenly I understand what her parents embedded in her name. Cheon He—川河—river and river, one Amnock, one Imjin, mother and father, heaven and earth, inseparable.

A man comes over and puts his hand around Cheon He's waist. "Mike," he introduces himself then points to the girl down the river, "Our daughter, ten years old."

His shoulders, waist, hips, and calves bulge with muscles. His green eyes spark with fire, like all the Irishmen I know. Cheon He leans her head on his shoulder, arm draped around his waist, bending like a river around a mountain, an image she created on the flag. He is her Baekdu Mountain range, and she is his Mississippi.

"Thank you for bringing Kinship of Rivers to Illinois," he says. "It means a lot to us. Really."

I take her flag with both my hands. It weighs a ton. I bow to them and place the flag on the grass to dry. The riverbank is now covered with drying flags, a quilt of colors and joy.

Inside the pavilion, the crowd is busy with action. The two baskets full of art materials are empty. The huge pile of fabric has vanished. The parents have joined in, making flags with their children on their laps or making their own flags. The grown-ups sprawl on the concrete floor, squeezing, splashing, spraying, smearing, and spilling the paint all over the fabric, laughing with their children. Their loud joy almost lifts the roof off the pavilion.

Erica opens the Dutch oven cover. "Cakes!"

As children and their parents devour the cakes, Immanuel and I spread the flags on the riverbank. There are about fifty, all wet and heavy from paint. One flag is covered with a child's handprints. I have watched him spray with joy. The hand is his entire being, ready to travel up and down the rivers around the world, until it reaches Everest.

That night, the bird with a human face and dragon scales visits my dreams. It flies out of the cliff cave, clutching a prey still flailing wildly to get away. The bird comes closer and closer, its wingspan almost as wide as the river. Our eyes locked. Its amber eyes glow like the sun, burning my retinas. The human in its claws has gone limp, his face ghostly pale, his ancient army uniform in shreds. Suddenly the bird grins, its jagged teeth gleaming against its blood-red tongue, before it vanishes into the city of Alton.

I wake up with a pounding headache in my temples. I know the bird is real. So is the man in the bird's claws. And Alton, the city where the Mississippi and Missouri converge on the Illinois side, is haunted.

22

BMW

His name is Wayne. People call him Big Muddy Water. I call him BMW. He's tall and lean. You can't squeeze an ounce of fat out of his six foot two frame. He doesn't have a bulging chest or biceps, but when he moves, he gets the best mileage out of his dark, mean muscles, like a good old BMW engine: efficiency, efficiency, efficiency.

He doesn't waste his words either.

"Meet me at my canoe company tomorrow at 5:00 p.m. I'll take you and Immanuel to Twin Island, where the Missouri meets the Mississippi. You camp there overnight, and I'll pick you up in my canoe at sunrise."

What a godsend! Or Erica-send.

The morning after our adventure on the dam, Erica took the whole group to Riverland, the state park across the lock and dam for kayaking and stand up paddle boarding (SUP). Both are new sports for me. Kayaking is easy. I sit low and close to the water, my torso and legs balancing the boat, my oars dipping in and out of water—and the boat takes off like a dragonfly. SUP is a different story. It looks super easy and cool: just stand on the board and paddle with a long oar. But it takes me fifteen minutes just to learn how to stand up on the rolling water. I kneel on it first until my knees becomes numb. So I try to stand, one leg at a time. I thought I have super balance, being a yogi, dancer, and martial artist, but SUP is a different animal since I have to deal with the waves. When I finally stand up, I feel humbled and triumphant. Then comes the next issue: I don't know how to turn. The currents are much stronger than I thought, and the wind picks up speed as soon as I stand up. I'm getting tired and want to get to the shore, but every time I get closer, the current and wind push me off toward the dam, and the guards on the security boat warn me of the danger through their loudspeaker and order me to turn around, and I have to start all over again. After my third try, I'm frantic, exhausted, and, worse, starving. My limbs shake, and my wrists have lost all sensation. I'm ready to give up when Cheon He appears out of nowhere in her kayak.

"Catch that current over there," she points at the waves far away, "and it'll bring you back to the shore in no time."

Really? That sounds so counterintuitive. I'm exhausted, and she wants me to go further away from the shore? I look up, but she's gone. My SUP is already drifting in the direction she pointed out. I stop struggling and just go with the current. "Looking good," people shout from canoes and kayaks. I beam and start enjoying my SUP for the first time. When I arrive at the spot where she told me to turn, I dip my oar to the rear left, and it turns effortlessly. Wow! So, in order to reach the shore, I have to get away from it first. Who would have thought of it? Cheon He must have learned this knowledge from her rivers in Korea and from the Mississippi. Within five minutes, I reach the shore. It almost feels too quick. The young man who sent me off on my first SUP adventure praises me. From the sandy shore, I look for Cheon He in her kayak, but she is nowhere to be seen.

Erica comes over. "The flags look fabulous, Ping, both last night and this morning. Everyone marvels at them."

Immanuel and I came earlier that morning and wrapped the pavilion with hundreds of river flags. They instantly brightened up the place.

"Thanks, Erica, for giving us this great opportunity. It's a dream come true. By the way, do people paddle beyond that?" I point to the dam.

"Not many. The current is swift and unpredictable. But there is one person who does it every day and can take you there if you're interested. Come with me." She beckons and walks to a crowd on the beach.

"Hi, Wayne, this is Ping, from St. Paul. Ping, this is Wayne, Big Muddy Wayne. He brought all the canoes for us today. He knows this stretch of the river better than anyone else. He's our river gator."

Before Erica starts her introduction, I already noticed him. He stands out in the crowd. His face looks weathered, tragic, and proud. His spine curves between his shoulder blades as if he has hidden wings. I have seen him somewhere before.

He takes my hand, and I know he can deliver me beyond the dam.

"So, Wayne, we would love to paddle both the Mississippi and Missouri around here and spend some time at the confluence. We're free tomorrow, before heading down south."

"Tell me why you want to be in the two rivers at the same time."

"Because the Greeks said it's impossible," I laugh. "Well, I would like to install our river flags on the confluence island and paddle the major tributaries of the Mississippi for the Kinship of Rivers project."

"You're Ping!" His eyes light up. He grabs my hand again and squeezes. "I've been following your project since last year. Beautiful project, beautiful work," he points at the fluttering flags on shore.

I have never felt so honored. Praise from this man is worth a million. And he no longer needs my explanation, since he has been following the project on Facebook.

"I know the Quapaw Canoes at Clarksdale will take you deep into the river. You'll be in good hands with those river gators. John and I have been partners for years, taking people into the Mississippi."

My chin drops. The Mississippi is mighty and long but crowded with miracles. What are the odds of meeting a man like BMW on Lock and Dam No. 26 through the Army Corps? And that he knows John, who will take me on a three-day paddling trip from Clarksdale to Choctaw Island, past the confluence of the Arkansas and Mississippi? I have never met John in person. We connected through the Kinship of Rivers group on Facebook.

"I have to teach my last class tomorrow. I'll be done by 3:00 p.m. Can you be at my office by 5:00?"

"Yes. What should I bring?"

"Just you and your friend. I have everything." He steps into the big canoe, where a dozen kids sit in two rows, still and alert. He gives an order. The twelve angels raise their oars, and the boat slithers into the water soundlessly.

I walk to the pavilion with Immanuel and start taking down the flags. We work quietly, both amazed by what has been happening to us since we started the journey. Wonder pops up wherever we go: Dave's offer to host us in New Orleans, the Great River Museum, Cheon He, and now, BMW and his offer to take us to the confluence island for camping. We're sailing on the river of dreams.

Let it run, let it run, I tell myself, just go with the flow of river gifts.

Immanuel gets lost on our way to BMW's place, and we arrive an hour late. BMW has packed everything for us: kitchen kit, water bags and bottles, life jackets, food. His office sits behind a cement factory.

"This place was covered by poison ivy when I bought it," he says. "I couldn't even see the house or its swimming pool when driving by. We spent two years cleaning it up, little by little, over and over, because poison ivy is stubborn."

Who are "we"? I look at his bare fingers and the oozing blisters around the wrists. He seems so alone, not lonely, just alone.

"My partner, ex-partner, plans to put in solar panels. Once done, our energy bill will be zero."

Where does he sleep? This house feels truly like an office, with all the camping and canoe supplies, giant stove and sink, giant cans of tomato sauce, boxes of pasta—well organized and clean but lacking a feminine touch. Though sunlight bathes the place and flowers bloom everywhere, the place feels heavy and dim and sad. I look up. Three concrete towers loom over us from across the road. Who's his ex-partner?

"We finally started making money this year. My youngest son is going to college on a basketball scholarship in the fall, just like his brother. So I'll have more funding to put into the business. Good timing. My wife just got laid off."

Wife? I would never have guessed this man is married.

He looks at his watch. "The sun is going down. We should go if we want to paddle to the Twin Islands before dark."

We pack everything into his truck, load the canoe, and drive to the landing through the flat landscape. The river rises fifty feet when it swells, says BMW. These fields used to be wetlands, the flood plains of the Mississippi, filtering and fertilizing the land along the river's path. Now, the levee keeps all the sediments from the upper Mississippi and its tributaries. Some are carried into the gulf and some stay in the river, creating huge islands that move with floods.

We gaze at the land stretching all the way to the horizon. Lots of the fields are vacant.

"The government pays farmers not to plant crops. The agricultural runoff is killing the gulf," he says.

We drive in silence until we reach the landing.

"If we hurry, we can still make it. We start from the Missouri, paddle four miles to the confluence, then eight miles to the campsite on Twin Island," he declares.

Swiftly, we get everything into his canoe, and just when I step into it, he asks, "Where's your life jacket, Ping?"

I look at myself, then Immanuel. Only BMW is wearing his. Neither Immanuel nor I have one on.

"Didn't I hand them to you?" he asks, totally puzzled.

Immanuel and I look at each other, and we vaguely remember the orange life jackets passing through our hands, but neither remembers where we put them. We run to the truck. Nothing.

"Well, we can't enter the river without it. It's the rule. So I'll go and get them."

He takes off in silence, no blame, no criticism. But I can feel the disappointment from him, not at us, but at himself. Immanuel and I walk back and forth in the fields, picking flowers, taking photos of each other, to kill time.

Forty-five minutes pass. BMW's truck appears at the horizon.

"We don't have time to go to Twin Island today. We'll just paddle to Duck Island and camp there. Do you mind if I join you on the island? I don't think I have enough time to go back to my office tonight either."

"Of course, of course, it's even better," I reply. This actually makes much more sense. He told me how he was going to paddle us to the island, leave us there, then swim across the river and jog back to his truck and spend an evening at home, then come back in the morning to get us. I tried to visualize his paddling, swimming, jogging, driving, swimming back and forth. It made me dizzy.

We launch finally. I'm itching to paddle so I take the bow seat in the front. BMW steps into the stern seat to steer. The river appears smooth on the surface, but I can feel the tug and pull through my oar. Big Muddy is a wild beast.

"There are many hidden eddies along the shores," says BMW. "They are fun to swim in."

What? My eyes widen. "Don't they pull you in and never let you go?"

"Only if you try to fight it. But if you relax and swim with it, all the way to the bottom, it will release you and pop you right to the top. You should try. You'll love it."

Hmmm, perhaps. I have to first unload all the horror stories of people drowned in eddies from my childhood memory. It was my grandma's favorite story, her way of keeping us away from dangerous rivers.

We pass by a few cliffs dotted with dense trees. As the cliff recedes from my view, I have a glimpse of a strange bird, the one that followed my car at Alton, into my dream.

"What's that?" I jump.

BMW looks in the direction I'm pointing. The bird has vanished. The painted cliff has also disappeared from our view.

"Oh, the Piasa Cave," says BMW.

Piasa, Piasa, I repeat the word. I have heard of the word, just as I have seen the creature associated with it. But I can't put my finger on what it is exactly.

"Is it a bird?"

"So you know the legend of the Piasa Bird? I thought it's only for the locals."

I have a million questions, and I don't know where to start. BMW points at the island on our left side. Two rivers meet at the tip of the island, then fork apart. It looks familiar.

"Here's the confluence," he says. "See that park? They spent two million on that tip, but the river just floods it every spring. When I came here in April, the entire place was submerged. Only the tip of the flagpole showed. I don't know how long that park will last. Two million . . ."

I recognize the spot where Immanuel and I stood in January snow. Now I understand why everything was soggy, flooded, and tossed about, including the parking lot, the path, the giant stone banks. The river overwrites everything mankind tries to do.

Soon, we close in on another island on our right, smaller than the state park but lush with trees.

"Duck Island, the real confluence island," says BMW, quietly, as if he doesn't want to disturb the spirits on shore. "Look up, Ping," he whispers, pointing to the two o'clock position.

The sun is setting toward the roots of the trees. The trees form a dark silhouette against the sky. "Look, look," he urges. I still can't see anything. Then I hear the sound of wings. A dark shadow flies over my head, and I catch a glimpse of its white head and tail. It flies past us, into the treetops. Now I see it. A giant nest. Over its edge, a baby eagle's silhouette, mouth wide open for food. The mother circles around, as if making sure there is no danger.

"My sacred place," BMW whispers.

"Thank you for sharing it with us," I whisper back. We watch in silence until both mother and baby enter the nest for the night.

"Time to make our own nest," declares BMW. He steers our canoe to the tip of the island, where the two rivers meet and part. We dock on the sand beach, dotted by driftwood trees that form a strange driftwood forest. Upon closer examination, I realize all the trees are erected in the sand upside down. The roots open against the sky, like crosses with figures hanging on them.

"John was here with me a month ago. We camped here for two days," says BMW.

That explains it. Though I've never met him, I have been feeling his energy. I look up and around. On my left, the Mississippi is lined with barges longer and wider than a city block. On my right, the Missouri flows by, joining the Mississippi at my feet. I'm immersed in a deep quietness.

If this is the real confluence, why didn't they build the park here? I want to ask but stop myself. It's obvious that the island has no access to the shore. Visitors would have to swim here or take a boat. Besides, there would be no more eagle's nest if this island becomes a state park.

It's getting dark. We unload our boat quickly. I make a fire, set up the pot to make dinner. Where's the water?

We look at the food pile, the empty boat, then one another. BMW turns gray.

"Sorry, I've been very distracted these days. This never happened before." He looks as if he was about to cry.

It's incomprehensible indeed. I remember filling our bottles and cans with water and transporting them to the truck. Apparently, we never packed them. We checked and rechecked the back of the truck for our life jackets, and we would have noticed the water.

We look at one another, at the fire, the empty pot. The only water we have is what remains in BMW's and Immanuel's bottles, which is not much. The sun has already set. It will be dark in half an hour.

"I can still make a good dinner with two cans of chicken soup, adding onions, carrots, potatoes, and tomatoes, which won't absorb water. We just won't be able to make coffee or tea in the morning."

Immanuel looks tearful. He loves coffee in the morning, especially when we camp. And he drinks water every hour throughout the night, to prevent dehydration. He keeps three mason jars of water under our bed for this purpose.

I burst out laughing. Perhaps it's the expressions on their faces, both disappointed, but for different reasons. Both BMW and Immanuel are highly organized people. What are the odds that they would forget life jackets and water? I roll on the beach, laughing, throwing sand into the air. "No life jackets, no water, no life jackets, no water." Soon, my guffaw infects BMW, and he joins in laughing and chanting, until Immanuel also joins in.

Finally, we stop. It feels good to laugh at our own folly.

"I'm going back to get water." BMW gets up, straightens his clothes, and steps into the canoe.

"It's getting dark. How are you going to paddle six miles up the river by yourself?"

"Not a problem. I do it all the time. I'll just canoe across, jog to the truck, then drive back to the office, and I should be back in one hour."

He looks determined. There is no point saying anything else.

"I'll save you some dinner, then," I say.

He raises his oar and vanishes into the river. The island feels too quiet suddenly. Immanuel shivers. I add more driftwood into the fire.

"We'll need a lot of wood for tonight. Let's gather while we still can see."

We walk in opposite directions and pick a huge pile of driftwood. The big pieces I pull out of the sand are soggy with water. Immanuel doesn't want them. They will kill the fire with smoke, he says.

"No worry. I can burn anything, as long as it's wood. I'm a fire witch, remember?"

He chuckles nervously. "When will he come back? What if he doesn't? How do we get back to the shore tomorrow morning?"

"He'll be back when our dinner is ready. If something happens, we can easily swim to the shore."

"What about my water for the night? I'll be so thirsty." His eyes and nose squeeze together, and he looks like a baby with a hundred-year-old face.

"He'll be back in no time," I say, handing him a cutting knife. "Would you please cut the vegetables into cubes before we lose the light? Thanks. He'll come back soon, and I want our dinner ready."

The task seems to calm him down. He kneels in the sand and starts cutting with great care. He's a good sous chef. After a day's hard work, we come home and prepare our meals together, a daily ritual of greeting, exchanging, sharing. Our dinner is always delicious, which is a good sign. Whenever I screw up a meal, it means either I'm stressed out or I dislike the person I cooked for. Immanuel is a small man with a big appetite. It amazes me to watch him eat: fast and furious in big bites as if he were reincarnated from a starving ghost.

When the fire subsides, and the charcoal starts glowing, I pour some olive oil into the pot, fry the onions, then potatoes and carrots, then tomatoes, then Napa cabbage. I add some black pepper but no salt. The canned soup has enough salt in it. My original plan is to add rice to make chicken rice soup, but that requires extra water. The air is now permeated with the fragrance of cooking. It's totally dark, but we have a good fire and plenty of fuel for the rest of the night. I pour organic chicken soup into the sizzling pot then put the lid on.

"There, when he comes back, we can eat."

"I want a real fire." Immanuel picks up a piece of driftwood. "It's too dark."

"Let it simmer ten more minutes. Then, I'll move the pot and we can have a huge white-man's fire. Let's lie down on the sand and find the Big Dipper."

We lie down, heads toward the Mississippi, illuminated by city lights. On the Missouri River side, the sky pulses with stars and the sounds of crickets. They have no connection or resemblance to each other yet are made of the same substance: carbon dioxide, the building block of all life.

"The Big Dipper, see?" Immanuel holds my hand. Ten minutes have passed and no mention of a big fire. The stars put his mind in a peaceful place.

"I wish I had the river flags on this island," I say to myself.

"Too bad we didn't pack the flags. We could have done a perfect installation here." Immanuel is reading my mind, and that means he's content, even happy. "I'll make sure we pack our flags for the Choctaw Island paddle," he comforts me, squeezing my hand.

I give him a kiss. "It's going to be a fantastic trip."

"It's already been fantastic."

I look into his eyes. They reflect the glowing of the charcoal. It's rare to hear him say more than two sentences continuously, more rare to hear him express contentment, even gratitude. At our social gatherings, he sits through the dinner without saying a single word, no matter how much guests try to get him to talk. It puzzles and pains them at first, then they get used to him, then they stop noticing him.

"If people want to talk to me, they can come and talk to me. Why do I have to initiate?" he says vehemently when I ask him why he won't initiate a conversation. He's a gentle speaking man with nice manners, but he can explode with anger, especially after I discovered his $19,000 credit card debt and made him pay it off every month. I bought his paintings to help him start the process with a $2,000 leap, cooked his dinners and lunches so that he could save money, and took away his credit cards so he could no longer shop for expensive underwear, socks, gloves, boots, clothes, and art materials online. I asked how he could spend $19,000 in less than a year; he said it was his business investment: become rich and famous by making expensive art and selling it fast and high.

"Thanks, Immanuel," I squeeze his hand. "It was your idea to make this trip, remember?"

I hear the sound of the oars—gentle, rhythmic, soothing. I can't see a thing on the river, but I know BMW is returning. I remove the pot from the fire, add some driftwood. The fire shoots up, illuminating the shore and BMW's shadow pulling the canoe onto the sand.

"Good timing. Dinner's ready," I shout as I divide the soup into three. A bit too thick for my liking, and the bottom is slightly burnt for lack of water, but it tastes good. We sit around the fire, sipping the soup, watching the sparks dancing in and out of the fire, a pot of water boiling for tea.

"This is my first meal of the day—Sooo good," sighs BMW.

I can tell he's starved. He rose at 3:00 a.m., organized his papers, prepared his lessons, taught, prepared our trip, paddled, ran back and forth for our life jackets and water. This is his daily routine, according to my phone conversations with John in Clarksdale, who also wakes up at 3:00 a.m. to write and paddle. This is river gators' flow. Their endless energy comes from water and sun.

He sips. I can feel his cells grab each fiber, each drop of fat, each particle of protein from the soup, and transform them into blood, muscle, nerves. I can feel the gratitude from his being and my gratitude of his appreciation.

"You know, Ping, I've always cooked for the people I paddle with. This is the first time my client cooked for me."

"Well, I'm not really a client."

"You're right. You're one of us."

We finish our dinner without speaking further. The island is quiet and full of sounds at the same time: the hum of the distant barges from the Mississippi shore, the crickets, an otter swimming across the Missouri, and the scuffling of tiny feet in the sand.

"Baby turtles, just hatched," BMW whispers. "Lucky timing."

Lucky indeed. Had they hatched during the day, seagulls and other birds would be waiting along their tracks to snatch them for meals. We listen with contentment. How often do people get to spend a night with two rivers flowing by their sides? Except for BMW. This is his job: bringing people here to listen to the pulse of the rivers and stars.

"Everything is equal here," says BMW, his words crisp under the stars. "Hobo or investment banker, Hollywood star or truck driver, same difference on this sacred island made by sacred waters. Here, we're stripped of illusions: money, fame, desire, greed, lust. That's why I bring people here, children, adults, rich, poor, locals, foreigners, every day, every week, every month until winter arrives. That's why John and I get up at 3:00 a.m."

I remember the same emotions I felt when my feet touched the Tibetan Plateau. Suddenly, nothing mattered anymore: fear, love, betrayal, aspiration, ambition, success. The only thing that counted was my breath, the air rushing in and out of my nostrils, filling my lungs with thin air, pumping blood to my heart, and the acute awareness of who and where I was, the need to return to that land every year, like a pilgrim.

I'm a pilgrim. So are BMW and his river gators.

"Wayne, would you tell us the story of the Piasa Bird? Where did it come from? Where is it now?" Immanuel breaks the silence, his eyes glistening in the dark.

I jump. He asked the exact question that has haunted my mind for the past three days. Did he also see the bird? Why didn't he ever mention it?

BMW sits in silence. I thought he fell asleep. But he inhales and words tumble out, high-pitched and fast as if he were possessed.

"The Piasa Bird is said to have flown over the 'Great Father of Waters' thousands of moons before the white man came, when magolonyn and mastodon were still living. *Piasa* means 'the bird that devours men' or 'bird of the evil spirit.' It is part bird, reptile, mammal, and fish. Its colors of red, black, and green symbolize war and vengeance, death and despair, and hope and triumph over death. Its image is painted on the limestone bluffs at the confluence of the two great rivers, near Alton.

"Before the village of the Illini, the mighty river swept to the south, clear and fresh. The surrounding woods were rich with game. The bluffs and the mighty trees shielded the Illini from the northern winds. Ouatoga, the old chief, had led his tribe in the ways of peace for most of his lifetime. One early morning, the young braves were leaving on a fishing expedition, some already on the river in their canoes, others preparing to embark, when the earth shuddered with a scream. Out of the western sky came a monster. Its body was the size and shape of a horse; long, white fangs stabbed upward from the protruding lower jaw and flames leaped from its nostrils; two white, deer-like horns angled wickedly from its head. Trees bent under its pounding wings. Its stubby legs held daggerlike talons, and its spiked tail wound around the body three times. Before the braves realized what happened, the beast swooped across the beach and carried one away.

"Each morning and afternoon thereafter, the Piasa Bird would come, shattering the village with its blood-chilling screams and the thunderous beat of its wings and wouldn't leave until it returned to its lair with a victim. And it seemed to prefer humans over animals.

"The Illini looked to their chief, Ouatoga, for a solution. He had led them through the trials of famine, illness, and the threat of warlike tribes. But Ouatoga felt helpless before this danger. The beast armored its body with scales, like a coat of nails. Nothing could penetrate it, not even the sharpest arrows from Tera-hi-on-a-wa-ka, the best arrow maker.

"Ouatoga appealed to the Great Spirit. For nearly a full moon, he prayed and fasted. In a dream, he found the answer. The body of the Piasa Bird was not protected under the wings. After offering thanks to the Great Spirit, Ouatoga called the tribe together and devised a plan. All day long, Tera-hi-on-a-wa-ka sharpened arrowheads and painted them with poison, while the tribe fasted and prayed. At night, Ouatoga and six of the finest braves went to the top of the high bluff overlooking the Great Father of Waters. When dawn came, Ouatoga stood on top of the bluff. The braves were hidden nearby behind a rock ledge, bows ready.

"Suddenly, the scream of the Piasa Bird broke the silence, and the winged monster swept into view. Sighting Ouatoga, it shrieked, pounced, and sunk its talon into his flesh. Ouatoga fell to the ground, but he held onto a tree root. As the Piasa Bird raised its great wings to fly away with its victim, the six braves stepped from their hiding place and shot six poisoned arrows into the unprotected place beneath the beast's wings. Again and again the bird raised its wings to fly. But Ouatoga held fast, and each time, six more poisoned arrows drove into the bird. Finally, the poison did its job. With a scream of agony, the Piasa Bird released its hold on Ouatoga, plunged down the bluff, and disappeared in the river.

"The braves carried Ouatoga to his tepee, where he was nursed back to health. A great celebration was held in the camp of the Illini. The next day, Tera-hi-on-a-wa-ka mixed paints and, carrying them to the bluff, painted a picture of the Piasa Bird in tribute to the victory of Ouatoga and the Illini. Every time an Indian passed the painting, he'd shoot an arrow in salute to Ouatoga and deliverance from the Piasa Bird."

Nobody says a word when the story ends. In the silence, only BMW's last words: *deliverance from the Piasa Bird, deliverance from the Piasa Bird, deliverance from the Piasa Bird.* I look at Immanuel. He must be hearing the echo, too, his face paler than a ghost, his body shaking. Why is he always haunted by so much fear? Fear of losing control, of making a fool of himself if he opens his mouth in public, fear of the end of the world. Our basement is piled with water jars, beans, rice, first aid kits, lighters, fuel—things he tried to make me buy, but I simply refused, and he ended up buying with his credit card, things now ridden with worms and moths.

"Did you say the bird disappeared from the river forever?" I break the silence.

"According to the legend, yes." BMW's voice has returned to normal. I detect his hesitation.

"What do you think?"

"Let me tell you this," he says after a long pause. "Alton, where the bird appeared and died, is haunted. The Illini knew. One of the reasons why they moved away. Later the city became a hub for the slave trade. Many of the arrivals died in the Enos Sanitarium, where the slave traders unloaded and restored their goods before the sale. Those dead souls have never left that building. And the Confederate Prison, on the corner of William Street and Broadway Street, hundreds of soldiers captured during the Civil War met their deaths at that location. Some died from injuries, some came down with devastating illnesses, some killed themselves, others were tortured to death. All the spirits, with their unfinished business, unfulfilled dreams, linger at Alton, searching for something."

His face contorts, as if ghosts seized him by his throat. I'm not surprised. The minute we met, I knew that he carried a world of pain on his shoulders.

"I knew the city wasn't normal. I knew it," Immanuel screams. "That's why I refused to eat lunch in that black building, remember?"

BMW looks startled. It's the first time Immanuel raised his voice. In fact, it's the first time he offered his opinion without being asked.

"Yeah, it's one of the most haunted places in America."

I want to tell BMW about the Piasa Bird that appeared in my dream and my rearview mirror when we passed through Alton, when we camped on Locks and Dam No. 26, when we paddled in the river. I want to tell him that the monster still lives, in the cave of the bluff, the bottom of the Mississippi, the shadow of our consciousness. But he must know. So does Immanuel, or he wouldn't have lost his cool.

"Isn't every place haunted by spirits in some way?" I try to lighten the mood. "Matter never dies, right? We are just as ancient as the universe, made by the particles that burst out of the big bang. My friend Allison told me never to whistle in the dark because you never know what spirits hang out there."

"I'm going to bed." Immanuel takes my hand. "Care to join me?"

I nod. "In a minute. I want to bathe in the river first."

He smiles at my routine. Growing up in China without water in the house, I could bathe only once or twice in the winter. Every night before bedtime, I would prepare a basin of hot water. First I would wash my face, my midsection, then my feet, a ritual that had kept me clean and sane throughout my childhood, then adulthood. I insist that my partner come to bed clean. We spend a third of our lifetimes in our beds, resting, healing, dreaming, so shouldn't we treat it with the utmost care and respect?

I walk into the river with a hand towel. The night air makes the water feel warm. The mud seeps through my toes like melted butter. I give a kick and start floating. The Big Dipper guides me into its swirling world. The brown water keeps me afloat, just like the Dead Sea keeping me afloat, together with Wei and Di. When was that? 2004? It seems so long ago. I still had some Dead Sea mud from that trip, but Aiden and I have gone our separate ways, and he married soon after. I float in the brown water. The Missouri and Mississippi are lulling me into a dream.

"Ping, are you coming?" Immanuel calls from the tent.

I swim back to the shore. My toes get muddy again, so I rub them clean in the sand. I haven't used my Shishedo moisturizer since I started the trip, and my skin feels extra soft and smooth. It has to do with the water, sand, and mud.

BMW lies by the fire, head propped in his left hand, his thin sleeping bag half zipped to his knees.

"Where's your tent?" I ask, swatting away mosquitoes.

"Oh, I like to sleep in the open."

"Bugs don't bite you?"

"Not much. I'm immune to them, for some reason. Perhaps they don't like my blood that much, too thick, or bitter, I guess."

I laugh. "Sleep well, then, sweet dreams under the stars."

"I will, I know I will, at least for tonight. May good dreams follow your sleep all night."

He lies still in the sand, propped on his elbow, eyes on the current that gathers the two great rivers, his body merged into the driftwood forest he and John erected in the sand, upside down, roots into the sky like praying hands.

My sleep is indeed riddled with dreams. First, it is fire, thousands of acres of ponderosa pines burning, seeds popping like machine guns. Then comes the flood, tsunami waves swallowing villages, cities, mountains. I watch animals and humans flee, but there is nowhere to go. I can't see Immanuel, only his voice reading Deleuze's *A Thousand Plateaus*. Stop, I scream, stop reading and just pull me out of this nightmare. But he keeps reading in his flat tone. I try to bust out of this nightmare.

"Ping, Ping, shhhhh." Immanuel's voice and his hand over my mouth. "Shhhh, don't wake up Wayne."

I open my eyes, grateful to be back in this world.

"Bad dreams?" He asks. How piercing blue are his eyes, and how thick his eyebrows! I turn my gaze away.

"My end-of-the-world dreams, nothing unusual," I whisper.

"Still early. Get more sleep." He yawns, turns off the flashlight and lays his head on the pillow.

"I'm good. The sun is rising. I'll take some shots."

A sliver of orange light opens a thin flaming path in the middle of the Mississippi. The Missouri is still wrapped in foamy mist. Do rivers dream? What about fish and clams? Do they desire, laugh, and cry like us? On the sand beach, BMW lies motionless, his head propped on his hand, exactly the same position I left him. The only difference is that his sleeping bag is soaked with dew.

I look back at our tent. The sun has set it ablaze, along with the river. Immanuel has gotten up, rolling up our sleeping bags then lifting the orange tent over his head to shake out the sand. He looks like a dancing sunflower.

Perhaps I have a Piasa lurking in my own shadow? I look at BMW, his shoulder blades pushed together like wings. Is there a bird in him too?

The sun rises higher, driving away the mist on the Missouri. Fire and water, sun and mist, dark and light, transforming continuously into each other. This is the way of rivers.

"Coffee, everyone?" chirps Immanuel.

The mother eagle flies out of her nest, as if answering his call.

23

The Fig Tree of Cairo

Since I was a child, I have been fascinated with Cairo at the confluence of the Mississippi and Ohio Rivers, not just because it had the same name as Egypt's capital but also because it was the destination for Huckleberry Finn and his runaway slave friend Evan. Every Sunday, when my family was sound asleep, I would sneak out and jog to the cave a mile from the public bathroom and tune my radio to *Voice of America*. At midnight sharp, the story of *Huckleberry Finn* would come on. I glued my ears to the static radio, laughing and crying with Evan and Huck, their adventures along the Mississippi. My heart jumped when Evan cried from his raft: "Dat's Cairo!" Reaching Cairo meant that he would no longer be a slave, no longer subjected to being sold and bought like an animal, no longer separated from his wife and children at the whims of his owner. I cried when a steamboat hit their raft just as they were about to step on the shore of Cairo. I laughed until my belly ached when Tom Sawyer put Evan through such ridiculous torments to escape his prison, even though Tom had the paper in his pocket that would free Evan from his slavery.

In my childish mind, Cairo stood as a symbol for adventure and freedom.

Cairo rises out of the sediments of the Ohio and Mississippi Rivers and sits at the lowest point in Illinois, where the two rivers meet. It marks the end of the upper and middle Mississippi, the beginning of the lower Mississippi, hence, the gateway to the South. Because it lies so low and close to the rivers, it is subject to floods, especially when both the Ohio and Mississippi swell at the same time. Over the years, the Corps of Engineers fortified the city with levees and floodwalls as high as sixty-four feet and built a floodgate known as the Big Subway Gate. It weighs eighty tons, measures sixty feet wide, twenty-four feet high, and five feet thick. When floods rise from the Ohio and Mississippi Rivers, the gate comes down, turning Cairo into an island.

I'm excited to reach the city and hang the river flags at the confluence.

From Duck Island, we get back to BMW's office before 8:00 a.m., covered with mud and dew from the Missouri and Mississippi Rivers. BMW rushes into the shower then rushes out to his school to close everything down for the summer. I almost don't recognize him. His white buttoned-down shirt and combed dark brown hair turn a river rat into a handsome teacher.

"Take your time to clean up. No need to lock the door. Church is here," he shouts, already gone.

I take three showers to scrub out the mud from my hair, nails, crevices, and cavities. No soap or shampoo or towel. The shampoo bottle in the tub is as dry as the Sahara when I wrench it open. How did BMW get himself so clean so fast? I use my dirty T-shirt as a washcloth, dry myself with my clean shirt and pants, then put them on wet. The sun will dry them in five minutes anyway. Does BMW live here? The bathroom is bare: no mirror, no toothpaste, no toilet paper. The only indication someone lives here is the empty shampoo bottle and a thin roll of paper towels. Did he mention Church? Who is he? A ghost?

We stay until 10:30, after we clean up, eat, sort our food in the cooler, rearrange the car, meet and chat with Church. He is more than real. He is the great-great-grandson of William Clark, the explorer, living with BMW to work on his dug out canoe from an old log, preparing for his trip following his ancestor's route. He knows the rivers like a river rat. He helps us map our route from St. Louis to Memphis via Cairo, back to Highway 55, the Great River Road. It will take us straight into Cairo in two hours and forty-seven minutes.

Immanuel is in a great mood. Church and his river stories have lifted his spirits. We talk about where we should stop for the night: Memphis or Clarksdale. Immanuel likes the idea of staying in Memphis. He and his ex-wife spent time there on their way to her mother's house in Nashville. But he objects vehemently to the idea of visiting Graceland. He hates Elvis, hates all the culture around the icon.

"But you love rock music! How could you love rock and roll while hating its origins? Besides, nobody had a voice like Elvis. Nobody!"

"I don't care. I just don't want to go near Graceland," he says, his eyelids quivering, his sign of distress. I shut up. He's sliding into his dark maze again. But why? Did he have bad experiences there with his ex-wife? She's a witch, he once told me, used her spells to foresee their union before they even met, to win his love and devotion to her and her two kids for two years. Did she foresee their final breakup too? Did she use her spell to stop him from walking out of their relationship? I heard of love potions but never the potion for heartaches.

"Shall we shoot for Clarksdale tonight?" I suggest. "We don't have a hotel reservation in Memphis. So we are free to do whatever we want: walk around its riverfront, take some photos, then take off, unless we feel absolutely crazy about the city and must stay overnight. Do you think you can handle that much driving today? It'll be about seven hours from St. Louis to Clarksdale."

He remains sullen.

"We can have a good dinner there," I try again.

He loosens his hands, which have turned blue from gripping the wheel. "We'll see," he says.

The closer we get to Cairo, the more desolate the scenery along the highway: crumbling gas stations, fallen barns, stores with boarded windows. When the gas light comes on, Immanuel stops at a gas station. I jump out with our empty thermoses. The heat from the highway has roasted us bone-dry, and our three thermoses of chai are long gone. I don't drink soda. Immanuel and I agreed that we would not buy bottled water or soft drinks during our trip, as our pledge to rivers. The station is dark and quiet. Let it be open, let it be open, I chant as I push the door. It's locked, and a small sign hung from inside: closed. Out to lunch? I peek in through the dark glass and see empty shelves, some knocked down on the floor.

"No gas here," says Immanuel from the pump.

"Well, let's fill it up at Cairo. It's only twenty-five miles away." I remap my GPS to see the distance between the current location and Cairo.

"Hope there's a gas station when we get there."

"Of course there is, and more than one." I suppress the doubt rising from my stomach. "Cairo is a big confluence city. It'll be as busy as St. Louis, if not busier."

The highway to Cairo cuts through empty fields steaming with heat mirages. The gas light turns red from yellow. Still, no sign of a gas station. I turn off the air conditioning to save fuel.

"You know it's really dangerous not to have water in this kind of weather," says Immanuel. "We should have at least some emergency soda."

Anger seeps through his flat tone. I can tell he's craving a Coke, icy cold, and he can't have it because of our pledge. I remember the coconut drinks I bought for the trip. I fish them out from the grocery bags. "Here's our emergency drink."

We each finish two.

"We should reach Cairo anytime now," he says.

I sit up and look for the city skyline: tall buildings, water towers, billboards. Could I spot the Big Subway Gate from the road? Like the Arch of St. Louis? There's nothing but eerie emptiness. Suddenly, a sign appears on the right side of the road.

Cairo, population: 2,831.

We look at each other. This must be a joke. I remap my GPS again: current location to Cairo: 0.3 miles. We are here, in Cairo.

"Could it be a suburb?" I mutter as our Honda CRV slows down through the city, no, the town, no, the ruins. I have imagined Cairo as a bustling city sitting at the confluence, where all the barges run up and down the rivers of the Ohio and Mississippi, horns blasting, trains rumbling, trucks and cars coming and going across many bridges, just like St. Louis at the mouth of the Missouri and Mississippi. There are traces of a prosperous past along both sides of the street: the broad sidewalks, the stately buildings with elaborate designs, banks, insurance companies, post office, hospital, library, museum—all the symbols of power and money. But every window is nailed shut, every wall covered by weeds and graffiti. The whole place is whitewashed, not the pristine painted white, not even bleached white from the sun, rain, wind. Something unspeakable has hit it, like the Hiroshima bomb.

I start shaking. Cairo brings me back to Xintian, the small town on the bank of the Yangtze, now under the water behind the Three Gorges Dam. I visited the "Nail," a euphemism for the lone house sticking out like a rusty nail in the rubble. The dam was to be completed in two days. The flood would come, and the entire village would go under. Everyone had been evacuated. Old Ran, the owner of the Nail, refused to leave.

"I'm going down with the house, with the river," he said in a calm voice.

And we went down together, into the local police station. The cops rounded us up and interrogated us for eight hours before they let us go; they couldn't find any evidence of me spying for the American government.

How's Old Ran doing? Where's he living, now that Xintian is under the water.

"This place is cursed," shrieks Immanuel, sinking into his seat as if he doesn't want to be seen by ghosts.

I shudder. He knows spells. He was married to a witch.

"Well, haunted or not, we still need to find gas, in order to get out of here. And this is the only way out. So let's keep moving, Immanuel."

At the end of the street, we see a café. It looks empty from outside. It doesn't have a "closed" sign, though, and it's our only hope to get water, perhaps some hot food, some information about where to buy gas, and, hopefully, the confluence spot. I haven't given up on this place. Not yet.

We park our car in the sizzling concrete lot. I walk around and see a fig tree in the back of the café with junk piled beneath it: old furniture, rusty car parts, rotting brushes. The tree leans against the wall as if standing on guard. I stroke the gnarly bark. It must be over a hundred years old, some of its roots pushing through the cracked concrete. In the lush leaves hide hundreds of figs, green, yellow, tear shaped. How does such an old tree support so much fruit? I close my eyes and listen to the sap flowing upward from the roots to the fruit, its leaves absorbing the sunlight and turning it into nectar.

"Where did you come from, beautiful?" I murmur to the tree.

Then I hear the hum, the most delicious sound of a working air conditioner. At home, unless it's above ninety-nine degrees, I never turn on the central air. I hate air conditioning as much as Immanuel hates Graceland. I sprint to the parking lot, shouting.

"It's open, the café's open. Let's go in."

Immanuel's face breaks into a huge smile as he runs. I smile, dodging the slamming door. In his excitement, he forgot his manners. The river has washed away his masks one by one, revealing the real Immanuel: competitive, compulsive, intuitive, spontaneous, sometimes funny, and much more alive, very different from the well-behaved, quiet introvert back at home. When we met, he told me all he cared about was manners, the mark of civilization and high culture. His goal in life was to be appropriate. It still puzzles me. To be appropriate is to follow norms. To be an artist, let alone a groundbreaking artist, one needs to break the rules. And none of his paintings has anything to do with being proper. He gets his inspiration from porn sites, downloading thousands of erotic images then selecting a few to paint. He uses the most expensive materials to paint a layer of the selected porn, mask, cut, and strip it, then paints another layer, repeating the process five times. Each painting is the equivalent of five paintings, with results totally depending on chance, whirling with chaos, anger, conflict, and contradictions until some kind of beauty emerges.

I open the door and step into the 1950s: the decor, tables, chairs, counter, the cash register, the blond middle-aged waitress who also serves as a cashier, the old couple eating grits, eggs, and bacon in the corner. We have entered a 3-D movie theater.

"Hello, do you have ice tea?" Immanuel's voice quivers a little as if he were talking in a vacuum.

"Yes, indeed. To go or stay?" She looks young and old at the same time, as if she, too, had been frozen in time and space.

Immanuel looks at the menu above the counter then back at the food the couple are eating. "To go, please. By the way, can we fill our thermos bottles with hot water?"

She raises her eyebrows as she eyes our humongous thermoses. "Sure you can, sweetie. But I'll have to boil it first, and it'll take a few minutes, okay?"

I smile at her southern twang. Not as twangy as I heard in movies, but it's a twang. I like her manner. She needs business desperately. Instead of sitting down to order a lunch like proper tourists, we are asking her to boil water for us. How much could she charge for the boiling? Yet, she remains genuinely friendly. Not a trace of anger or disappointment. That is manner.

"Perhaps you want a burger here?" I turn to Immanuel. He often orders burgers when we travel.

He sucks down the ice tea fast. Already the cup is empty.

"I would rather wait until we get to Memphis. Oh, dinner will be my treat," he adds hastily, taking out his wallet to pay. "Can I have another tea, please?"

Wow! Did I just hear him right? This is the first time he offers to pay for anything, his tea, our dinner. What happened? I gaze at his glowing eyes and pink cheeks. Oh, no, sugar rush! I turn to the waitress.

"How's business?"

"Still alive." She smiles. "You can see we're the only eatery still open in town. Folks have to eat, whether from here or far away, right? The state park also helps. Occasionally people come to see the confluence."

I practically jump over the counter to hug her. "The confluence! Where's the confluence?"

She points to the left. "Just keep going on that gravel road for less than a mile, and it'll take you straight to the Fort Defiance Park."

I can't believe my good luck. In St. Louis, I asked BMW and Church about the confluence point for the Ohio and Mississippi Rivers, and they just stared at me until I started doubting my sanity. Did I make myself clear that I meant Cairo, Illinois, not Cairo, Egypt? Now, this Fort Defiance Park sounds like a state park, and if it is a state park, it must have decent facilities for visitors to view the confluence, for me to hang the river flags.

“Thank you so much! Why is your café the only business open? What happened to all the other businesses? What happened to all the people in town?”

Her smile freezes. So does her hands on the register. Tears roll down her marble face.

“Please, no need to apologize,” she says before I open my mouth. “Every stranger comes in with the same question in their eyes, but you're the only one who actually asked. So thank you for giving me the chance to tell the story, our story of Cairo.”

She pauses then points to the window. “You drove through that street, our history of glory and shame. What you saw is what you get: rubble, wasteland, ghost town, whatever words that rush to mind, but no words can tell the real story. Cairo used to be a great city of port, railroad, and ferry. Nearly all the steamboats from the Mississippi and Ohio passed through our place, carrying food, metal, coal, oil, minerals between South and North. There was no bridge at that time. Everything had to be ferried across. During our busy season, we would ferry over forty thousand railroad cars every month. Just imagine all the traders and businessmen living and passing through our city. My great-grandfather ran a hotel, the biggest in town, and the finest restaurant that hosted the wealthiest merchants, shippers, and high politicians from the nation and around the world, including President Roosevelt. Did you see the museum, one of the seven remaining buildings by Alfred Mullet? It was used as the U.S. district court for many years, the customhouse for all the steamboats and trains, and the post office. In our prime, it was the third-busiest post office in the United States, right behind D.C. and NYC. Who would have guessed it walking through the town now? After the Civil War, lots of slaves came and settled here. Yes, there was tension and violence between white and black folks. The most infamous lynching took place here. You may have heard of Will James, hung and chopped up at Eighth and Commercial, not far from here, by a mob of ten thousand. Well, the same mob also lynched a white man a few hours later. How do you explain that? Racism? Mob momentum? I don't know. All I know is since the big flood of 1937, since the Big Subway Gate sealed Highway 51 to stop the Ohio River flood, something bad happened. My dad used to say it chopped off the serpent's head, the big serpent that lifted our city out of the swamp and turned it into a crown jewel. He suspected that the two brothers from St. Louis cast some black magic into that iron gate. You know St. Louis had always been our rival. They were jealous of our prosperity, had been plotting to take it away from us. You Chinese probably know more about this, your feng shui theory?

I actually read a little about it, and it totally made sense to me. After the gate shut our artery, the levees and flood walls rose higher, turning Cairo into an island, cut off from the rest of the world, the roads, the rivers, the money. After that, barges replaced steamboats. Those monsters could carry everything they needed for the entire river, fuel, food, and supplies. They no longer stopped at Cairo. Then the two bridges, another two chokers around our artery, cut out our ferry business. All the vehicles passed over our heads on the bridges, leaving us to die slowly.

"But what really killed us were the riots in the sixties, followed by boycotts and white flight. We used to have over fifteen thousand people. It seemed that overnight, we had only two thousand left—the poor, the sick, the old. Why didn't I flee? Because I promised my father at his deathbed that I would keep this place open and alive, as long as the fig tree lives. It's been standing in the back of our house for over 112 years. My great-great-grandfather brought it from Egypt in 1900 for his bride and planted it as the witness of their love. It's been giving us the sweetest fruit through good and bad years. It's the last witness of our story, my last friend. Every night, I dream of shutting down this restaurant and starting a new life in New Orleans. Every morning, when I see the tree, I feel my feet deep in the earth like the roots, and I can't leave. So I do whatever to keep the place going: selling my antique furniture, old photos, and jewelry to dealers and collectors. A promise is a promise. I'm a southerner, a river folk. Our oath is worth a diamond. As long as the fig tree stands, I stand. Oh, your water is boiling. Can I have your thermoses?"

She runs into the kitchen. I look around the restaurant, dazed and awed. What have I done to deserve this precious gift? Her story is worth a diamond, priceless, like her oath. The old couple have left the restaurant. Immanuel sits at a table, sucking on his ice tea.

"Here it is, the hot water. Anything else you need? Can I give you another ice tea, sir, before you go? It's on the house," she calls out to Immanuel.

He jumps up and hands his cup to her for the refill, then sprints out with his tea, slamming the door behind him. I tuck a ten-dollar bill under the tray.

"Thank you for the story. Thanks for the fig tree. I'd love to have a cutting from your ancestor's tree, if not for our Minnesota winter. But it'll bear fruit in my memory."

Her face glows. "Thank you, my dear. Come back when the figs are ready to eat. They'll turn yellow, juicy, soft, and sweet. The best figs on Earth."

"I'll try." I wave and turn to leave.

"And I'll be here," she says. "By the way, the gas station is around the corner. You won't find another one until you get close to Memphis. Just so you know."

I turn to thank her for another timely gift. She stands behind the counter, her frail body in the shadow, her chest and head held high like a southern belle, her blond hair catching fire from the light that seeps through the window. She is glowing in the lava of her history, the last witness of the swamp city. For a split second, Old Ran, the nail from the Three Gorges Dam, and Kelisu, the Muslim woman from the Lhasa diner, come alive next to the waitress.

I bow and close the door as gently as I can.

Immanuel has turned on the car, waiting, blasting the Raveonettes on the stereo. I walk across the parking lot and pick up a fig leaf from the concrete. The scorching heat has shriveled it. I will moisten it with a wet towel to smooth and open it up, then make a print on the river flag. The story and tree will travel with us down the Mississippi then up the Yangtze until it reaches Tibet. From there, her story will spread to the entire world.

We find the gas station, fill up, then drive toward the confluence in silence. The park is easy to find. Big cottonwoods and oaks shade our path. I see the watermarks around the tree trunks. They have been under the water during the flood seasons, a sight that brings me back home to St. Paul, where the trees at Fort Snelling, the confluence of the Minnesota and Mississippi Rivers, go under the water in the spring, then reemerge with similar rings of watermarks. I can't believe I'm homesick. I glance at Immanuel. Does he remember last spring's record-breaking flood that put downtown St. Paul, Fort Snelling, and Hidden Falls under deep water? Does he remember the evening when we walked down to the Mississippi? The familiar path had turned into a swamp, a lake. Ducks hunted for fish around grills and tables. I took a shot of Immanuel walking on a downed tree, shafts of sunlight on his head through treetops, and he looked like Jesus walking on the water. Does he remember?

Breezes from the two rivers. The green clear wind is from the Mississippi and the heavy one from the Ohio. The Ohio River may not be the longest but has more tributaries than any other river and contributes the most volume of water to the Mississippi. I run to the bend where the rivers converge. There is no marker. No need for it. I can see, smell, and feel the rivers' weight. By the time the Ohio reaches the Mississippi at Cairo, it has received so much water along its path that it is even bigger than the Mississippi. I can hear Evan's tearful cry from the raft: "Dat's Cairo!" My heart leaps with joy and gratitude. How many people can stand at two great confluences to meet three mighty rivers in North America within three hours?

I open a banner of river flags made by the fifth graders from Horace Mann Elementary, St. Paul, and walk down the rocky beach with Immanuel, each holding one end of the rope. The banner is long enough to include both rivers. The wind blows it up and down, sending children's wishes along the waterways, toward the gulf.

"What are these?"

I look in the direction of the voice. A tiny man with a giant head gazes up at the flags. He's wearing a T-shirt with NIU on it. He has a thick mop of brown hair and penetrating brown eyes. Behind him, a group of young men and women appear out of nowhere, throwing sticks and rocks into the river, at each other. The middle-aged professor writes in his notebook. The beach is filled with laughter.

"River flags, made by folks from the upper Mississippi and its tributaries, St. Croix, Minnesota, Des Moines..."

"And you're displaying them along the lower Mississippi and letting them absorb the energy from the water?" he says.

I kneel down to shake his hand. He just named the deeper meaning I have tried to pinpoint. Yes, every time we open our river flags, something magical happens. Could it be a blessing from the rivers? From the artists? What is a blessing? A transfer and exchange of energy, from one place to another, one body to another, one time to another. The waitress at the café just gave me her blessing. This confluence, this banner, this college student with penetrating eyes, these rivers . . . is this magic?

"What are you guys doing here?" I finally ask.

"Studying the ecosystem of the confluence." He points at his T-shirt, then at the professor. "Northern Illinois U."

The professor raises his notebook above his head, and the students start gathering around him.

"Great to meet you. Good luck with your travel," he says.

"Would you take a picture for us, please?" I hand him the camera.

Before we leave the beach, I sprinkle the flags with the confluence water, a habit I started at Lake Itasca when I took my class there. Let the flags absorb the water, air, and soil from the places they traveled to.

We fold the flags and roll them up, tie them with the rope, then climb the tower to see the confluence from a higher perspective. From the tower, the students looked tiny on an island flanked by big currents: one green, one brown, one narrower, one wider, both powerful and wild, joining hands at the tip of the land. I looked in the direction of Highway 51, hoping to catch a glimpse of the Big Subway Gate that cut off the dragon's head and choked Cairo to death. There is nothing, except for a metal and stone sculpture in the shape of a compass, with its needle pointing to the west. We go down and discover that it was built in memory of Clark and Lewis, who camped here for six weeks to study navigation via stars and constellations from the locals. I take a photo with my phone and send it to Church Clark. He will be delighted to discover this place where his ancestor stayed. What other treasures does this island hold? I Google search on my phone and find General Grant, President Jefferson, Roosevelt, Huckleberry, Evan . . .

Immanuel touches my shoulder. "Shall we head to Memphis for dinner before it's too late to drive to Clarksdale? Again, my treat."

He lifts my hand and holds it tight against his ribs. I feel the thump of his heart, the sound of blood surging through his body. It's the artistic and warm Immanuel I fell in love with at our first encounter. I squeeze his hand.

"Memphis it is," I say.

V

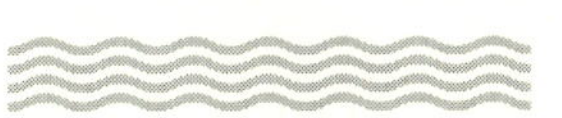

Five Tastes of the Mississippi

24

Memphis: Ribs, Pyramid & Magnolia Grandiflora

The driving distance between Cairo and Memphis is two hours and forty-four minutes via the Great River Road, almost the same as St. Louis and Cairo: two hours and forty-seven minutes. That makes Cairo the very center between St. Louis and Memphis. Who named the cities after Egypt, Cairo, the modern day capital, and Memphis, the ancient capital in ruins? Did it have anything to do with the Egyptian shipping giants? We pass the exit to Graceland. Immanuel tightens his grip on my hand. Is he nervous about something? I glance at him. Crap! His eyelids are fluttering rapidly.

"Are you okay?" I ask, pulling my hand out. It's numb.

"I probably shouldn't have drunk so much tea."

"We'll find a good place to eat soon. Look, Memphis."

Skyscrapers of glass and steel, bridges, billboards flashing on and off, the usual skyline of big cities. A silver pyramid glistens on the riverbank.

"Wow, they really made the city look like Egypt!" I shout, relieved that Memphis is nothing like Cairo. That means decent food. Immanuel says nothing. He seems to be slipping into another storm, fueled by his beloved Raveonettes and ice tea. I have tried to listen to the local music from the radio stations. We are traveling along the Great Road of American music, for Christ's sake, and now we're in the heart of this cultural icon, Memphis, the city that made Elvis, Johnny Cash, BB King, and many others. Isn't he ever curious? He allowed me to turn on the radio twice, for about three minutes, before he turned it off and said he needed quietness. Three minutes later, he went back to his Massive Attack, Raveonettes, and Dark Dark Dark. I do love those albums. After five days, however, my love turns into nausea.

"Can we please turn off the music as we enter the city?"

He pushes the button, his hand shaking. In the sudden silence, I can hear the storm blowing inside his brain, his chest, his abdomen. I regret my request. Perhaps there is a reason why he has to drown himself in the blast.

In silence, we enter Memphis, just as we exited Cairo, but the mood is different. He clasped my hand to his chest when we left Cairo, now he is cold and distant and angry, a chasm between us, with no bridge for crossing.

We drive around to find street parking along the riverfront. There is none. So we enter a public parking ramp. Warning signs everywhere about car thefts and break-ins. We have a carload of stuff, and we can't take our valuables with us. We lock our bags in the trunk, cover the boxes in the back seat with sheets. I take my laptop. It contains everything: my writing and photos. Losing it will be losing my life.

"You're not expecting me to carry your laptop, are you?"

"Nope!" I walk away.

He locks the car and passes me in strides. I try to keep up in my decomposing flip-flops. I have been wearing the same pair for three years. They could fall apart any time. I was hoping to replace them in Cairo. Perhaps I can find a pair of slippers in Memphis. The city is hilly, the streets are broad and long, lined with galleries, museums, banks. The sun has set behind the buildings. Everything lurks in shadows. Where are the drugstores and restaurants? Please don't let me trip, I pray to myself. Immanuel stops at China Buffet, turns to me, a deep frown on his face.

"Want to look at the menu first?" I ask.

He gives me a look as if I had said the most odious thing then opens the door. I follow him in. Not a single soul. The interior is fancy but cold. I grab the menu. Cold and stiff. I've lost my appetite already. A Chinese man slithers out from the kitchen.

"Is there any local food around here?"

"This is local food."

"I mean the ethnic cuisine of Memphis. What's the most famous local food?"

"The ribs, barbecued. We have it here, see?" He points to the barbecue ribs with his long, pointed fingernail.

I hit my forehead. Of course! Barbecue. Memphis holds the world barbecue contest every year, in conjunction with the music festival. In mid-May, the whole city turns into a carnival of food, music, drink, dance. Tickets are sold a year ahead of time. A VIP ticket costs $600. We just missed the festival, but barbecue should still go on.

I look at Immanuel. He already walked out. Sorry, I say to the manager and run after him. He walks as if being chased by a demon. What's up with him? What happened to his warmth and promised romance—a dinner in Memphis? I just want to sit down, get some water, eat whatever to fill my stomach, then get the hell out of this town.

"Hey, beautiful!"

I turn to my right where the voice came from. Haven't heard catcalls since I had children. Three men sit against a tobacco shop window smoking cigars, one black, one white, one with a cigar and a T-shirt that has Cuba in red print. They look so content that my heart feels lifted. I stop. Screw Immanuel. Let him run to wherever the demon takes him.

"What's a good place to eat in this town?" I ask, flashing a smile to the three old men.

"Everywhere!" they say in unison.

I laugh. "What's everywhere?"

"Depend on what you want to eat," says the man with the cigar hanging between his lips. He looks like he just walked out of a Cuba poster.

"The most authentic barbecue that will make me remember Memphis forever."

"Ah!" They exclaim in unison, eyes sparkling with pride, and start telling me where to go, all at the same time.

"Shut up, will you, my good men?" shouts Cuba. "Let me explain to the niiiice young lady from the Orient how to get to the right place." He points to the right. "Just follow this street until you hit Beale, honey bunny. Y'all pass many barbecue places but don't pay them no heed no matter what they say. Just go straight to the corner, and on the left is Blue City Café. Dat's the place you want. Y'all hear? Dat's the place y'all never forget after you leave Memphis."

I laugh, nod, put my hands in front of my chest to thank Cuba and his friends. His accent brings Evan and Huck to my memory. Maybe he's even a descendant of Evan. Who knows! The world is only six degrees away! Immanuel is almost out of my sight. I take off my flip-flops and sprint after him, hoping he will not turn and vanish into the crowd around the corner. I have never been to Beale, but my instinct tells me that it has a different scene from the empty street I am on. Barbecue joints zoom by, all boasting the world's best ribs. But I ignore them as Cuba warned me, eyes focusing on the corner restaurant ahead. Oh no, Immanuel turns the corner. I dash as fast as my bare feet allow me. Turn left, and there he is, ordering a beer from a bar smaller than a closet, a shelf displaying half a dozen liquors, a counter with three taps for draft beer, and a girl in black lingerie lying on top of the counter serving Immanuel a beer. Yes, the girl sprawls on the countertop like a mermaid, in her fishnet lace "uniform."

"Five, please," she twangs. Immanuel slips a $100 bill into the crease of her breasts and murmurs something to her ear. She opens her red lips and cackles. Since when is he so funny? Oh, yes, he was voted the funniest man in the produce department. The whole street is lined up with minibars like this, each equipped with a girl in a flimsy "uniform." Music blasts out of windows and doors from both sides of the street. So this is the famous Beer Street. No, Beale Street.

"Oh, thank you, sir," says the mermaid, fishing the $100 bill from her bra and kissing it before slipping it into the drawer behind the counter.

Blood rushes to my face. This is how he got his $19,000 credit card debt and why he penny-pinches me so that he can tip the "mermaids" with $100 bills? Three hours ago, at the Cairo gas station, he asked me to reimburse him fifty cents for a box of matches he bought. My stomach heaves. I want to throw up. He must have felt the heat behind his back. He turns, his eyelids fluttering like moth wings.

"Oh, hi, here you are. I thought you were still chatting with those men at the tobacco store. So I thought I would buy a beer to kill some time. Oh, what happened to your shoes? Why are they in your hands? Since when do you do hand-walk?"

He is showing off his humor talent. The mermaid cackles again.

I walk away and enter the restaurant adjacent to the mermaid bar. It's crowded inside but much quieter. I sit down against the wall and ask the waiter for a glass of water with lemon, no ice. I wipe my soles with napkins before I slip into my flip-flops. My feet burn as if I had walked on hot coal.

Immanuel comes in and sits across the table. What did he do with his beer? Pour it in the drain? What a pity! If I spent $100 on a beer, I would take my time to enjoy it.

"What's the matter? Tell me how you feel—sad, angry, jealous?" he says in a monotone as if reciting a quote from some textbook. He prides himself on being an expert at reading and expressing emotions, having taken many therapy sessions with his ex-wife when they lived in Viroqua, Wisconsin.

I feel like slapping your face, you jackass! I want to tell him, but of course, I don't. That wouldn't be Minnesota Nice, would it? I look across the crowd and focus on the graying braid on the back of a Harley Davidson biker, his leather jacket covered with pins.

"You were very rude, you know, to the bar girl."

I look at him, speechless. Did I hear him right?

"She thought we had a fight or something, thought you were going to smack her. You made me look bad. You made her dislike me."

He looks like he is about to cry.

"Say something, Ping. I told you how I feel. Now it's your turn."

I feel sick, I want to say. Focus, just focus, Ping, I order myself, on the sweet side of Immanuel. He brings home expired fruit and vegetables, sometimes steaks, from his co-op. He cuts fruit into pieces and feeds me on a fork while we watch a movie. He bikes home every day, stops at the library to pick out a movie, washes dishes and cleans the kitchen before our movie. He's punctual, reliable, and faithful.

"You're being very rude to me, Ping."

"So you want her, a perfect stranger, to like you," I say slowly, word by word.

"Yes, I like girls, all kinds of girls," he blurts, his eyes steely blue.

"So you like all kinds of girls," I repeat his words, a method I learned from him during our arguments. The words sound so ridiculous that I start laughing, my heart crumbling in ruins like Cairo.

"Well, I don't mean like that," he blushes. "You know what I was trying to say."

"What do you two folks want to order?" The waiter appears with my lemon water. He looks like he has lived all his life in the restaurant. He must have been watching us. He must have seen all sorts of strange things in his restaurant.

"Anything you want, my treat," says Immanuel, resuming his calm appearance. He wants to impress the waiter. He wants everyone to like him, except for me.

"I'm not hungry. Just get what you want."

"Well, how about the combo? It has ribs, gulf shrimp, baked beans, right? It comes with a salad, right?"

"A combo it is," says the waiter and takes off.

I pick up my camera and start shooting: the signs, posters on the walls, the Indian biker, the crowd—there is beauty in everything, every person. Every person? Including the man-child who just revealed his mean side? The food comes and goes into his mouth. He eats like a hungry ghost.

"Have some beans, at least," he says, pushing the saucer-sized dish toward me. His meanness subsides a little with the food in his stomach. He wants to reconcile.

I shove a spoonful of baked beans into my mouth. It tastes sweet, salty, spicy, and creamy all at once. It tastes like the South.

"It's all yours. I'm really full. This may be our last chance to eat. I don't think we'll find this kind of food on our way to Clarksdale."

I eat another spoonful, but my stomach still hurts. I walk out of the restaurant to breathe. For the first time, I see the sign of the restaurant: Blue City Café. Cuba is damn right. I will never forget the place.

"Where are you going?" Immanuel comes out after me.

I point to the river. "I need to walk along the shore and take some photos. You're welcome to come along, or you can hang with the bar girls here, and I'll find you later."

He brushes past me. I know I'm being mean-spirited but don't feel like apologizing. He huffs and puffs toward the river, and I follow in my loose flip-flops.

We reach the river and turn right onto a well-contained path along the bluff. Below us, the river shimmers in the last rays of the sunset. Down the grassy slope, a bride and groom pose for the photographer in their wedding attire. The bridal gown trails behind her, leaving a path of foamy waves. The slanting sun renders her transparent, her hair, torso, limbs. The only solid thing is her heart, red and delirious with happiness. I cross my fingers for them. May their love flow like the Mississippi and never dry out. Immanuel is watching too, leaning against the railing, his shoulders no longer heaving. Do the newlyweds remind him of his proposal, before he moved in with me? He said he wanted to be with me on a daily basis, not because his landlady kicked him out of his basement apartment. I said we should probably wait to see if we could live under the same roof for a year or two before we made that leap. I didn't want to repeat my marriage that lasted less than three weeks. My ex-husband proposed to me on the phone from Berlin, flew to Beijing the next day to marry me, and we split on the peak of the Emei Mountain during our honeymoon, after I refused to wash his underwear.

And I refused to sign a prenuptial agreement to marry Aiden, even after we had two kids together.

I pride myself as a good observer. But Immanuel defies all logic. Like his paintings, he hides himself behind layers of masking tape, allowing fragments of an eye, tip of a nose, parts of genitalia, fingers, or toes flickering from behind the quarter-inch strips that he cuts meticulously with a razor. Phantoms of his face and spirits. Why does he put himself behind the bars? To feel safe, to attract viewers and buyers? He seems sweet, reliable, and punctual, coming home every day at 4:00, waiting for me to take a walk and make dinner with him; yet, he complains that I demand him to have dinner with me too often; therefore, I hinder him from painting, his ambition to become a great artist. I know he spends 99 percent of his free time hanging out in his favorite cafés in Minneapolis: Peace Coffee, Common Roots, Seward Café. I asked him once why he didn't go to his studio to paint, and he said he needed to work on his artist's statement. Well, his statement changes every week, and each version makes less sense than the previous one. He is anticapitalism, anticorporation, anticonsumption; yet, he hunts online for the most expensive silk underwear, gloves, boots, paint, books, foods, porn. He claims to be a peace lover, talks in the most gentle, barely audible voice; yet, he once chased me out of the house with a pair of scissors, just because he didn't like a word that I had said.

"Hey, Daddy, look, look!"

A most lovely girl in a white dress points up at a giant, creamy white flower floating in a sea of dark green. Immediately, I smell it: a lemon-citronella scent that permeates the dusk along the bluff, a scent that feels just right for this beautiful veranda, river, and the smiling girl. As soon as I see the first one, the second, third, and fourth pop out of the green canopy. I follow the flowers into the thick foliage, down to the brown trunk. The tree is so thick that I can't see the roots. What tree is it? The flowers look like lotus, but lotus grows only in the water.

"It's magnolia," says a man behind me. I turn and see a shockingly handsome man pushing a stroller, an equally tall and handsome white woman next to him, carrying a baby in a pouch in front of her, a ball of fuzzy blond curls sticking out of the pouch.

"Wow, this is the biggest and most beautiful magnolia tree I've ever seen!" I exclaim.

The father looks at me, his brown eyes speckled with blazing green.

"It's our state flower, and it's everywhere in Tennessee and down the Mississippi." He smiles as if I were praising his children. "In fact, my dad voted for it in the fifties. Its official name is magnolia grandiflora, because it is the biggest among all magnolias, and the tallest, as tall as ninety-six feet. But we call it southern belle, for its beautiful flower, scent, and rose-colored seeds. We also call it bull bay because its young leaves look like bay leaves and bulls love to eat them, especially when they feel sick. My favorite part of the tree is its trunk. The wood, hardy and cream colored, makes the most endurable, most beautiful furniture. No bugs eat my wool sweaters in my magnolia trunks and closets. We have three trees around our house. No mosquitoes bother us when we sit outside."

I nod. "In China, we use magnolia buds to open sinuses and clear sinus infections. We use the bark for bloating and indigestion."

"Animals know what's good for them," he agrees.

"Daddy, are they angels?"

The father laughs and bends down to hug the child. I laugh too.

"Yes, they are angels, God's gifts for us," says the father.

"Oh, oh, oh, look at that one. She got wings, see?" cries the girl.

I follow her finger and find it in the tree. It's still in the state of budding. Two petals open halfway from the root of the oval body, like angel wings. It is by far the least dazzling of all the flowers, smaller, dimmer, its tip damaged; yet, it grabs our attention the most. We all stare in silence, holding our breath. Is it because it's hidden deep, in the earliest stage of blossoming, therefore, full of potential and hope?

Far away, the glass and metal pyramid glistens with an orange glow.

"What's that?" I ask the father, pointing beyond.

"Oh, the Great American Pyramid," he replies with a faint sneer.

"Hmm, what's the story?"

"It was built in 1989 as the sixth largest pyramid on Earth, the symbol of our city, like the Arch for St. Louis, the Statue of Liberty for New York. It kind of made sense, since our city was named after the ancient capital of Egypt and close to Cairo. The city collapsed so suddenly that Memphis got scared. People wanted to do something to stop the bad luck coming down the river. The pyramid might do the trick. And the statue of Ramesses the Great, one of the most famous Egyptian pharaohs, made from the model of the actual statue in Egypt, would surely bring power and fame to Memphis. But my dad went nuts since the groundbreaking. Stupid, stupid thing to do, he muttered. The pyramid doesn't belong here. The evil king has no business standing on our ancestors' land. My dad was a quarter Cahokia. He believed the site chosen for the pyramid was the base of the burial mound. He wrote letters to the government, but nothing was ever returned. Nothing. On November 9, 1991, the pyramid's grand opening night, he circled around the house as if mad, chanting words I couldn't understand. I remembered the day because it was my birthday, and my friends wanted to take me to the new arena for the grand opening concert, but the tickets were long gone. My dad wouldn't have allowed me to go anyway. Well, when we turned on the TV that night, the first thing we saw was the flooded arena and sandbags piled around the perimeter to save the electric wires under the stage. Some idiots had shut off the pumps during the day while loading in the Judds' concert equipment and forgot to turn it back on. My mom ordered me to turn off the TV so my dad wouldn't see. But he knew. He kept shouting fire, water, fire, water, Sun God, water serpent, curse, mercy. I didn't know what he meant at that time. But later, I found out that Ramesses the Great was the sun god Ra. Well, that was just the beginning of disasters. The arena was assumed to be NBA ready, but when the Grizzlies came to town, they discovered they couldn't use it. The upgrading would cost more than building a new arena. The Grizzlies left. So did the University of Memphis men's basketball team. The pyramid remained empty, leaching millions of dollars every year from the city. My friend is a feng shui master. He said a leaking faucet could drain money like crazy. Now, imagine a big flood on opening night. If it's not a hemorrhage, what else would it be? The last event held in the pyramid was 2007. I was there for the concert by Bob Seger and his Silver Bullet Band. Well, well, well, how more symbolic could it be? After the concert, no one used the arena ever again. The silver bullet killed it, like killing a vampire. Pow!"

He aims at the pyramid with his hand in the shape of a gun. I jump. The baby starts crying. The mother hums and rocks then opens her blouse to nurse the baby. The girl slumps in the stroller as if the story weighed on her. How much can she understand? The orange glow has vanished. The pyramid now stands in a deep shadow.

"The pyramid truly became a pharaoh's curse, a haunted place. No business would go near it. Not even a casino. You would think one could fight evil with evil! Someone came up with the idea of turning it into an aquarium. But the fire from the Sun God just killed it in the bud. The city finally decided to remove the pharaoh. So in 2012, the statue was leased to the University of Memphis for one dollar. You can see it on the campus if you are interested. Well, it did kind of lift the curse. The Bass Pro Shops finally signed a fifty-five-year contract with us. It's now being renovated into a mega–shopping center for outdoor sports, with workshops for fishing and hunting and archery, and a river museum."

"How do you know all this?" I ask.

"My father died of brain cancer soon after the pyramid was built. So I have been obsessed with the curse conspiracy. After I graduated from Emory, I started working for the city planning, where I met my beautiful wife." He hugs her with one arm. "So I know all the past and future of the pyramid. It took five years to negotiate with Bass Pro Shops, back and forth, back and forth, and it was the removal of the statue that landed our contract."

He makes a gesture of wiping his forehead and laughs. "Hey, what brought you here, if I may ask? By the way, I'm Anthony. Welcome to Memphis."

I shake his hand and tell him about the Kinship of Rivers project, our travels down the Mississippi, our river flags, our plan to bring two thousand flags to the Yangtze River from the Mississippi River. The smile on his face gets bigger and brighter, spreading to his entire body, to his wife and children. He grabs my hand again.

"Beautiful, sister, just beautiful! What a great idea, what great deeds! I wish my dad could meet you. I wish I could go to the Yangtze with you! But my spirit, our spirits, will travel with you down the Mississippi and up the Yangtze. God bless you. God bless our rivers and land. May I give you a hug?"

I open my arms. What else could I have done but receive the blessing from this beautiful man and father. The mother also hugs me, their baby between us, suckling milk. Their warmth opens my blocked channels.

The young girl raises her arms, wanting a hug. I lift her to my chest. Her fuzzy blond hair feels like the morning sun, and she smells of fresh lemon, the scent of a budding magnolia.

Immanuel is looking in our direction. I wave, calling him to join us under the canopy of the southern belle, the magnificent magnolia grandiflora, in the city of Memphis, at the confluence of the Wolf and Mississippi Rivers.

25

The Great Crossroads

Yazoo Pass could easily be the hottest café in Manhattan. Its wall-to-wall windows let the sun into the entire café, furnished with glass chrome tables and chairs, lush brown couches and loveseats, booths with leather seats, outlets for laptops, and of course, wireless service. Food is local, organic. It would have been Immanuel's café if it were in Minneapolis.

It sits in the heart of Clarksdale, a small blues town in Mississippi.

Immanuel is immersed in wireless bliss, a steaming mug of cappuccino made of organic raw milk, two toasted croissants, a perfectly fried egg over-easy on the glistening porcelain plate. When he finishes the feast, he pours himself a glass of milk from the jar that cost $15.95. The waitress apologized profusely for the price but guarantees its supreme taste because it's organic and raw, from a farmer she knows. She even petted the cow that produced the milk! I'm lactose intolerant, but I buy it anyway, for Immanuel. Spending makes him happy. When the plastic swipes through the machine, his chest lifts, his eyes brighten, even his voice deepens. The breakfast—two cappuccinos, three croissants, two eggs, and a jar of milk—costs fifty dollars. But it's worth it. His blue eyes sparkle as he sips his milk, reads and types on his laptop, a contrast to the stormy Immanuel on our drive from Memphis to Clarksdale last night.

I had never heard of Clarksdale before this trip. The only reason we came this way is John Ruskey, a river guide I met through the Kinship of Rivers Facebook page. John promised to take us to Choctaw Island in Arkansas in his voyageur canoe, through two confluences: the White River and Mississippi and the Arkansas and Mississippi. We would camp on the sand beach of Choctaw Island.

"You'll see the heart of the lower Mississippi, Ping," he sang in his Mississippi twang, as we sealed the deal over the phone.

I sip Earl Grey and watch Immanuel chuckling as he scrolls his screen up and down, down and up. He needs this moment of peace and joy. Our drive from Memphis to Clarksdale was ghostly. I thought he hit the bottom in Memphis. But it is nothing compared to last night.

The distance between Memphis and Clarksdale is only 77.1 miles along the Great River Road, Highway 61. According to my iPhone, it takes only one hour and thirty-five minutes to reach our destination. That means we should get there before 10:00 p.m., and hopefully, we can find a decent motel. John also mentioned that we could camp at his Quapaw Canoe on the bank of the Sunflower River, if we need to.

Immanuel was in a bad mood when we got back to our car from the river walk.

"Did you have a good time with the black man?"

"Yes, I did, also with his family. I wish you would've joined us. Anthony and his wife Cristal told me such amazing stories about Memphis."

"Well, you didn't introduce him to me."

I was speechless. He saw me waving at him, but he walked away. Why was he so stubborn about making people go to him?

"Never mind. I just thought if we traveled together, we should work together as a team. Now would you please stay awake and direct me out of the city and to Clarksdale? I don't want to get lost again just because you doze off."

I laughed, not knowing how to respond. So I shouted GPS directions from my iPhone, adding my own interpretation just for the fun of it.

"Turn left to the Riverside, then onto Highway 61 South, the Great River Road of America. Distance from Memphis to Clarksdale: 77.1 miles, one hour and thirty-five minutes. The whole road, 1,400 miles from Minnesota to New Orleans, is also known as Blues Highway, with great musicians from Dylan and Prince at the headwaters, to Elvis Presley, Johnny Cash, BB King, and many blues singers in middle and southern Mississippi. It's a road along great music. Now let's turn off the CD and listen to local blues on the radio."

"Why are you talking like this?" he pinched his right ear shut.

"This is my work voice. I am trying to stay awake to give you directions."

He turned up Dark Dark Dark to the highest volume. We drove without a word. Every fifteen minutes, I shouted out the remaining distance over the blasting music. I pinched myself to stay awake, as the loud music kept shutting down my system and sending me into a slumber. When we reached Lula, my GPS went blank.

"Uh oh," I muttered.

"What!" he jumped. How did he hear me through this blast? A sign for Highway 49 zoomed by us then vanished in the dark.

"What road now? Highway 61 or 49?" he screamed.

I was alarmed by the hysteria in his voice. Was he having another sugar attack? He looked as if we were lost in a jungle.

"I believe we should stick to 61. It should take us to Clarksdale. But my GPS is not working for some reason."

He snatched my phone from my hand.

"Strange," he muttered, as he scrolled the screen in disbelief. "Nothing but blankness. What happened?"

The car rumbled and shook as if in a convulsion. We were off the road and driving on the rough line designed to awaken sleeping drivers. He swerved to get the car back on the road but went off the side again. For a second, our car seemed to be falling off the road. He turned the wheel, and we spun around until the car screeched to a stop, and the engine died, along with Dark Dark Dark. The silence pricked my ears with hundreds of needles. I couldn't see where we were, but I felt the vibration of a deep hum from the fields, the road, the sky, as if we were in an earthquake bubble, then came a wailing with an impossibly high pitch. I had the urge to jump out of the car, chase after the sound, troll, writhe, and wail with that sound that no human could make.

"Did you hear that, Immanuel?"

"What are you talking about? You're hallucinating. It's not real. There's no blues. You know I don't listen to this stuff. Besides, the car is dead, and the radio is off."

He must have heard it too. Or how would he have recognized the sound was blues? He clutched the wheel as if hanging on for dear life. Did he also feel the urge to walk into the darkness? Where were we? I flipped on the interior light. It came on. The Highway 49 sign appeared.

"Where the heck are we?" screamed Immanuel. "What's that Highway 49? You never told me we should be on it."

"I have no idea how you got on 49. I said we should stick to 61, remember?" I took my phone from him and rebooted it. "As long as we stick to 61, we should arrive at Clarksdale very soon. Oh, look, the GPS came back. We're not far, about ten miles."

He started the car, and we followed the green pulsing circle pointing to the red dot, our destination. In about fifteen minutes, the green and the red almost merged. We were at Batesville. The GPS told us to turn left, onto the service road.

"Batesville, hmmm, could it be another name for Clarksdale?" I muttered, checking my GPS over and over, resetting the route to make sure: 291 Sunflower Avenue, Clarksdale. The GPS insisted that we turn onto the service road. John said his canoe company was on Sunflower River. Could it be on the other side of the highway?

Immanuel took the phone from my hand to check it himself then turned left without hesitation. If the GPS said so, it must be right. Pretty soon, the green dot passed the red one, and the road ended at the Comfort Inn. We stopped at the front door. I knew this couldn't be our destination. We didn't drive all the way to end up in a motel.

The front desk was empty. I rang the bell. A blond woman came out. I showed her the address.

"Oh no, hon, this is Batesville, not Clarksdale. It's a twenty-minute drive from here. Just turn right on Highway 6, hon, toward the river, and it'll take you to Clarksdale."

I thanked her and ran back to the car. I told Immanuel what she said.

"But the GPS said it was here."

"Well, do you see Quapaw Canoe and the river?"

"No. But we'll find it in the morning. The GPS said . . ."

"This is Batesville, twenty minutes away from Clarksdale."

"What about the GPS?"

"Screw GPS! It's just a gadget. The woman lives here, drives here every day. Do you believe this damn thing can compete with her?"

"Human flesh makes tons of mistakes, Ping."

He was right. We did make mistakes all the time, including following the gadget to Batesville. How on Earth did we get here? Highway 61 was supposed to take us straight into Clarksdale. When did we get off 61? I remembered seeing the sign 61 and 49, in a flash, which pointed to Clarksdale, then my phone and car went berserk. Something must have happened at that crossroad that led us astray. But then why did my GPS so stubbornly point us to Batesville instead of taking us back on the road to Clarksdale? It just didn't make sense. Suddenly, the low hum, the wailing music, and our spinning car came back to me. I froze. Were these all related?

"I'm not staying here, Immanuel. We're going to Clarksdale. If you're too tired to drive, I'll drive. The woman from the hotel gave me good directions."

He sped out of the parking lot and turned right on Highway 6. The road was empty and dark. Not a single light on either side or ahead of us. Where was Clarksdale? The woman said it was only twenty minutes away, and we had been driving twenty-five minutes. We should at least see some lights, an indication that we were approaching the city. It was only 10:30. There was no way a city would go to bed so early. Even though I couldn't see a thing, I had a weird sense of déjà vu. If we turned left into the Comfort Inn, then turned right to get out, that meant we were back on the same road we had come in. If it was the case, then we were driving back to the crossroad of 61 and 49. Had Immanuel noticed it? He should have. But he showed no sign. Was he under a spell? Were we?

The car stopped. I lurched forward, then I heard him say, "You may have heard it wrong. She may have said turn left instead of right. I'm going back to where we came from."

I didn't protest when he spun around and drove back toward Batesville. I knew the woman had told me to turn right on 6. "Toward the river, hon," she said. But doubt crept up on me. We would find out soon anyway, I told myself. I rechecked my GPS, and it was pointing to Clarksdale in the direction of Batesville. Very, very strange. Suddenly, I remembered John Ruskey. I had his number. Why not call him and ask for directions? It was late, but it was an emergency. He said we should call him when we arrived.

I dialed John's number. "Please leave a message. May the river be with y'all."

Well, we were certainly driving farther away from the river. I waited three minutes, dialed his number again, and left another message asking for help. The darkness felt impenetrable. Where would we end up tonight?

Batesville reappeared. Same gas station, same motels, and this time, I saw the road signs: 55 North to Memphis, 6 East to Oxford. Oxford, that was the campus of the University of Mississippi. Immanuel seemed to know we shouldn't go beyond the intersection. He turned left onto the service road and drove toward the Comfort Inn, as the GPS directed us.

"I don't want to ask for directions again. She'll think we're stupid."

He slapped the wheel with his palm. "Why can't we just stay here for the night? I'm so tired. I need to lie down." He sounded like he was crying.

"Can I drive please? I promised John we would get to Clarksdale tonight. It couldn't be far away. John is a river guide, owns a canoe company, remember?

So it has to be close to the river. I can feel it. If we keep going to the west a little further, we'll find Clarksdale."

"I am not going back to that road," he hissed.

"There's no other way, Immanuel. Please give me the keys." I looked him in the eyes. His pupils dilated and scattered. He looked on the verge of a nervous breakdown.

"Absolutely not. I am driving." He started the car.

I buckled up, something I do when I sense danger. He snickered and hit the gas pedal. The car shot out of the parking lot for the second time. We were not coming back here no matter what, I said to myself.

Same darkness, same emptiness, same bewilderment. Where were we? Where were we going? I dialed John's number. Again, no answer, just his voice: "May the river be with y'all." Was he real? Was this road real? And Clarksdale? And the river? How could it not be real? We had driven, canoed, camped, and walked along it since we left home. But now we seemed to be in a different universe.

Immanuel drove like a maniac, slamming down the brakes at each sign. Our car lurched back and forth, back and forth. My stomach churned. I dug into the palm side of my wrist, an acupressure point for nausea.

"I'm getting carsick. Please slow down."

"I can drive however I want," he screamed, hitting the wheel with his fist. The car lurched forward with a roar. The speedometer went up to seventy.

"Immanuel, this is a country road. The speed limit is under forty."

"Shut up, just shut up!" he screamed, hitting the wheel. The car honked. I heard the siren, then the flashing light of a police car in the rearview mirror.

"Cops, Immanuel."

He turned pale. His hands shook so much he could barely steer the car off the road and park on the shoulder. A cop came to the driver's side. Immanuel lowered the window.

"Good evening. Do you know why we stopped you?" he asked.

"Speeding, sir?"

"Well, you sped through two stop signs at seventy-five miles per hour. May I see your license, please?"

He went back to his car to check Immanuel's record. We sat in silence. I didn't want to tell him that it was good he finally got caught. It could have cost lives, his, mine, others. Hopefully, he would start paying more attention. Would he? He already had gotten caught going through red lights three or four times before, but that didn't stop him from doing it again. It was shocking to watch him drive so recklessly while he cared so much about being appropriate, obeying rules, and so on. Once behind the wheel, he became a beast. No more Minnesota Nice, no more yield to other drivers who wanted to exit or enter.

The cop was taking a long time checking his record. Oh, God, I hoped his last fine for going into a one-way street didn't show up on his record yet. How much would the fine be this time?

The cop came back. He shined his flashlight into our car, on his face, then mine. "So you're from Minnesota. What are you doing in Mississippi? What's in the back?"

"We're traveling along the river for an art project, sir," I said. "And the boxes in the back hold a thousand flags made by river folks from the upper Mississippi. We're traveling down the river to make another thousand flags with the folks from the lower Mississippi. Next year, we'll take them as gifts from the Mississippi to the Yangtze . . ."

He listened, his face relaxed, then slowly, a big smile.

"What a good thing to do!" he said. "What's your next stop?"

"Clarksdale, sir. And we are having trouble finding the place. We've been driving back and forth along this road, and it didn't get us anywhere. We're frustrated and tired. Perhaps that's why we failed to notice the stop sign, sir. We're not excusing ourselves, but we're very sorry, sir."

"Hmm, I see. You know if you just keep driving to the west, you'll hit Clarksdale. Are you staying with friends there? Did you say you have a guide to take you down the Mississippi?"

"Yes, sir, John Ruskey from Quapaw Canoe Company is taking us to Choctaw Island tomorrow morning. That's why we have to find Clarksdale tonight."

"Oh, the Driftwood! Why didn't you say so earlier?" The cop smiled. "Just keep going west on this road, and you'll see the city in fifteen minutes. It's about ten miles from here. Once you see the McDonald's sign, turn left, and you'll be in the business district. The Quapaw Company is on the Sunflower River, not very far. Do drive safely, sir," he turned to Immanuel. "I'll just give you a warning this time. Make sure you slow down and stop at every sign. There are other officers along the road."

I couldn't believe our luck. A Mississippi policeman let us go without a fine? Didn't he say we had two charges: speeding and going through stop signs? Wow, the magic of river flags and John Ruskey. If the cop knew him, then he must be real, and Clarksdale must be real too.

We reached Clarksdale shortly. For some reason, we missed the McDonald's sign and ended up in a different part of the town. It looked ghostly in the dark, bleak like Cairo. We drove by a motel. The sign read the Riverside, Open, but the ivy-covered building looked abandoned. Something had happened there long ago, I said to myself. Immanuel slowed the car. I shook my head, and he moved on. At the corner, I saw the street sign: Sunflower Avenue. We must be close to Quapaw then. Where was it? Before I could say anything, Immanuel had turned and Ground Zero appeared around the corner. At first glance, it looked like another abandoned structure in a desolate parking lot. It was lit inside. Shadows flickered through the graffiti-covered windows. Minneapolis also had a Ground Zero, an S&M joint Immanuel frequented and had once dragged me to to watch girls in leather bras and thongs stamping on a naked, legless man in a metal box, moaning with pleasure as blood sputtered from his pale fat body punctured by the stiletto heels. I felt sick for three months after that visit. Music seeped through the door and walls, a song similar to what I heard from the wheat fields at the crossroad of 61 and 49. The singer's voice glided along the guitar strings—a thin wail of sorrow, a thread of longing. What was this place? Why did it look so bleak and cheerful at the same time? I wanted to check it out, but Immanuel had made another turn.

We passed on the street lined with boutiques, a furniture store, restaurants, and a very modern looking café. Immanuel parked the car and jumped out. He pulled and pushed the café door, but it wouldn't open. He kept trying until I told him it was closed. He threw himself upon the glass and looked in.

"We're coming here for breakfast," he declared in a croaking voice.

I looked up. Yazoo Pass. "I bet they're wireless," I said.

We moved on and reached State Street. Just as the cop said, it was lined with McDonald's, Taco Bell, Days Inn. Immanuel looked at me, and I just pointed at a motel ahead of us. It really didn't matter. Everything would be just the same. We pulled up. I ran in. It was full, to my surprise. The clerk told me to go to the Presidential Inn.

"It's behind the mall, hon," she said sleepily. "You won't see it from the street. Just enter the mall and go to its very end, and you'll see it. I just checked for you. They still have two rooms left."

Interesting. This seemingly bleak town was busy. I directed Immanuel to the inn and checked into a room. Immanuel went straight to bed without a word. I washed and stretched out next to him. What happened to us tonight was beyond my comprehension. Tomorrow John was taking us to Choctaw Island, but where was he? The phone rang. John Ruskey. I tried to jump out of the bed to grab the phone charging in the bathroom, but my body was so heavy as if chained to the bed. It rang four times. I listened to the voicemail as John's voice flowed. He had just come home from an event. He was sorry we got lost. He wanted to know if we arrived in Clarksdale safely. He wished us good night. I slid into a deep sleep, with his last words lingering in my ear: "May the river be with y'all."

By 8:30 a.m., Yazoo Pass is ablaze with light and sounds, the southern dialect, German, French, Italian . . . The whole world seems to gather here for a good breakfast. Immanuel is also ablaze in the light. I have never seen him so peaceful, so illuminated. This fleeting glimpse into his soul—is this what binds us?

As if answering my question, he looks up and reaches for my hand. "I love you," he says, his eyes tearing up. "So sorry about yesterday. I should never have had the ice tea at Cairo. Those sugar crashes. Will you forgive me?"

I squeeze his hand. "Will you forgive me for dragging you to Clarksdale? We could have stayed in Batesville last night. I don't know why I was so stubborn."

"Thank God you did! Or we wouldn't be sitting here!" He smiles, his eyes warm like the spring sky, melting the iceberg in my chest.

"Would you tell me what happened to you in Memphis?" I regret my question immediately. You idiot, why are you ruining this moment?

"Well, a bad fight with my ex-wife that broke our marriage. Back at home in Viroqua, we had a band. My wife was the singer, and I played drums. The men in the band started flirting with her. She did nothing when they kicked me out of the band, well, not exactly, but they told me they got a new drummer and I could play guitar if I wanted. I like playing guitar. I mean I am good at making up songs when I just strum and fool around. You heard me play in the bedroom every night. I hate those songs they were going to perform for their upcoming gig in Memphis. I could have done it as a drummer but not as a guitarist. So basically they kicked me out by assigning me to an impossible task. My wife didn't stop them. She let them bring in the new drummer, let them come to my house for rehearsal every night. I left whenever they came over in the evening. I couldn't stand their laughing and flirting in my own house. I spent more and more time in coffee shops and the library, less and less time at home, and she never tried to bring me back. When we passed Memphis on our way to Nashville, the subject came up, and we argued. Then I told her I was going to spend a week with my ex-girlfriend in Oregon during her Memphis gig, and she screamed she hated me. That just did it. It severed the last string of our marriage."

"So sorry to hear that."

A shiver runs through my spine. Immanuel hardly spends any time at home except for eating and sleeping. What does it mean then? What about our fight in Memphis? Does it sever our string? It was pretty thin in the first place. On Facebook, he has just changed his profile as an artist living in Minneapolis.

I look up and see a bearded man in a black felt hat entering Yazoo Pass. He is thin and sinewy, medium height but appeared taller, and he walks as if floating on water.

"John!" I jump up. He's already striding toward our table. We have never met, but I know it's him. Who else could move through a crowd like a fish in the river? A northern pike, a walleye, a catfish? No, he has more elements than just fish. Before I could come up with the right species, he grabs my hand, shaking it up and down.

"Hi, y'all!" he calls.

"Hi, y'all!" I call back, laughing. I know immediately John Ruskey will take us to the most magical place in the deep of the Mississippi.

"So Big Muddy Wayne has trained you well," he laughs.

Yes, indeed. During our morning coffee on the confluence of the Mississippi and Missouri, BMW made me practice the call until I got it right. Our river greeting, he said. With that, you will get all the help you need along the Mississippi. Y'all, he hooted, and the river rippled with rings of laughter.

"Would you like some raw milk from the local organic farm?" I ask John. Immanuel frowns. It's too casual and too personal to offer this to someone I have just met, but John won't give a damn whether I am being appropriate or not, as long as my offer is genuine.

Sure enough, he sits down, pours himself a full glass and drinks it in one gulp, just like a Chinese man bottoming a glass of seventy-five-proof spirits. He takes off his hat, his graying hair flying over his shoulders, and his brown eyes lighting up with speckles of green from under his thick brows. I think of Anthony, the black Cahokia from Memphis, BMW from St. Louis, Bob the ranger from the St. Croix River, Brent the wandering magician at the Horseshoe Lake, Tom the midget in Cairo, Fay the southern belle, Mr. Ren from the Three Gorges, Mr. Kang, the descendent of the Great Canal builder . . . These people look as different as night and day. They are, however, connected with similar spirits: wild, untamable, primordial, the spirits that light up their souls and come out through their eyes. I know I'm going to meet more spirits like this as we travel down the river. I remember Ranger Bob's words as he flew me down the Namekagen River in his canoe: "River people are different, Ping; we are another species."

"I brought you a river map I made," says John, spreading it on the table. I recognize the brilliant watercolors and the zigzagging Mississippi right away. BMW has a similar map in his office. He said John made it while canoeing with him in March. He would paddle a few strokes then draw or write on his sketchbook in his lap. I laughed, thinking he just made it up. Now that I'm face to face with John, I realize BMW wasn't joking.

"How many days do you have and how far do you want to paddle?" he asks.

"Three full days. I want to paddle as much as possible, and I want to spend some time on Choctaw Island. We're both strong paddlers. Thirty river miles a day is easy."

He looks me in the eyes, as if checking how serious I am, then he nods, and points to the map.

"Normally, we start from the Helena Harbor, a 115-river-mile journey, camping on Island 62, Smith Point, and Choctaw Island. It takes about ten to twelve days, depending on the paddlers. But in your case, we will start at the Rosedale Landing, paddle to Choctaw, camp there for two nights, then come back on the third day. Most of the paddling will take place today, about forty river miles, depending on the water level. The lower Mississippi is wild and open. Its channel can vary from half a mile wide to three miles at the mouths of the White River and Arkansas River and can fluctuate fifty vertical feet. Landings, boat ramps, islands, campsites, sandbars, and other landmarks change from week to week. But you'll see all the wildlife and wonders that few have access to. We can paddle up some back channels to reach the Arkansas three miles above its mouth, and then paddle back down the Arkansas to rejoin the Mississippi near Ozark Landing. However, forty river miles through giant boils, whirlpools, and hydraulics is a lot to handle, even for advanced paddlers. The route has no service along the way. If we capsize, it means a long swim to the shore. So think about it. Take your time before you answer me."

I turn to Immanuel, just to make sure that John hasn't scared him off. He can handle it. He took me to a six-day canoe trip in the Boundary Waters. We paddled, portaged, and changed our campsites every night. It was my first trip to do most of the paddling. I learned fast. I had to. We paddled for days without seeing a person. A slight mistake could have put us in danger. Could the lower Mississippi be more difficult than the Boundary Waters? Didn't the SUP instructor in St. Louis say: "It's all water. Everything you learned about it can be applied?"

Immanuel gives me a nod.

"We can leave any time, John."

He sits up, looking pleased. "All right. I'll stop at my house first, check on my daughter. Haven't seen her much lately since the paddle season started. I may take her with me this time. I miss her so much. She's five, my angel. I'll also pick up our dinner for tonight on the island. Spanish chicken, made last night. Then we'll go to Quapaw Company. My crew should be there very soon."

My eyes open wide. So he has already arranged everything for the trip. Then why did he ask me all those questions to scare us away? Just to make sure? Did he anticipate our determination and capability? He must. He posted a welcome note on the Kinship of Rivers page while I was paddling with BMW in St. Louis: *Ping, I can feel you're flowing closer to Clarksdale, Mississippi.*

We stand up to leave. I take the milk jar, still more than half full. We can use it for camping. Immanuel closes his laptop with reluctance.

"Can we come back to Clarksdale on our way home?"

I laugh, knowing he wants to come back to Yazoo Pass. "We'll try. It's out of our way, but it's possible, depending on what happens in New Orleans."

We follow John to his house. He has a lovely garden with flowers and herbs. His wife must have a green thumb. John brushes his hand over a rosemary bush. "I used it for my Spanish chicken," he says then shouts for his daughter. "Emma, Emma, Daddy's home."

He looks sad when there is no answer. "Well, my wife must have taken her to daycare. Perhaps you'll meet her when we come back."

He grabs a cooler and starts pulling out stuff from the refrigerator and pantry: spice, salt, potatoes, tomatoes, pepper, lettuce, pasta, salami, sausage, cheese, butter, jam, eggs, bacon, olive oil, and finally, the Spanish chicken he roasted the night before. Just from a look at it, my mouth starts watering already. "Wait until I cook it again with potatoes and tomatoes and peppers over slow fire, in a Dutch oven." He winks.

His house is full of colors, blue, orange, yellow. A large engraved print catches my eyes: a figure in the clothes and posture of an ancient Chinese sage, with a dog head.

"What's that?" I point. The figure looks strange and familiar at the same time.

"Oh, my father's work. He called it *Blue Dog Buddha*."

"He's really good."

"He worked as an engineer all his life. Very strict about his routines, very strict with us too. His parents came to America from Russia. They opened a butcher shop and did pretty well. During the Depression, my grandpa gave credits to the poor who couldn't afford the meat. It left him no money to pay the bank for his shop and house. The morning the bank came to possess everything, he shot himself. He was a proud man, couldn't face his wife and children. My father had just turned five when that happened. He was never the same again, never let himself forget what poverty could do to us. I had lots of conflicts with him as I grew up. He wanted me to master a trade, something more practical, but all I wanted was to follow the river. For years, we hardly talked. In his later life, however, he started seeing images like this," John points to *Blue Dog Buddha*. "This piece was his last work, and he gave it to me before he passed away."

We gaze at the image. The more I look at it, the more it looks familiar. This Buddha of half-human, half-animal, this blend of civilization and wildness, this harmony of authority and benevolence, awe inspiring yet humble, far away yet near, strange yet familiar—is it the Piasa Bird? Perhaps. But the bird carries too much destruction. *Blue Dog Buddha*, however, vibrates with kindness, peace, and wisdom.

I turn to John and almost jump when I see his face. No wonder the Buddha looks so familiar. It's a portrait of John, or a portrait after John's spirit, the river spirit I feel from all the river people. His father knew. Of course he knew. John was his son, after all, the artist his father had wanted to be all his life.

"Your father was an artist, and he passed his torch to you, John."

"Thank you, Ping." His voice rumbles deeply.

"Are we leaving?" Immanuel comes out of the bathroom.

"Yes. Follow me to the Sunflower River. You can park your car at our company."

We pass the Riverside Motel again. It looks more cheerful and alive in the sun.

Quapaw Canoe Company, a three-story brick building, stands on the bank of the Sunflower River on Sunflower Avenue. I notice the beautiful stones on the ground, colorful and smooth in all kinds of shapes. John must have collected them from different rivers he explored. He invites us into the building. It is a museum: a vast display of driftwood and mud fossils in the most impossible shapes and colors: dragons, fish, flowers, plants, and stones with eyes, mouths, hearts. Water is the most nimble artist of all. No human hand can compete with her.

How many rivers has John roamed? And why only driftwood and fossils? Suddenly the cop who stopped us at the crossroad comes to my mind, his big smile when I mentioned John's name, and his remark about John.

"Are you the Driftwood?"

He laughs, and I double over laughing.

"So what made you settle in Clarksdale, Driftwood?"

He smiles from ear to ear. "I met my wife."

Of course. What else could it be? I point to the sign that hangs above his collections. "What's the meaning of Quapaw?"

"Downstream people. The Quapaw followed the rivers from the east all the way to the mouth of the Arkansas and Mississippi. Their headquarters are now in Ottawa, Oklahoma. Their land, Tar Creek, was mined for lead and zinc for many years. The mining companies made billions of dollars, but the natives got nothing, and their land is now the most toxic place in the United States, their children with the highest level of lead poisoning."

"The film *Tar Creek Superfund Site*, is it about them?"

He nods. We stand in silence. Why did every place touched by money end with a tragic story?

"How far down the stream do you go with your crew?" I ask finally.

"All the way to Nola, to the end of the Bird's Foot." His face opens like a sunflower.

"What's Nola?"

"New Orleans, Louisiana."

I smile. I saw Nola signs everywhere but had no idea what it meant until now.

We come outside to pack. John says we can take our laptops, which makes Immanuel immensely happy. I have no heart to remind him that there is no electricity or Internet on the island. I'm also surprised that we can take as much as we want to make ourselves comfortable: clothes, food, books, and other necessities. The canoe can carry a lot, John says. Well, we don't have to portage from island to island like our trip in the Boundary Waters. I pick out ten rolls of river flags, three boxes of fabric crayons and markers, a small print-making kit, and a dozen pieces of fabric.

"Here's Mark River, our bowman," says John.

Mark looks like a boulder in the current, dark skin glistening in the sunlight, muscles rolling like waves. He moves like a bullfrog, smooth and strong and ready to jump ten times higher than his body weight. We shake hands. His bulging eyes shine as he pats the canoe on the trailer.

"We're taking this babe?" he asks, as he cleans the smudge off the name *Junebug II* with his fingertips.

"Wow, where did you get this beauty? It's just gorgeous!" I say, stroking the red trim along the canoe. It looks familiar. I've seen it somewhere, recently. I have paddled it.

"John made it," Mark says. "In fact, he made all the boats we have here: *Kingfisher*, *Grasshopper*, *Ladybug*, *Water Ram*." He points at the building. "All stored there. I'll show them to you when we come back. Our biggest ones are twenty-nine-foot cypress strip voyageur style canoes. They can take an army down the Mississippi. But this babe is special. It has a twin, in St. Louis."

My brain lights up in a flash. Yes, I did see its twin at BMW's place. He took me in it to camp on Duck Island at the confluence of the Missouri and Mississippi. Now I remember its name: *Junebug*. "So the Big Muddy Wayne has a sister."

Mark nods. "John made *Junebug I* and *II* side by side, after he finished his apprenticeship with Ralph Frese, the legendary canoe master. He chose John as his last apprentice, to pass down all his knowledge. The *Junebug* twins were John's graduation thesis."

I stroke the smooth wood along the intricate patterns. "What kind of wood?"

"Louisiana bald cypress," John says. He has come over with ropes to secure the canoe to the trailer. "I use red oak for stems, and a variety of other woods throughout, but mostly cypress, from the Atchafalaya Basin."

Another man comes over, smiling and slapping John and Mark on their shoulders. His movements are bouncy and relaxed as if he were dribbling a basketball. He is Ellis, our driver to the landing.

"Aww, I want to go to the island too," he whines, smiling at me.

"Why can't you?" I ask.

He laughs, shaking his head. "But who's gonna pick you up in Arkansas at the end of the trip, gal?"

I laugh and ask him if he played basketball. He did for his college then worked as a beer salesman for thirty years. Now, he's just enjoying his retirement, driving vans for the Mighty Quapaw and the canoe paddlers from all over the world.

"Life is goooood!" he sighs.

As we chat, John and Mark hook the canoe to the truck and board the western windows with Styrofoam boards. "The best air conditioning," John says, locking the building then looking around for a final check. "Let's go."

Our truck passes Riverside Motel again.

"What's that hotel?" I point to the ivy-covered place. It looks so quiet outside, but I feel the heavy energy inside.

"Aww, you don't know?" Ellis shouts. "The famous hotel that hosted the greatest musicians: Sonny Boy Williamson, Duke Ellington, Bob Nighthawk, Muddy Waters. Ike Turner lived and rehearsed his Rocket 88 there. It used to be a hospital. Bessie Smith died there when her car got hit at the Crossroads."

"Oh, wow!" I say, then it hits me.

"The Crossroads!" I almost yank Ellis's hand off the wheel. "What crossroads?"

"Easy, easy, miss. It's the famous crossroads of highway 61 and 49, where the devil tuned Robert Johnson's guitar and made him the best blues singer and player instantly. And of course, the devil took his soul as payment. Ever heard his 'Crossroads Blues'?"

He opens his mouth and sings:

I went to the crossroad, fell down on my knees
I went to the crossroad, fell down on my knees
Asked the Lord above: "Have mercy, now save poor Bob, if you please"

I shudder. This is the music I heard rolling back and forth in the fields when we got lost at the conjunction of 61 and 49, the music that gave me the urge to jump into the dark night to go after that echo. I didn't hear the words then, but the tune is the same, the pining, the wailing and pleading for mercy. That is when my GPS went berserk and pointed us to Batesville, and then Immanuel went berserk afterward.

Yeoo, standin' at the crossroad, tried to flag a ride
Ooo eeee, I tried to flag a ride
Didn't nobody seem to know me, babe, everybody pass me by

Mark joins in. His voice, deeper than Ellis's, adds weight to the song.

You can run, you can run, tell my friend Willie Brown
You can run, you can run, tell my friend Willie Brown
That I got the crossroad blues this mornin', Lord, babe, I'm sinkin' down

The song ends, but echo lingers in the silence. Immanuel sits frozen in his seat.

"Here it is, the Crossroads!" Ellis points to his left.

I look up. We are still driving along De Soto, at the edge of the town. On the grassy island where Ellis points, I see a baby-blue post with two guitars: one pointing north toward Highway 61 and one pointing east toward Highway 49. Below the guitars is the sign "The Crossroads."

I stare at the sign and the two guitar replicas. Nothing like the crazy energy I felt last night at the conjunction. Is it because of the daytime? No. I'm sure we didn't get this close to Clarksdale. Is there another crossroads of 61 and 49?

"Before he sold his soul," says Ellis, "Johnson was a mediocre musician. But after his deal with the devil at the Crossroads, he suddenly sang and played like a fiend, and women went nuts about him. He traveled from town to town, playing music wherever he felt like stopping. No woman could turn him down when he said, 'May I go home with you tonight?' He died young, in his twenties, poisoned by a jealous husband. Aww, what a life! To sing and play like that, to have women love him like that!"

"Would you die like him?" asks Mark.

Ellis thinks about it then shakes his head. "I heard it took him three days to die, crawling on the floor in agony as the poison ate through his guts. No way I'll die like that. When I'm ready to go, I shall have my last breath in my own bed, in my old lady's arms. She'll be yellin' like a fiend for leaving her behind, but what the heck! Still better than dying from rottin' intestines." He laughs, slapping his lap.

"Ellis's brother is Super Chikan," John says. "He tours around the world."

"Why Super Chikan? He loves chickens?"

"You bet he does," laughs Ellis. "Our family had a farm, with lots of chickens. And Jimmy would walk around talking to them all day long as if they were pals. We used to call him 'Chikan Boy.' He must have been a rooster in his past life."

"He's good. His name may go into the Hall of Fame someday." John points to the brick building nearby.

"I didn't know Clarksdale is such a center for the blues. Last night as I drove through the town, I thought this place was another Cairo."

Everyone laughs hard. "We fooled you, didn't we?" Ellis says between his guffaws. "Yeah, we keep our town rustic just the way it used to be. Germans and Japs love it. They have all the fancy buildings back at home. This is what they flock here for, the original flavors. Have you been to Ground Zero yet?"

"We drove by. That's what made me think of Cairo. I should have known better. Is everyone a musician in this town?"

"Pretty much so. Mark sings, and John has recordings of his own music. Really good stuff," Ellis says. "That's all we do in Clarksdale: work hard during the day, go to the blues club at night, drink cold beer, dance with women to the best music. Wouldn't live anywhere else. No devil can wrench me away from Clarksdale."

We all laugh.

"Did Bessie have her accident at this junction?" I ask. I'm still not convinced that this is the real Crossroads.

"Nope. It was north of town, on 61 South from Memphis where it meets 49, at Lula, near the White River. That's the real Crossroads, where Johnson sold his soul to the devil, where Bessie had her accident. This one in town was made for tourists. Good for business, you know." He winks.

I nod. Everything comes together now: the weird energy that messed up my GPS, the echoing singing, Batesville. Does everyone have the same experience when they pass the Crossroads?

"Don't you worry. Not everyone can encounter the devil," says Ellis, as if reading my mind. "It has to be mutual: both you and the devil are ready to trade. I bet Bessie got scared when she saw the devil and tried to run."

I look at Immanuel. Such terror in his eyes. Who did the devil come for, me or him?

"Enough bullshit, bro," Mark interrupts. "You're scaring our guests."

"We were already scared last night." I start telling them what happened. When I finish the story, no one says a word until Ellis breaks the silence.

"Damn Devil, I say! I'm glad you didn't get trapped at Batesville. Who knows what he may have done to you there. You got some good spirits protecting you."

I nod, thinking of John's voicemail message: *May the river be with y'all.*

Ellis drives into a gas station. "Hey, I'm going to get me some chicken wings. Would you like some?" He looks at me.

I shake my head, even though I'm hungry again. Immanuel will not approve of fried, conventional food. Ellis jumps out, hooks the pump to the truck, then runs in, and comes back with a small bag. Grease drips through the wax paper.

"Want some?" He offers it to everyone. It looks like chicken nuggets. I shake my head again. Mark and John both take some and start chewing heartily. A delicious smell fills the truck. I sniff, listen to the chewing sound, and my mouth suddenly floods with saliva.

"What exactly are you eating?"

"Chicken gizzards." Ellis winks.

"Can I have some?" I extend my palm. Ellis bursts out laughing.

"Haha, I knew you'd want it. I saved my last three pieces, sis." He drops the bag in my palm.

I fish one out, examine it in the air before I pop it in my mouth. Chicken gizzards are my childhood delicacy. Whenever we slaughtered a chicken, the gizzard was cleaned and sliced into thin pieces then sautéed with chicken heart, liver, and scallions. I would not eat the meat because I had raised the chickens from the beginning: watched them hatch, grow, lay eggs, mate, then become the meat for my family. The only thing I would eat was the gizzard, which is not meat, tendon, skin, or organ, just a sac where corn, husk, worms, stones, grass, and seeds are ground into mush. I suffered from frequent stomachaches as a child. For some reason, the gizzard soothed the pain. Later, I learned that Chinese medicine called it "chicken inner gold" and used it for indigestion and stomachaches. So I must have intuitively known its medicinal function, like an animal.

The southerners fry their gizzards whole, wrapped in corn flour peppered with spice. I chew slowly. Its greasy, spicy, firm, crunchy, and savory texture and flavors flood my stomach with peace. Immanuel is watching me. I can't tell if he's judging my manner or simply wants some. I hand him the bag. To my surprise, he takes one and pops it in his mouth. He better like it. It's the last piece. He chews and nods. I smile.

We arrive at the Rosedale Landing around 10:00 a.m. John and Mark jump out of the truck and start loading the canoe with provisions. The three giant coolers sit in the middle, then the tents, tables, chairs, and water bags. We each receive a waterproof case for our computers, camera, and cell phones. Soon, our canoe is bulging with things.

What if the canoe capsizes? How are we going to fish all the stuff from the bottom of the river?

"No worry," says Mark, as if reading my mind. "Nobody can steer the lower Mississippi like John."

When the canoe is all ready to go, John takes out a gigantic watermelon from the back of the truck, chops it in half, and cuts one half into slices. "Eat as much as you can, our water and food for the paddling," he says. Everyone plunges into the melon. I walk into the woods. I love watermelon, but it makes me pee like crazy. If we're going to sit in the canoe for six hours, I better not indulge myself.

When I walk back, Ellis is backing the canoe into the river. John stands in the chest-deep water, guiding Ellis. The canoe slides off the trailer then floats on the river, ready to take us. My heart jumps as I watch John swim to the shore pushing the canoe like a toy. This is going to be a great trip.

We step into our boat. Ellis waves, shouting that he will pick us up in Arkansas three days later. Mark sits in the bow seat in the front, massive like a mountain, wiping away my doubt that our canoe might tip over, losing all the gear and bags. We settle in behind the "mountain," holding a beautiful oar in our hands. It's light like a feather, curved slightly to go with the movement of the water.

"You know how to use this kind of oar?" John asks but stops as soon as he sees us dip it in the river. "You're indeed veteran paddlers," he says, a smile in his voice. "Well, you two will be the engines. Mark will set the pace."

I look back. He's standing on the back tip of the canoe as if he were on a SUP. Is he going to steer like that all the way to Choctaw Island? How does he keep his balance? But our boat isn't tippy at all, with all the weight in the middle, with Mark in the front as our anchor. He paddles like a canoe racer. Well, almost. His strokes are strong and precise, and he alerts us before he switches sides so our oars won't crash. It isn't so easy in the beginning because Immanuel's pace is a bit slower and longer than Mark's, so they clash often.

Mark reminds me of Todd, the always-smiling canoe racer I met while paddling the 252-mile river with the St. Croix River Association, a two-week journey along the most beautiful and cleanest river in the United States. Todd and his partner passed us one day. When I saw their canoe flying against the strong current, my curiosity fired up. We were going with the current, and we were exhausted. They went against it; yet, they had ten times more speed and a hundred times more fun. When we camped on the shore that night, I saw him again, setting up his tent right next to mine. I asked him about his canoe and how he made it fly so. He laughed, took me out into the river, and gave me a crash course. Swish, swish, swish . . . hut . . . swish, swish, swish, hut . . . For half an hour, we rode the currents with fish, turtles, butterflies, birds, and wind in the sunset.

"Can we say 'hut' when we switch sides?" I ask Mark. He laughs and practices it a few times, slowly at first, then faster, and soon we get into the rhythm. Swish, swish, swish . . . hut . . . swish, swish, swish . . . hut . . . Our boat glides like a bird.

How wide is the lower Mississippi? It depends on the season and the year, says John. It's about a mile from shore to shore now, but last year, when the water rose fifty feet higher, the same river doubled its width. It put lots of places under the water, shifted shores, wiped out old beaches, created new ones. Rivers have their own ways of doing things. Any attempt to tame them will end badly. As John talks, I think of the Three Gorges Dam that put thousands of years of history, thousands of homes under the water, and a million and a half people out of their ancestral land. Five years after completion, this man-made lake continues to have its own way, causing massive landslides on both shores, earthquakes, snowstorms, leaking, forcing more people out of their land.

How many locks and dams on the Mississippi? Some say twenty-six, some say twenty-nine. How many dams on the Yangtze? In 2006, she already had about twenty-eight thousand dams around her neck, torso, waist, limbs, wrists, and ankles, and the frenzy for hydraulic power had just begun. Everybody, from the local villagers to the central government, is thirsty for money from the dams. A river runs like blood. If one of the veins is blocked, it causes swelling and pain. If the blockage happens in the brain, it causes a stroke. If the channels don't reopen, it dies. How many times have we killed our rivers?

Swish, swish, swish . . . hut . . . I close my eyes to listen to Mark's rhythm, the heartbeat from his chest and ours, in sync with the heartbeats of the Mississippi, trees, fish, birds, rocks, soil, sky. I feel the heat from Immanuel's body. His heart is finally beating together with the river, and it is beautiful. I open my eyes and scan the river's blue-gray horizon, hazy, misty, mystical, and breathtaking. I feel Todd's heartbeats too. Is his spirit flying with us now? Three months after our encounter on the St. Croix, Todd drowned in Lake Mille Lacs. It was a cold and windy fall day. His sea kayak flipped and drifted away in the waves. The sun was setting fast. His kayak partner should have towed him back but decided to row back alone to get help. When he looked back for the last time, he saw Todd floating among the waves in his wetsuit, gazing at the twilight. He looked calm and happy.

On both sides, large circles of water rise like sunflowers, smooth in the center, rippling petals around the rim, as if a giant catfish were blowing water from the bottom, inviting us to jump in and play. These are not eddies. They don't have the hollow sucking mouths in the center, swallowing everything into the deep bellies. I look back, but John is nowhere to be seen. Is he sitting down? I crank my neck to look. He is not in the back seat, standing or sitting.

"John!" I shout. "Where's John?" Mark looks back with a smile and goes on paddling, as if nothing happened. I look at Immanuel. As a pro swimmer and lifeguard, he might need to jump in to rescue John.

"Hi, Ping." A voice bubbles out of the "sunflower," then half of his body rises as if he was standing on the water, in the center of the boil. I laugh, together with Immanuel and Mark. How did he get into the water so soundlessly? He waves to invite us in. I shake my head, remembering BMW's invitation to swim in his eddies. The boil looks friendlier, but I won't know how to get back into the canoe without flipping it. You go, I nudge Immanuel. He shakes his head, probably thinking of the same thing: how to get back into the canoe with grace. John disappears under the sunflower, and within two seconds, he pops out next to the canoe, leaping and frolicking like an otter. Before I see how it happens, he is standing in the back again, and the boat doesn't even tremor.

"What are those?" I point to the "sunflowers."

"Boils, the opposite of eddies. Instead of spinning inward and pulling things in, a boil pushes the water up and out from the bottom. The river is welcoming you with its bouquet. Very special. I saw such boils when we paddled here for our honeymoon."

"You got married in this river?"

"Ceremony in Clarksdale, then we stepped into our canoe. We cheated a little," he chuckles. "We stopped by an island so my wife could take off her bridal gown and change into something more suitable for paddling."

We sail through one sunflower after another, the bouquet that celebrated the union of John and his wife. How auspicious! Our canoe zigzags from shore to shore, following the river's bends. This is how all rivers move, the Yangtze, the Yellow, the Mississippi, and hundreds of others. In fact, I've never seen a straight river, unless it's a canal made of concrete. Why don't they go straight to the sea? And why do we have to zigzag with the river? Isn't a straight course a fast course?

"A straight course is not always a short course, Ping." John says, sensing my doubt from the frequent turning of my head. "The river wants to make a bend at every five to seven folds of its width. And no one knows why. If you drop a rock, it falls straight by the gravity, yet the river disobeys that rule. It just wants to meander, taking sand, rocks, soil, and trees from one shore and bringing them to the other, then taking the equal amount from the other shore across. Each side loses and gains, and in the end, everything evens out. I guess that's the nature of water: the greatest equilibrium. As I said, a river has her own way of doing things, and we're much better off working with her instead of fighting her. So if we want to go faster, we follow her bends and let her current take us from shore to shore. The more we fight her, the slower we'll go, and we'll only be exhausted and end up nowhere."

"How do you know which current to follow?"

But I already know the answer. It takes a river spirit to know the river. So we meander, around the bends with mud and sandbars on one side, giant rocks dropped by the Army Corps on the other side, man's efforts to stop the river's erosion.

"Those are hunting clubs." John points at the mansions hidden in the dense woods along the shore. "There are more wild animals than you could imagine on the islands. When winter comes, the clubs put out bait to attract them for the hunters who pay phenomenal amounts for deer and bears. Kind of cheating. But money can buy anything these days—almost."

"Look," Mark cries, "the mouth of the Arkansas!"

At the blue-gray horizon, an island with a giant sandbar stretches before us. Immanuel perks up and quickens his strokes. But it takes us almost an hour to get there. Just as we come close to the beach, John steers the canoe to the right, into the backwater channel. Suddenly, we enter a different world. Everything is still and quiet: the clouds, wind, ripples, and reflections of cracked mud. The only things moving are flocks of red-winged blackbirds darting in and out of black willows, and the white turn-leafs in and out of the water, uttering shrieks of delight. I have been in this world before. Yes, it was the Cahokia Mound, similar vibrations of energy, invigorating and calming. We paddle in silence, our oars dipping in and out of the river, making no sound.

John slips into the river again, swimming upstream like a salmon. He passes our boat and climbs on the pile of driftwoods that block the stream. He walks on a shaky tree limb as if he were on a tightrope. When he reaches the end, he dives in and swims away. Soon he appears on the other shore, running along the muddy bank like a black willow spirit. He is a frog, a turtle, a dolphin, a merman, living in two worlds, land and water, human and beast. He laughs when I tease him.

"It's a great compliment, Ping. I wish I were a full beast. Hey, look at this soil," he shows me a handful of the sand from the shore. "The most fertile thing on Earth. It looks sandy, but any crops, trees, grass, fish will thrive here."

I pinch some between my fingers and smear it on my face. A musky, muddy smell, the smell from a freshly cooked carp and catfish and other bottom feeders. People may say whatever they want about bottom feeders, but I love the taste of the earth and water, especially when the fish is fresh and cooked with ginger, garlic, wine, and soy sauce. Since I started paddling down the lower Mississippi, the richness of this soil has entered my hair follicles, pores, blood, and bones. I have since stopped using my expensive Shishedo tonic water or moisturizer. They no longer feel right in the South. In fact, they feel murky and clogging. The sandy mud massages and moisturizes the skin, grinding off the dead cells and filling the cracks in my heels. This is the best skincare on Earth, and it is free.

"We've got to go," says John. "Lunch at the confluence? And toilet break? We'll have another two hours of paddling after that."

He steers the boat out of the calm water and enters the turbulence. The Arkansas and Mississippi Rivers meet here and let us know their power. Our canoe tosses up and down, side to side, waves crashing from all sides. John sits down to steer. Mark paddles at a furious beat, thick muscles rolling along his arms and torso. We follow his pace. Even Immanuel manages to keep up with Mark's strokes. Nobody talks. No time for words. We need every breath we have to get out of this combined force from the Mississippi and Arkansas Rivers before it consumes us. Our boat lunges forward to the shore. We are almost there.

"Watch out," John shouts. I look up. A high wave comes right at us, roaring like mad, its mouth wide open, white fangs and white tongue gurgling with a white appetite to swallow us whole. "Keep still and keep paddling," he shouts, then we go under. For a second, we are in the belly of a whale, dark and cold and silent. This is it, I tell myself. We capsized! But we come out of the water, our canoe shooting forward like an arrow.

"This is fun! Again, again, again!" I shriek. Everyone laughs.

"We may not be this lucky next time," says John. "Perhaps it was a good thing you didn't know. But this is one of the places where you can feel the entire force of both rivers, actually three rivers, squeezed together. We're lucky there's no barge going upstream. The turbulence would have been ten times bigger. A nine-time canoe race champion paddled here once. She said some invisible force kept pulling her oars in all directions, and she nearly capsized many times. She never came back to this river again."

"That's why you come back again and again?" I ask.

"You truly have no fear, Ping." He laughs. "Who's your guardian angel?"

"You!" I cry, pointing to John, Mark, Immanuel, water . . . "Each and all of you!"

Everyone laughs. We have now reached the shore. John jumps out to pull the canoe onto the rocky beach and tie the rope to a boulder. Our boat is filled with water. We scoop and sponge it dry, have a quick snack on the black rocks, relieve ourselves in the black willow woods, and then prepare to get into the river again.

I have an urge to bow, not out of arrogance or ignorance. I want to try this beautiful canoe made of bald cypress and feel the river at the very front of the boat. John points to Mark.

"Ask him."

Mark looks me up and down then walks to the middle seat.

"I'll switch after our next break," I say.

"Our next stop will be our last stop. But you can do it. I know."

I step into the bow seat.

"Are we going back to Clarksdale, John?" I ask, alarmed as our boat heads the way we came.

"Just paddle, Ping; you're going to like this."

We paddle toward the current. From where we are, I can see how the two rivers actually meet: one brown, one slightly green, one coming from the west, one from the north, both fast and furious, unforgiving. When they touch, they create so much force that the current rises a few inches before it levels out and rushes toward the south. John steers the boat in such an angle that by the time we reach the current, we are quite far away from the island.

"Ready, Ping?" asks John, and we enter. Our canoe makes a sharp turn as we get into the current, and immediately, I feel an invisible hand tugging my oar, not downward or sideways or backward, but forward, toward the south. Our boat shoots down the river like a bullet. Within seconds, the mouth of the Arkansas is barely visible behind us.

"Wow! How did you do it?"

"We are riding the current of two rivers, Ping, actually three. The White River is not far from us."

We are all smiles. Even Immanuel is smiling hard. How can he not? We are riding a primordial force.

"We're gladiators," I hoot. I have no idea why. I know a gladiator was a Roman arena fighter, but the image of gliding and dancing with the wind feels right for us.

"We're river gators," shouts Mark.

"Yeah, gators gladiating with the river and wind!"

To bow is to set the pace. I stroked quads for my rowing team in Minneapolis, and Todd also showed me how to move a boat. Reach far, paddle, and stop the oar at the hip. To paddle a big river, conserving energy and making each stroke as efficient as possible are the keys.

Swish, swish, swish . . . hut . . . so we sail, crisscrossing the Big Muddy. My face cuts into the breeze. Fresh air pours in through my nose, mouth, skin. My lungs and heart move with the river, in the river. I open my mouth and let out the songs from the Yangtze:

A long river flows to the East
Fragrance of rice rises from both shores
At dawn I listen to boatmen's calling

At dusk I watch white sails downstream
This is my home on the bank of the Yangtze

When I finish, Mark starts singing the blues from St. Louis, Mississippi, Memphis—some full of sorrow, some full of joy, passed down from his father and grandfather. John tunes in with his whistling. Our sounds become part of the symphony of birds, fish, trees, wind, and water.

It is a confluence of river spirits.

26

Choctaw Island

From the air, Choctaw Island looks like a fat seal swimming upstream, belly full of food from the river. The seal is so fat it even expands the Mississippi into the shape of a stomach. Sitting across from Arkansas City, the island has every floodplain landscape possible: giant beaches like the Caribbean Sea, sand dunes and sandy plains as dry and hot as the Sahara, and the grasslands of the Serengeti. Its forests are a mixture of various hardwoods along the higher ridges, hackberries, oaks, sweetgums, sycamores, and cottonwoods, falling away to the willows lower and thick privets bunched and overhanging in the wooded wetlands. It's a paradise for birds, fish, and paddlers.

We arrive at Choctaw Island with the sun at the 4:00 position above the tree lines. This time, we land at a giant sandbar. We pull up the boat, take out our gear, and set our tents under black willows. John and Mark put up a big tent for the kitchen and dining then line it with tables, chairs, coolers . . . Immediately, we have a home. John starts a fire on the sand between the kitchen and water and boils a giant kettle of water. "Coffee, tea?" he asks. We opt for tea. I make a thermos of chai, mixing it with the raw milk. It tastes heavenly. John washes and chops potatoes, throws them into the cast iron with the roasted chicken, then whole tomatoes and Spanish peppers. The fire has burned out, only cinders glowing in a circle on the sand. John puts two pieces of driftwood side by side, with the fire in the middle, and places the Dutch oven on top.

"Dinner will be ready in half an hour," he announces, and walks up the sand dunes. Within seconds, he is gone, only a track of his bare footprints.

I sit by the fire with Mark, watching the twilight dancing on the river. Immanuel is swimming butterflies, his specialty when he swam for his high school team. The Mississippi vibrates with the sound of his torso flipping in and out of the water.

"He's strong," Mark says.

"He is, and so are you. Immanuel thought you were a football player."

"I played for the New York Giants for a year, then in Canada for five. All my brothers played football and got scholarships playing football. I guess I just followed the current."

My eyes pop wide open. "Did you grow up in Clarksdale?"

"No, east St. Louis, the poorest black neighborhood. Everyone has scattered. I left by playing football, just like my brothers, playing basketball and soccer. No matter where I go, I always end up in the river. So when I came to Clarksdale, I changed my name from Peoples to River. It just felt right. Mark River."

I nod. It does. Mark River. How many rivers has he marked with his oars? Like Mark Twain, who immortalized the Mississippi with his pen.

"How did you meet John?"

He hesitates. "Well, through a friend. I was taking people up and down the Mississippi in St. Louis before I met John. When I came to Clarksdale a year ago, I knew it was the right place for me. My dad said our family came from Mississippi State, and I don't think he made this one up. He's told so many lies in his life, especially about women and to women. You would laugh if you watched him flirt. Oh man! It's in his blood, in my blood, too, from his father and my grandpa, the biggest lady's man in the neighborhood, until his wife, my grandma, stabbed him in the chest and missed his heart by 0.2 inches. When Grandpa came out of the hospital, he was a born-again Christian, never flirted with women again, never even glanced at them. I wish my mom had done the same to her man. She might still be alive. Oh well, my dad has kind of settled in the woods, one hundred acres with a spring-fed lake, his latest wife watching him like a hawk. I guess she's the knife in his chest now. It's pretty funny if you know the history of my old man."

"Do you miss St. Louis? Do you miss football?"

He gives me a long look. "St. Louis is a city with pockets as dark as black holes. Once you're in, it's impossible to get out. Well, almost. I was the lucky one. Many of my friends are either dead or in jail. When I was five, my mother bought a house near the river, a white neighborhood with the best football program for youth in the entire nation. I was the only black kid on the team. I knew this was my way out, my chance to go to college, especially after my mom died of a brain tumor two years after we moved to that neighborhood and my father's mistress moved into the house the day after her funeral. So I played hard, and I got a full scholarship to play for a private college. As for playing football, I just have one thing to say: we die young. Again, I'm lucky I came out alive. The river saved me. I'm alive when I'm paddling and writing my River Citizen blog."

I know exactly what he means, about luck, about being alive. "You're a river person. So is John, so is Immanuel, so am I. We are river people."

He stares at me until I realize I have just linked his original family name, Peoples, to his new name, River—River Peoples. We are all River Peoples. We are kin.

"Dinner's ready!" John appears out of nowhere, holding a turtle he found on the other side of the island. No one but us on the island today, he declares. How did he cover this big island, barefooted, in such a short time? He looks like he just climbed a few trees, with willow, oak, and alder leaves stuck in his dripping hair. Of course, he has swum too.

"She had just laid eggs when I found her." He pinches the turtle between his fingers.

The turtle's mouth opens and closes, gulping, claws swimming in air, eyes full of tears.

"Let her go, please!" I beg. John sets it down on the sand, facing the beach. It takes her a while to realize her freedom. Then she starts running, tripping and flipping, but always running to the river. Within a few seconds, she vanishes.

The twilight hits the sand and lights up tracks of tiny footprints from the hill to the water. "Baby turtles," John crouches down. "Most of them never make it. See?" He points to the tracks that end in the middle then to the bird footprints along the turtle tracks. "They waited here for their snacks. Gulp, gulp."

He looks up and sees my sad face. "Hungry? I'm starving. Hey," he shouts, "Let's eat!" Immanuel comes running from the river. He has never looked so happy.

The chicken is tender and juicy, the potatoes creamy. The peppers, tomatoes, and rosemary are a perfect combination. I eat a huge plate, John and Immanuel gobble two, Mark has three. John scrapes the leftovers into a container. Mark will eat this with eggs and bacon for breakfast, he says.

For the first time in my life, I feel anxious about cooking. Tomorrow, it will be my turn to make dinner. How can I surpass this?

Immanuel washes the ceramic plates in the river. I go over to help. At home, we do the same thing: cook, eat, and clean up together. The moon rises over

Arkansas. From the south, a towboat pushes barges upstream toward the north. We count. Sixty-three barges, longer and wider than a street block. I feel their humming vibrations. We are really lucky that we didn't encounter them at the confluence.

When we get back to the base, John has laid out two black necklaces on the sand, each made of a beautiful mud fossil from his collection.

"Congratulations for having paddled forty miles today. These are your badges. Few people have earned this honor. I usually give the badge at the end of the trip. But you two are phenomenal paddlers. So here."

"That's right," Mark cuts in. "Last time we took two men out, they paddled for ten minutes at the beginning of the trip, put down their oars, and never touched them again."

"And Mark had to paddle the entire way to the island," John chimes in.

"And they claimed they were pros," says Mark.

The whole Choctaw Island shakes with our laughter. Now I understand why John gave us so many tests before our departure.

We crawl into our tent. Immanuel falls asleep right away, the necklace rising and falling on his chest. He earned this, as John said, and he looks so proud and peaceful. I gaze at the red eye in the stone. Would this be my entrance into his heart? His eyelids flutter rapidly. What is he dreaming? Through the plastic ceiling, I see the moon over our tent. It's half full, shaded by mist, which means a windy day tomorrow. And the Big Dipper in the sky turns slowly across the river.

I wake up with geese clunking over the tent. The sun is just poking out of the tree line. I walk to the beach. The blue kettle sits quietly on the sand, next to the glowing cinder. I touch it. Super hot. I make myself a thermos of chai. Birds are flying out of their nests, gracing the sky with their silhouettes. The sun, thick and orange like the yolk of a pickled duck egg, casts a golden path across the river. The wind is blowing hard.

"There'll be a sandstorm today," John says from behind. I turn. He looks like he has just flown, run, and swum around the island three times, his hair wet, covered with sand and leaves, his feet bare, one hand clutching the camera case, the other the notebook that contains his writings and drawings. Does he ever sleep?

"I'll make breakfast soon, before the sand gets really hot and blows things everywhere. We can nap in the afternoon when it's too hot to go out."

I go back to the tent to see if Immanuel has woken up. I look in from the gauze window. I freeze. A black snake coils around the red-eyed stone on top of his heart, rising and falling. I close my eyes, count to five, look again. The snake is still there, its triangular head up in the air, a tiny, exquisite tongue flicking in and out. Suddenly, our eyes lock. It sees me. A flicker of light beams up its tiny eyes. If I make a wrong move, it might bite Immanuel. I breathe gently, in and out, in and out. It seems to calm down the snake, and its tongue starts flicking again. What should I do now? I can't alert Immanuel, can't shoo it away. A snake is not a fly. What is it doing on his chest? Why coiling around the black stone? I wanted that stone, but Immanuel picked it up first. I shiver as I remember the sound of music at the Crossroads. Is it the same spirit? Will John or Mark know how to get it off his chest? Even if they do, I can't just go find them and leave Immanuel alone with the snake on his chest. How did it get in? I don't remember seeing anything when I got up. I know I zipped the fly when I left the tent. Aiden trained me well on this. Suddenly, the snake tenses up again, its head lifting high as if sniffing the danger, its coil tightens around the necklace, ready to strike. I'm about to shout when a black shadow flies over our heads. Powerful wings slapping the air. The Piasa Bird? No, bald eagle. I look down. The snake has vanished, only the stone on Immanuel's chest.

I unzip the tent and start beating around the tent with a piece of driftwood. Hopefully, it will scare the snake out.

"What are you doing?" Immanuel sits up.

"Lots of mosquitoes got in last night and moths too." I keep beating the ground with my stick. I don't want to scare him. If the snake is still inside the tent and if Immanuel freaks out and starts thrashing about, the snake might attack. I need to get him out.

"Coffee is ready. John is making eggs and bacon."

He yawns and stretches, taking his time.

"A scorpion may have gotten in too."

He leaps out at the speed of light. As soon as he's gone, I start dragging the sleeping bags and clothes out of the tent. No snake. Where did it go? Am I hallucinating? I put things back, one at a time, making sure the snake doesn't hide in any folds, creases, corners. I zip the tent and join in the breakfast. How did the snake get in? How did it get out? What could all this mean? The black snake around the red-eyed black stone, the bald eagle . . . I need time to process what just happened. No one will believe me if I tell them. Maybe John would, and Mark, but not Immanuel.

The breakfast is delicious, but I play with the scrambled eggs in silence. John gives me looks but says nothing. The wind blows forty miles an hour in gusts. Columns of sand rise from the sandbars and push across the beach, through our tents, trees, and hair. On the other shore, farmers are burning harvested winter wheat fields. Black smoke rises above the tree line, crosses the river, and joins in the sandstorm. They are magnificent to watch, but soon, our noses, eyes, and throats clog with sooty sand.

Immanuel and I hang the flags on a pile of driftwood near our tent. Their natural contours are perfect for the banners. Immediately, the island is transformed into a joyful place. Flags dance in the gusty wind, each like a child jumping and clapping hands, shouting songs into the air, water, and sunshine. John jumps from driftwood to driftwood, picking up each flag to examine the poems and art. The wind blows his hair here and there. The tree limb trembles terribly in the gusts, but his bare feet clasp like bird's talons. This is his home, Driftwood upon driftwood, wind upon wind.

"It's very, very beautiful, Ping." He jumps down from the pile, his eyes wet with emotion.

"Would you make some flags on this island? I'll bring them to Everest."

He nods. We go to the kitchen table and spread out our supplies: fabric I cut, dyed, and ironed, fabric crayons, fabric markers, and plants I picked after breakfast: black willow, cottonwood, wild oak, and a blade of unknown grass. John picks it up.

"Wild oat, my favorite. When the wind blows, it bends and makes a circle on the sand. It makes me feel calm, centered."

I take the leaf and ink it, put it on the fabric, fold it over, and ask John to rub it twenty times. When I open the fabric, we have a mirror image of wild oats. John draws a stream between the oats, and now, he has an oat reflection. He writes: "Wild oat, wild oat, making circles in the wind."

He holds it high with both hands. The wind blows it up and down, and the plant comes alive on the fabric. I have never seen him so still, so content. My heart is also filled with peace. Is this all we need to be happy? A blade of grass? A grain of sand? A gust of wind? A drop of water? John sighs and puts it down to sign his name. Then, he asks if he could take a flag home for his daughter. I hand him three.

"One for Emma, one for your wife, and one for the three of you together."

I print willow twigs on the rest of the fabric. The black willow leaves, as I suspected, make the most stunning prints. I can shape the willowy stem into any angle I want. Mark takes a black willow piece and finds a shady place to write his words on it. Immanuel takes a blank one. He doesn't want anyone else's hand on his work. He is a pro artist.

"Come with me, Ping," says John. "I want to show you something."

I look up. Mark is sitting under a willow, writing furiously on his notebook. Immanuel is painting at the kitchen table. John motions at me to follow, his eyes bright with a mysterious light. I walk barefooted, like John. My flip-flops will not last an hour in the sand. John, of course, never wears shoes. I follow him across the vast sand beach, into the meadow with draping grass, then the thick shrub of raspberry and other thorny plants. My feet and legs burn with pain. I have no time to look or attend to the lacerations. John walks ahead of me without stopping, as if the thorny shrubs were soothing sand or soft cotton. I follow, afraid of losing him. The meadow seems so vast. Finally, we enter the woods, with water up to my ankles, its cool mud sucking away my pain. Ahhh, may we walk in the woods forever, I sigh. But it ends abruptly. Ahead of us is a beach covered with gravel, brown, white, red, black rocks. I groan. I have the most sensitive soles. Any uneven objects will make me jump like a jumping bean. Why is he taking me to this place?

"Look down, Ping," whispers John.

Between my feet, a yellow stone. I pick it up and shriek. It's a tree fossil.

"Oh, John, oh, John, how did you know I love fossils!"

He smiles, picking up a black stone from the ground. "This is for you, Ping."

It is a mud fossil in the shape of a canoe, exquisitely beautiful. I remember the museum-sized collection in his office. "Is this where you found all the fossils?"

"Most of it, but not all. There's another big beach near Helena."

I start walking, my eyes glued to the ground. Never mind the sharp stones. My soul only feels the bliss. Soon, I find my first treasure. A giant mud fossil ring. I put it on my finger and show it to John.

He laughs heartily. "Bride of the Mississippi, Ping."

I raise my ring to the sun. It sparkles like a black diamond.

"When I graduated from high school, I decided to raft down the Mississippi from the upper river to New Orleans, with my best friend, Keith. We made our raft with barrels and scrap timber at La Crosse. It took us a few months to get everything ready and learn what we could learn for the trip. 'Take your time to prepare,' said every river rat we met. 'On the river, slow is fast, and flow is the key.' We started our journey before the upper Mississippi froze. Once we passed St. Louis, the river was open forever. The float was slow, so we played chess to kill time. We cooked, slept, and did our business on the raft. Not easy to do, without the modern equipment like we have now, no wetsuit, no good sleeping bags, no cell phones, nothing but our youth and passion. When we reached Mississippi State, actually not far from this island, we got so used to the slow, easy motion of the river that we became careless. We were playing a chess game on the raft, and when we looked up, we were ten feet away from a pylon. We paddled like mad, but it was too late. We rammed into the post, and the raft lifted, wrapped around the bridge like a piece of toilet paper, then crushed like a potato chip. Everything we had, books, clothes, radio, food, including the chicken we had just roasted, slid into the water in front of our eyes, and we could do nothing but hold onto the pylon like dummies. We managed to swim to a sandbar nearby and made a fire. It was windy and cold, one of the coldest Februarys in the South. Shivering in the dark, I made a vow: oh river god, if I survive the night, I will devote my whole life to you."

He pauses. The wind gusts, as if putting a period to his story.

"So you've been wed to the river ever since."

He nods. "So have you, Ping, all your life, like me, like Mark, and many others. We're river spirits."

I want to ask him if Immanuel counts as one of us. I want to ask him about the black snake coiling around the black fossil necklace on his chest. But I check myself. I already know the answer. Immanuel has his own path to complete.

"Locals believe Choctaw is made by the *Indiana*, sunk in 1875." John's voice seems to come from the bottom of the river. "The Mississippi has sunk many steamboats. The sediment accumulates around the wrecks, making islands over the years. But I think it's older, judging from the name Choctaw."

I want to tell him that Dave Brinks, the poet from New Orleans, is a Choctaw, and his ancestors are buried on this island. John looks up at the sun and said, "We should get going. The sandstorm is heating up the dunes like the Sahara."

He is right. On our way back, the sand scorches my soles so much that I run and scream my way to the river and jump in to cool my feet. By noon, the whole island shimmers in a heat wave. The only place still cool is the black willow grove. We bury ourselves in the cool sand under the shade. Even John joins us, after another expedition through the sandstorm, his legs and feet bleeding from thorns. He watches flocks of blackbirds in the thick of the black willows on the riverbanks.

"No willow, no blackbirds, no birds, no trees, no island . . . they're the foot soldiers. Their roots dig deep to stabilize the shifting sand," he points to the willow grove in front of us. "If necessary, they'll form a second tier to secure the land," he points to the willow grove where we are resting. "After that, anything will thrive," he points to the thick canopy of trees inland. "Cottonwood, birch, then oak, maple, pine . . . it's the order of the world."

He sniffs the air. "Do you smell their fragrance? Aspirin is extracted from willow leaves, bark, roots." He plucks a bug from a leaf and holds it to his nose. "Sand fly nymph, born on the willow, eating the willow, and turning into a fly from the willow. Smell it," he hands it to me.

A spicy, cool smell enters my nostrils, and immediately, my enflamed nose from the sooty hot sand calms down. Even my headache disappears.

"I ate one last week, and my tongue was numb for a whole day. The bug is filled with painkiller substance."

"That's why the beavers never have headaches. They chew willows all day long. No pain will go near them," says Mark.

We all laugh. John looks up at the willow canopy. "Exactly a year ago, the river is fifty feet higher, three times wider, and this whole beach is under the water . . ." His voice trails off, and he seems to be floating into a dream land.

Mark continues. "Just two weeks ago, the willows were covered with sand fly nymphs, millions of them, like stars in the sky, and all the birds in the world gathered here to feast. I was lying right here, under this tree, watching the birds eat and mate . . ." His voice also trails off, as if he were following John into dreams.

The willows shiver in ecstasy. I shiver, too, inhaling the medicinal fragrance, listening to the symphony of the air, the waves, the birds, the hot sand, and the duet back and forth between John and Mark, their bodies molded into the cool sand under the willows. I open my laptop, trying to capture the sound, smell, and touch of everything in words but find it impossible. My body is melting into the sand and willows and waves.

We are paddling, me at the bow seat, Mark and Immanuel as the engine . . . John steering . . . into the rolling sea . . . our hair open like a sail, our chests full with wind . . . the Choctaw and Quapaw elders leading the way . . . their headdresses and shoes beaded with fish, snakes, gators . . . palm with a black eye in the center . . . coiled by a pair of black dragons . . . Grandpa and Grandma . . . I shout . . . phoenix and dragon . . . dancing in the air . . . leaping toward the sea . . . toward home . . . in the river, turtles, catfish, sturgeons . . . over our heads, eagles, blackbirds, turn-leafs, Piasa Bird . . . the sea is a brown green meadow covered with flowers . . . children laughing and rolling with beasts . . . barefoot in thick prairie grass . . .

I wake up. The wind is still blowing, the air thick with sheets of sand and smoke. Under the willows, men are sleeping. In my lap, an Apple, my fingers poised on the keys . . . I enter the sea meadow again . . . same black dragon, birds, children, turtle . . .

This is Choctaw Island, home of the Quapaw and Choctaw. We're here as their guests, as children of the Mississippi.

27

The Basin Keeper from Atchafalaya

The minute I set eyes on John Ruskey's cypress canoes, I know I'm going to visit their home, the Atchafalaya Basin, where Louisiana bald cypress lives. It's the biggest swamp in America, home for alligators and cypress, and it holds 30 percent of the Mississippi water. If not for all the levees and spillways built by the Army Corps of Engineers, the river would have jumped its course, flowing west into the gulf via the Atchafalaya River instead of Baton Rouge and New Orleans.

I ask John if he knows people there. He gives me the name of Dean Wilson.

"I don't have his email or phone number. But everyone there knows him. He's a basin keeper."

"Basin keeper for trees and water? How will I find him?"

"You'll know how, if you really want to meet him."

We drive to New Orleans early in the morning. We stop at Natchez, walk along its bluff to stretch our legs, and eat at Pig Out Inn: ribs, beans, thin-sliced roasted beef, the must-try southern goodies recommended by Bob. We met Bob on Natchez's street. He is from St. Paul, graduated from Highland Park High School. Forty years ago, he came to Natchez for an archaeology project. His fiancée came along. When the digging ended, so did their relationship. She went back home to Minnesota, and Bob stayed, restoring antiques for a living.

Dave Brink is waiting on the terrace when we arrive in New Orleans. He stayed up all night working in the Gold Mine Saloon, then waited in the morning for our arrival. He brings our baggage into the house. It's new inside and tastefully designed. The walls are covered with large paintings, some hung, some leaning against the walls. Built-in bookshelves line the walls of his study, ceiling to floor, filled with books from all over the world. His manuscript *Secret Brain* lies on the big table. The poems come with charts and illustrations and oracles from I-ching. The Black Widow Press is waiting for his final revision.

"I have been throwing I-ching to arrange the order of the poems for the book," he says.

How does he find time to read and write? Perhaps he is like John and BMW, getting up at dawn. The overflowing library looks modern and newly updated, despite the weathered exterior of the house. Its foundation also seems compromised by some big force.

"I salvaged this house from Katrina," he says, seeing what's on my mind. "I bought it when Megan was pregnant with our first child. In fact, that was the year when you came to read at the Gold Mine Saloon, remember? With Brenda and Simon? You were staying on the second floor, and Simon walked in when you came out of the shower, and you freaked out? Simon still laughs like crazy when he tells the story. Well, that was one of the reasons Megan urged me to buy this house. We got everything ready for the baby, and six months later, Katrina came. I drove Megan and our baby to Natchez that night, where her mother lived. I'll never forget the desolation and terror. We had hurricanes every year, always threatening to breach the levee but never did. But this time, I had this awful feeling that it would, and I wanted to stay with the house. It was everything I had worked for. My Gold Mine Saloon would be fine. It stood on the higher ground of the French Quarter but not this house. In Natchez, we watched the levee break on the news, watched the water rise all the way to the street signs. The watermark is still there. Want to see?"

He takes us outside and points to the faint yellow mark on the sign. "I can't believe it's still here after all these years. The sun and wind couldn't erase it. Mother Nature doesn't want us to forget. Strange, eh? You know what's even stranger and really creepy when I sneaked back home by myself? Coffins, hundreds of coffins from the cemetery nearby. They rose from the crypts in the flood, floated out of the cemetery, and swarmed the streets. I stood here," he points at the street sign. "In the water that reached my chest, watching my house surrounded and attacked by those damn coffins, big, small, fancy, plain coffins with corpses and God knows what inside, and I just lost it. How could this happen? And why?"

He pauses, his face to the sky, in the direction of the cemetery. I want to tell him about Choctaw Island, the elders I saw in my dream, who might be the spirits of his ancestors, the eye in the hand, the snake and dragons surrounding the eye. Dave turns to me, his eyes filled with tears.

"After the flood left, my magnolia died. The tree was my grandfather, very old and wise and very comforting. I used to sit under him when I came home from the saloon at dawn, watching the flowers bloom. It takes exactly forty minutes for the buds to open, no more, no less, and I just sat and watched them blossom, petal by petal, first like a shy girl, then a naughty teenager, then a passionate lover, then a mother giving her milk and heart. Oh, I felt so blessed during the forty-minute sitting, meditating, writing, dreaming. All the other trees got to live after the flood, the palms, cottonwoods, cypress, but not my magnolia."

We stand in silence, paying homage to Dave's grandfather and all the other magnolias that died in Katrina. Finally, Dave turns to the garden with raised beds. They seem to follow a certain pattern.

"I built that after I removed the old tree. I tossed coins for an I-ching oracle, and it gave me *zhong fu*—inner truth." He picks up a stick and draws six lines on the ground. "See this? The two solid lines at the bottom symbolize the water, big water like the Atchafalaya Basin, or flood. The two solid lines on the top indicate the sky and the wind that stirs the water. In the middle, two broken lines, forming a hollow center, like an egg, a vase, void of the universe, or the heart free of judgments, therefore open to truth, peace, and life."

I look at the hexagram, then at the garden. It feels peaceful and centered at the same time. So does Dave. He looks strong and gentle in the core. I know this I-ching sign is an advantageous one, with all the forces one needs to restore life after the great flood: the water and ground on Earth, the wind and sun in the sky, but these outside forces will not work without the gentle force from inside. In order for the life to be awakened, there must be a seed in the hollow. What a great idea to create a garden where the old magnolia stood, according to the pattern of zhong fu! The Chinese character for inner truth was an image of a bird's foot over a fledgling, a baby bird that depends on its father and mother for survival and yet full of potential.

"Isn't it strange," says Dave, "that nothing would grow in the first two years after Katrina, nothing but sunflowers and watermelons. They grew like crazy. But no one would eat them. They say these plants pull toxins out of air, water, and soil and turn them into sweet water and seeds. I wouldn't have minded if I hadn't seen all the coffins floating around my house. I don't know what was in them and what leaked out. But now the soil's clean again. I have carrots, cabbages, garlic; when you guys return from the gulf, I'll make the turtle soup, recipes from my grandparents, and will invite all the poets and artists in Nola. I just left a message for my uncle. He has a boat, can take you to the gulf. How many days do you have? And what's your plan? I got you two tickets to Sasha's concert for tonight. She's a young, beautiful, and talented singer. You'll like her. I also booked seats for a secret concert at the Music Box for tonight."

"Secret concert?" I glance at Immanuel for his reactions. He's a snob when it comes to music. He likes Massive Attack and Dark Dark Dark and a few other bands. The rest are dregs.

"Ahh, it won't be a secret concert if I tell you, right?" Dave laughs, his eyebrows flying like wings. "But come here," he gestures at us to get closer. "It's Thurston Moore," he whispers in my ear.

"Who's that?" I ask.

Immanuel already pounces on him and grabs his hand.

"Yes, yes, we'll be there. Thank you, thank you so much!"

Dave looks shocked. Immanuel hasn't uttered a sound since we arrived. He must be thinking Immanuel is mute, as many of my friends thought.

"Who's Thorston?" I ask again.

"Thurston!" Immanuel gives me a contemptuous look.

"Oh, but he knows you and your work," Dave cries. "He loves poetry. He collaborates a lot with Anne Waldman and other poets. I told him you're coming to New Orleans, and he said 'wow.' He wants to meet you, Ping. He's going to teach at Naropa in July. I see that you're going there too, right?"

"Yes. Perhaps we can do something together there. I've been looking for musicians for collaborations."

Immanuel is going wild, his eyes, eyebrows, nose, and mouth jiggling and dancing and making funny faces. I have never seen him this excited. Now I'm curious about Thurston.

"We'll be there, Dave, for sure. Thank you so much for everything. I don't know how to thank you enough, but thank you," I say. "Is there a café nearby? Wireless?"

Dave points the way and goes to bed. We bring everything from the car to the guest room, hang the river flags around his terrace on the second floor, across his yard, over his inner peace garden. Megan comes home with their three-year-old daughter.

"Wow, these are beautiful," she exclaims. We hug and chat. We have not seen each other in ten years, and now Megan is a mother of three.

The café is just a block away from Dave and Megan's house. The temperature is almost reaching one hundred degrees. By the time we get there, we are drenched in sweat and panting like dogs. It's a big relief to enter the café with air conditioning. Immanuel orders his breakfast and opens his laptop right away. I join him after paying the bill with my credit card. We don't talk to each other for the next two hours, each immersed in our emails and Facebook updating.

I find lots of information about the Atchafalaya Basin: cypress, alligators, and swamp tours, each promising the best experiences on Earth: high-speed boats, fishing, hunting gators, catfish. I call them one by one. Some are booked until July 4, some just answering machines. I'm about to give up when the Last Wildness Tour comes up on my screen. It catches my eyes with its simple design and brief message. I scroll down absentmindedly until I reach the bottom, and the Basin Keeper Dean Wilson's name jumps out at me, with the phone number and place: Bayou Sorrel.

"I found him, I found him," I shout.

"Who, Thurston?" Immanuel looks up. "Have you realized what a big deal it is to meet him at his concert? Let alone that he knows you and said 'wow' when he learned you're in town?"

"Really? I didn't know that. But I found Dean Wilson. We're going to the swamp, to see bald cypresses." I pick up my cell.

"When?" he frowns. "Remember we have the concert, and we need to go to the gulf too. Besides, I really want to spend a few days in the city. We've been driving and running. I'm tired. I want a break. This is MY vacation, my first time to New Orleans."

I raise my hand to stop Immanuel. Dean Wilson is on the phone.

"Hi, my name is Ping. John Ruskey said I should call you. I just paddled the lower Mississippi with him. I would like to paddle the basin with you."

He laughs. "I'd love to take you into the swamp, Ping." He has an accent, but I can't tell where he is from. "I'm on the road and won't be home for two weeks. My son Al can take you. He's very experienced. When would you like to go? Tomorrow? Today? When is the sunset? Around 7:00 in the swamp. 5:30 for sunset shots? Maybe. So you want the 5:30 p.m. tour? Here's Al's number. Call and tell him you've talked to me about the tour. He'll tell you where to meet him exactly."

I shut the phone and look at Immanuel. "We're going to the swamp today!"

"We are not. We have Thurston's concert."

"Yes, we are. The concert starts at 9:00. We'll be back by 8:30."

"No, we won't. Something will happen, and we won't make it back on time. Eight thirty is way too late. We need to be ready for the concert by 6:00."

I laugh. Something will happen if one expects it to happen. Besides, why on Earth would one need two hours to get ready? It's just a concert, not a prom.

"Immanuel, I need to go to the swamp. I must. It's part of the Mississippi, part of Kinship of Rivers. It's my job. The grant covers the project, not the concert."

He sighs. "Can we go earlier? Like noon? I want to be back by 5:00."

"That's the worst time for shooting. Nothing good will come out of it."

He stares at me as if he were dying. I sigh.

"How about we get there at 3:30? The tour is about two hours. If we rush back, we'll be back at 7:00. We still have two hours to eat before the concert. I really can't go earlier than that. I need to bring home a few good pictures to prove to the grantors that I have done my job. Good compromise? I'll call Al to change the time."

We meet Al at Bayou Sorrel Bait Store. He looks gentle and confident, finished high school and will start college in the fall. He takes us to the river behind the levee. A boat with six seats is parked at the dock. We jump in. Al starts the motor, and immediately, we see an alligator cruising along the shore.

"This rarely happens! The alligators like you guys," says Al.

A white bird flies over our heads, legs tucked in, wings spread wide, its long beak pink against the sky. White heron?

"Not heron. It's ibis. In the mating season, they come in large flocks. The sky becomes a white concert hall with their singing and dancing. Again, the birds are also welcoming you."

I smile. Al is a good tour guide. He knows how to welcome his guests.

White houses line both shores among thick woods, elegant, even romantic looking, at the first glance. As we come closer, I notice they are all crumbling. Dark patches of mold and yellow rings of watermarks map the shingles, and plants crawl through the windows. I turn to Al.

"Last year's flood, bigger than 1937's," he says. "The Mississippi is overdue to jump its course. The Army Corps opened the Morganza Floodway, the second time since its construction, to divert the water into our river, to keep the Mississippi in the old channel, to keep New Orleans and Baton Rouge safe from the flooding. Small price to pay, right? All the houses inside the levees were flooded, beyond repair."

Small price to pay, small price to pay, I chew the words that sound so familiar. Yes, I have heard them indeed, in Chinese, at the Three Gorges. *Forsake your small home for the big family*, a slogan that displaced almost two million people in the dam area. Two million. That "small home" could make the entire Gambia, two Switzerlands, five Icelands. And for what big family? Who constitutes that big family?

"Well, at least we avoided another Katrina, right? And we kept the oil pipelines and other industries intact," he adds.

"Did you get compensation? Did you know your houses were subject to floods when you built them?"

"Yes, we knew. That's why we built them high, on concrete or wood stilts, without basements. We also thought the lock and dam was supposed to protect us, not to drown us. But the Army Corps had something more important to protect, I guess. As for compensation, well, when they cleared the water and land for the levee, they just told us to pick up our things and get out. For those who could prove their ownership of the land, they were offered $2.50 for an acre. Take it or leave it. They just want us out of the levee, out of the swamp, so they can take whatever they want from this place."

Suddenly, his voice shakes with anger. "Oh no, not this, not this again!"

In the water along the shore, a giant white thing floats. An alligator tangled in a fishnet, belly up and bloated like a balloon, a black hole in the chest gaping at the sky.

"Somebody shot it, just for the fun of it. Probably from one of those damn tour boats from other bayous." He bites his lips, eyes flooded with sorrow.

"I'm so sorry, Al." I want him to smile that joyful smile again. But words crumble in my throat like the decomposing alligator.

We turn around the bend in silence. A tree appears in the middle of the river, wide at the base, thin at the waist, and from there, it expands gracefully toward the top with branches draped with Spanish moss. It looks like a woman with an hourglass waist, her full green hair decorated with a flowing silk scarf. For a second, I thought I was seeing the Three Gorges Goddess wrapped in the morning mist, coming down to the river with the afternoon rain, the goddess who appeared in the dreams of kings and young men, filling their hearts with love.

"Louisiana bald cypress," I whisper.

"Yes, it's our state tree, treasure of our basin," Al smiles, light back again in his eyes. "Without it, there'll be no bayou, no New Orleans. You'll see what I mean when we reach the forest."

The river forks. Al takes the right. How does he know where to go? What if we get lost in this swamp? There is no way I could find my way back. Al smiles.

"No worry. My dad took me to the river before I learned how to crawl. My first words were fish, tree, water. I learned how to tie a boat before I learned how to tie my shoes. I caught my first fish when I was three, gutted my first fish when I was five. This is my home, our home. How can anyone get lost at home? The only danger is engine failure when you're deep in the swamp. It happened to my dad once, when his engine died in the place that could be found by only one person on Earth, his best friend. Fortunately, his cell phone still had juice. He called, and his friend was just leaving for a two-week trip. Boy, he was lucky!" Al laughs, turning another bend.

A black shadow blocks our path. I thought it was a cypress, but no, it is a metal structure with a platform in the middle, a black pipe reaching out and into the river.

"Shell's oil pipe, long abandoned," Al hushes his voice as if he were afraid of awakening some evil spirits.

"Why is it here?" A stupid question, but I'm genuinely shocked to see oil pipes here. How much pollution has drilling caused in the swamp? Isn't the Atchafalaya Basin the last wilderness in the South, like the last wilderness refuge in Alaska? Why have I never heard of the drilling here, unlike the intense debate on Alaska?

"Lots of oil and gas under the swamp. When it was discovered, companies swarmed here like mosquitoes, and rigs mushroomed. They cut the cypresses, some about two thousand years old, and dredged the swamp to clear a water pathway for big boats and barges. Sorrel was also used as the storage because of the Sorrel Lock, I guess. Every time a hurricane comes, we know there'll be oil spills in the bayou."

"That could be lots of spills!" I exclaim.

The boat turns again. On the left appears a giant oil structure, half of which is built on shore and the other half on the water. It is rusting and rotting all over, but its metal and concrete structure stands like a fortress. Nearby, a boat is sinking, its windows half submerged in the water. An orange ring of floaters circles the boat, like the police mark around a corpse.

"One of the storage infrastructures," Al says. "And that boat sank completely last week, but somehow came out of the water again two days ago, together with the oil from the tank. We informed the authorities. Someone put that floater around the boat, as if it could stop the spilling."

We stop by the boat. A thick layer of oil floats on the water, emitting sinister rainbow colors. Under that layer, nothing will grow. I think of the BP oil spill in the gulf, its much larger scale of destruction.

"How could they just leave everything here? Aren't they obliged, by law and conscience, to take things down and clean up when they leave? They've made tons of money from the drilling, right?"

Al snickers. "Are you kidding me? It's expensive to clean up. Who's going to pay? Not Shell, not Halliburton, not any of the oil companies. They've divided the profit among themselves. Nobody is going to spit it out for this. The government never has enough money to pay for the clean ups. Yes, there are laws, plenty, to protect the water, the watershed, the trees, fish, and birds, but who's here to enforce it?"

The air is thick like the brown water. My heart aches as I watch the scowl on Al's face. The boat turns, and I gasp. Before us floats a forest of Louisiana bald cypress. These southern giants, second only to sequoia, the tallest tree in North America, rise out of the murky swamp and tower above a carpet of water plants. Light comes through the clouds, and everything is illuminated: the brown pleated skirts around the trees' waists, the green crown of their spiral foliage, the pale gray headdress of Spanish moss, the lilac blossoms that weave an intricate pattern across the green and gold carpet of plants on the water, and the brown pathway opened by our boat that attracts birds looking for fish. Al stops the engine and lets the boat drift into this enchanted forest, this floating fairyland.

"My father came here as a young man from Spain," he whispers, as if afraid of breaking the dream. "He came here to acclimate himself in the swamp for his mission to fight the destruction of the Amazon rain forest and learn all the skills he would need to survive in the jungle. For six months, he lived entirely on the fish, frogs, raccoon, and other animals he caught with a spear. He never made it to the Amazon."

"This is his Amazon," I say. That explains Dean Wilson's accent.

"His paradise. He truly believes that gods live here, and we're keepers of this Eden. That's why when the thieves swarmed here to take down cypresses for mulch, he fought back. Without the cypress, without the swamp; without the swamp, without the last garden on Earth. He went to the legislators, environmental offices, but nobody cared, even though the swamp and cypress are protected by law. No money, they told him, to collect evidence. No evidence, no prosecution. So my dad followed the trucks, from the swamp all the way to the mill where they mulched the trees. He brought tons of photos as evidence, but the government still wouldn't do anything. He tried to get help from the Sierra Club and other environmental groups. The support finally came from one of the tourists, a man connected with the Kennedy people, and his proposal to form the Basin Keeper went through the official approval. Volunteers came to help him with the tracking, by cars, boats, and helicopters. And they got Walmart to stop selling Louisiana cypress mulch. Guess what those crooks did? They labeled their mulch bags as Florida cypress. My dad followed them to their sawmill in his car, then a pilot volunteer photographed the mulching in the mill from above, and he took the crooks to court. Oh, they hated him. They sent him death threats, shot at him, and poisoned his dogs, our dogs, our friends . . ." Al pauses, his eyes wet again.

"Were you born here?" I ask, after a long silence.

"Yes. When my dad decided to stay here, he invited his friends from Spain. One of them was my mom. She never left." He smiles.

"Have you been to Spain?"

He shakes his head. "I'll major in Spanish and environmental studies in the fall, when school begins."

"Are you coming back home?"

"What do you mean? Oh, when I graduate? I don't know. I want to be involved, but there are no jobs here, I mean paying jobs. There are plenty of things to do, to keep our swamp alive, but it's all volunteer work. I'll be back to help my dad in the summer. Most tourists think of the swamp as taunting gators and shooting them for fun. I want to show its beauty and magnificence. I'll be back. The swamp is my home, no matter where I am."

Al restarts the engine and takes us to a big cypress.

"Guess how old it is." He resumes his role as a tour guide. "I'll give you a clue. The older the tree, the slower it grows."

I look at its brown skirt. Could I count the pleats like the rings for its age? There were so many of them. "Hmmmm, six hundred years old?"

He laughs proudly. "Nobody could guess it right. This tree is at least fifteen hundred years old, if not older."

My mouth opens wide. I've seen five-thousand-year-old Chinese antiques in museums. But to face and touch a millennium-and-a-half-old living tree? I put my hand on its trunk. A warm stream flows out of the brown skin into my palm. The mother tree is nursing me with her milk. I bow my head in gratitude.

"There used to be more, older and bigger than this one, all cleared for timber in the last century. See that?" He points to a stump next to the mother tree. "See that mark? They cut a ring and tied a rope around the tree, to kill it. After two years, they would come back and take it down."

"Why?"

"Because cypress is so heavy it just sinks to the bottom if it's cut alive. It's the most water resistant of all the trees. Never rots and too hard for the bugs to gnaw through. That's why it's so valuable as timber. The only way it will float is to strangle it and dry it out for two years."

I stroke the noose mark around the stump. I can hear the mother tree being choked to death, while her children watch helplessly. Why did they tie the rope so high?

"Does she continue to grow after the strangle?"

"No, she's been dead for a long time. They came in the high-water season to tie the noose and used the high water to float the giants out of the swamp, the only way to harvest the trees then. They took only the big ones then, for construction and furniture. So at least we still had something left, no matter how small. We still had some hope. Now the trees are just ground into mulch for gardens, the most coveted mulch because it doesn't rot and it keeps bugs away from the garden. So size no longer matters, be it two years old or two thousand years old. They come in trucks, in the dry season, taking everything, roots and saplings, dead and alive. A complete wipe out and no hope for rejuvenation. A mature cypress is hard to kill, but a sapling is a different story. The seed falls into the water, waiting for the dry season for germination. It stays alive in the water for a year or two, then dies. When it sprouts, it has to grow fast in the first year, really fast, faster than the flood, so that the treetop can stay above the water. Those that can't grow fast enough will drown. After that, it has to compete for the sunlight. Oh, yeah, it needs a lot of sun to make sugar for food, and it's not easy in a swamp. Lots of competition. Every species wants to take as much room in the sky as possible to get the light and squeeze out other species. Without the mother cypress, a sapling has no chance to fight the invasive trees for the air space. That's why they grow in clusters. That's why they grow so slow. You see those stumps around each cypress? We call them knees, roots that come out of the ground above the water, to breathe during the high-water season, to give the ground support to the tree."

I gaze at the "knees." They form a large ring around the cypress, in all kinds of shapes, slender and elegant, attentive like the fairies under the Buddha's lotus seat, some deep in meditation, some ready to burst into singing or fly into the sky to dance.

A flock of ibis fly over, their wings so gentle and graceful. My eyes sting with tears.

Al whispers, "The natives believe that ibis is the last to seek shelter before a hurricane, and the first to emerge after the storm. They are a symbol for danger and optimism. Dad believes they're guardian angels of the sky."

So are you, Al, and your dad, Dean Wilson, Bob the ranger, BMW, John Ruskey, Mark River Peoples, and many other folks I met along the Mississippi.

"Thank you, Al, for everything." I bow.

The basin is quiet and still. The only movement comes from the bird wings. Al gazes at the sky, his face melting into this eternal stillness. I glance at Immanuel. He was also watching, his face serene, no shadow of darkness or desire. If there is indeed a garden for gods, then this must be it, except for the evil lurking under the water. Is it true where beauty lives, evil is not far?

The water splashes as if someone threw a handful of sand in the still water. Rings of ripples form a dance on the swamp. Al laughs. "Ah, the mullets, those tricksters. They are my dad's favorites, though they seem useless for the fishermen, too small, impossible to catch. They just make him laugh. Make me laugh too."

The air now ripples with joy. Suddenly, a huge splash then a thud in the back of the boat. Al's eyes bulge with excitement.

"Ping, we got a silverback!"

The fish jumps again, its silver body arching like a bow in the air, falling with a heavy thud on the boat's plastic surface. Al runs over and catches it with both hands.

"This has never happened to my boat. I mean silverbacks do jump a lot, but it's rare to see them fall in the boat. The swamp really likes you, Ping and Immanuel. She's offering you a gift."

The carp is still and taut in his hands, its slick back lined with intricate shiny scales, its round eyes ringed with pink as if it were crying. We gaze at each other. Do we know each other? The fish came from China. We are kin, in that sense. How did it cross the Pacific and end up in the Louisiana swamp? What story does it want to tell me? The fish blinks, and I remember the old man from the Three Gorges, standing quietly in the angry crowd. Everyone was shouting for justice. The corrupt officials had robbed their land and homes in the name of the super dam. Only he looked at me, eyelids pink from wind and too much crying, a roll of paper in his hand. He was panting hard too, like the fish, because he had just run from his apartment building to fetch his petition.

As the taxi driver tried to pull me away from the mob, the old man presented the paper to me, just like Al presenting the silverback.

"I want you to take the story to America. I want everyone in the world to know what happened to us, to our river."

He thrust the paper into my hand. As we sped away, amid the shouting that the police were coming, I unrolled the paper. It was a petition signed by the entire village that was now under the water, by hundreds of people now landless, homeless.

I take the carp from Al. It lies still in my hands, only its mouth opening and closing. We look at each other, and my eyes smart. I will cook this gift from the swamp at Dave's turtle party and offer its tender meat to the guests from New Orleans, the country, and the world. As the fish enters our mouths and blood veins, it will tell its story of the Yangtze and Mississippi, of all rivers and mountains, of all sentient beings, and what we, humans, have done to them.

28

The End of the Bird's Foot

"Americans are eating their evidence," roars Mike Waddle, thrusting two freezer bags under my nose. Each has a shrimp inside, one shiny and firm with pink flesh, an orange line bulging from its head down the spine indicating fertile eggs; the other shrimp looks pale and limp, tar balls under the shell, inside the head.

"This one was caught before the spill." Mike points to the pink shrimp, then the pale one. "This was caught last month, two years after the spill. The oil and dispersant they sprayed to cover the spill had infected its brain."

I nod. I'm not an expert on seafood, but anyone can tell that the skinny black-headed shrimp is sick.

"I haven't touched seafood since the spill. The dispersant is toxic. It changes living things at the cellular level. When BP hired me for the clean up, I was required to wear rubber gloves and suits. They said it was just for caution and there was no real harm, but I know better. The exposure to dispersants, by air or touch, can damage the nervous system, blood, kidneys, and liver. How do I know? Because everything it touches rots away, my rubber boots, gloves, pants. My ship is rotting, and all the fishing boats that sailed in the toxic soup. If it can eat away the steel, imagine what it can do to a living thing. BP sprayed over a million gallons of the chemicals on top of the ocean, into the leaking well five thousand feet deep, at the bottom of the sea. The chemicals break down the oil and turn the thick goo into billions of droplets that look transparent, almost like the lens over an alligator's eyes. It made the ocean surface look cleaner, no longer so gooey, dark, and sickly orange, but the oil still remains. You see, those billions of droplets sank just below the surface, hang like walls in the top thirty to fifty feet of the ocean, turning our gulf into a dead zone. And guess what? Venice is one of the last few spots where blue fin tuna and other marine animals come and lay their eggs in the warm water in May and June. The gulf used to be their nursery, but it's now a graveyard. Fish are dying, shrimp are dying, birds are dying, reeds are dying, cypresses are dying, and we're dying from mutations and cancers. All the seafood I catch have strange growths in their brains, on the skin. You see the black spots in the shrimp's head? They should be eggs, red and orange like this shrimp I caught before the spill, but now, it's nothing but tar, like the oil slick, and there are some half-formed eggs on the legs. Poor thing, she lost her sense how to make eggs and where to keep them. Can you blame her? No! Because the dispersants turned her brain into tar balls. And if I eat this, my brain will turn into the same shit."

Mike pauses to breathe, his face red and puffy from talking in one long breath. I can tell that he has hypertension, that his blood pressure has risen to at least 160, unless he is taking meds, but judging from his trailer home, I have a sense that he doesn't have health insurance, which means he can't afford the meds. He opens his humongous refrigerator lined with packs of Coke and beer and pulls out a can. His sugary diet won't help his hypertension, either.

"But you're still going out shrimping tonight. And all the other fishermen. Who is buying seafood? Who is eating it?"

Mike smiles. "Well, the Chinese buy most of it. Our shrimp are the sweetest and juiciest and not farm raised. People are willing to pay for the wild thing, and it's worth every penny."

"Do they know it's tainted?"

"Oh hell, they know. The dealers know it damn well, too." He laughs. "But what do they care as long as there's money to make? And it's big money because there are lots of rich Chinese nowadays, and they love seafood, the best kind, the wild kind, and only they can afford our gulf shrimp."

"What about the toxins?"

"Our tarnished shrimp is still a thousand times cleaner than the seafood in China. You know that already, right?" He looks at me with his bulging eyes.

Yes, indeed. And that is why I am here, with a thousand river flags made by a thousand folks who care about water. I grew up on the biggest fishing island in the East China Sea. Every morning, I walked five miles to the market, standing in long lines for our daily food from rice to tofu to meat, and the only thing that didn't require waiting was seafood. Piles and piles of them from the sea, yellow, silver, red, shrimp, crab, squid, and fish of all kinds, fresh, abundant, cheap, a few cents a pound. They were clean because there was hardly any industry on the fishing island then. As a child, I paid no heed. I took the abundance for granted. If the land failed because of drought or flood, which happened often, the ocean always had plenty for us. The first time I heard that fish were getting scarce and the price was shooting up on the island, I laughed in disbelief. Then, I heard that fishermen started fish farms because there was too little to catch in the sea; I was appalled. Then, I heard of the horrible pollution everywhere: the land, the air, the sea, the complete collapse of fisheries in the China Sea, and the fish men had to sail all the way to Africa and South America to catch fish, my heart broke. How could this happen so fast, in twenty years?

I look at the shrimp in Mike's hands. I grew up eating shrimp. My favorite way was to blanch it in boiling water for thirty seconds, no salt, no spice. The shrimp tasted like sea flowers, nectar of the salty wind. And that was why I bought two pounds of the gulf shrimp from Coastal Seafood before my departure, and Tony, my favorite fishmonger in St. Paul, guaranteed they were the best shrimp one could have. Never frozen, straight from the gulf. The heads were snapped off, so no one would see the tar balls.

"Look at the poor thing." Mike caresses the sick shrimp in his hand. "It no longer knows if it's a she or he, laying eggs everywhere, legs, shells, going crazy . . . If you put it out in the sun, even flies won't touch her or lay larvae on her. Too toxic. So this is the food for the fish, the birds, and us nowadays. No wonder we all go crazy like the shrimp, no wonder we don't know who we are . . ." His voice thickens with sorrow. "I try to alert people, the local fishermen, the traders, the Coast Guard, the government. I try to show them the evidence. But nobody wants to hear it. They want to move on, keep fishing, selling, buying, as if nothing bad had happened, like the dispersants that turn the oil into transparent droplets in the sea. They name me the 'Bug Man' because I can't stop telling people how no flies would lay eggs on the damn shrimp. They laugh as soon as I show my face on docks, those fishermen, white and Asian. But I don't mind. They know exactly what I'm talking about. They won't eat the seafood themselves, like me. They keep fishing, too, like me, because we've got to make a living, right? We have to pay loans and interests for our boats. What else could we do? There's no job around here, apart from the oil rigs. And it's backbreaking work, literally. I broke my back twice working for BP. They patched me up and sent me back to work until I am no good for them anymore. Can't lift the heavy equipment with my crooked spine. Pension? Insurance? Are you kidding me? Why would they invest money on a broken man? Especially a broken man with a big mouth? I'm on their blacklist. They make sure I will never get a goddamn job with them again. They know who I am in Venice, in the whole parish, the whole gulf. There are lots of drug addicts around here. Lots of oil and hurricanes. My home has gone underwater so many times, Katrina, Isaac, and many others. You see the levee outside the window? The Army Corps fortifies it every year, but we know better. We've seen the water rising, rising, rising, jumping over the levee and boom, everything goes under. Man conquers nature? Poof! Hallucinating. The more we meddle with nature, the worse off we are. It's a scheme, I tell you, like the Mafia from New York. They kill people, grind up their bodies, and stuff the evidence in the hotdogs. We eat them and say hmmmm delicious. The government and corporations take our money, brainwash us through schools, commercials, drug us into zombies so they can rob us blind, and we say hurray, thank you, Uncle Sam and Oil Man. But not me. My eyes and mouth are wide open. That's why they hate me. The Coast Guard harasses me like crazy, those scumbags, paid by my tax money. They hope I go away. I want to go away. This place has too much oil, too many drugs, broken spirits, too much everything except for hope. Lili wants me to move to Seattle, where her folks live. But I can't. This is my home, no matter what happens."

He stops, out of breath again, his face scarlet red, almost purple, his eyes bloodshot. I worry that he might keel over and drop on the floor. But he stands tall and still, the only thing moving is the Coke in his hand, shaking involuntarily.

A Katrina in his brain and heart. No medicine can calm this hurricane.

Outside the trailer, Lili is barbecuing chicken and brats in a tiny clearing of the woods. I go out to help her, but the clearing is big enough only for a small grill and petite Lili. No room for a chair. She squats over the fire, turning the meat with long chopsticks. An overturned crate serves as a tabletop. No seafood on the grill, as Mike said. Fragrance rises with the roasting meat. I'm suddenly hungry, very hungry. It's 2:30 p.m., and I haven't eaten since 7:00 a.m., when we said goodbye to Dave and drove to Venice.

Since our arrival at New Orleans, Dave Brinks texted and called his uncle in Venice many times, but no response.

"He must be working on the oil rig. Fishing really sucked after the spill." Dave frowned. "Do you have to visit Venice? I heard there's nothing left after Katrina and the BP spill. Pierre Joris and his wife tried to find some Vietnamese fishermen to interview for an opera. They were commissioned to write the libretto. They drove all the way to Venice, but every town along the shore was empty. Even when they did find someone, those Vietnamese either pretended they did not speak English or simply refused to talk. Perhaps you're better off just hanging around in New Orleans. I can try to get more concert tickets for you."

Immanuel nodded. He was still wrapped in the ecstasy of Thurston Moore's concert. He played in a ghetto house backyard converted into a giant music box, with spiral staircase, barn, and toy houses filled with musical instruments. Thurston flowed in and out of the toys like a fish, tinkering with different instruments and making crazy sounds that drove the audience wild. I knew Immanuel was eager to meet him. So I asked Dave to introduce us after the concert. Thurston was indeed going to Naropa, arriving the day after I finished my teaching there. And he was indeed collaborating with Anne Waldman. In fact, they were going to perform together at the Boulder concert hall. Immanuel stared, gobbling down every word Thurston uttered.

"Thanks, Dave. But I really need to bring the flags to the end of the river, into the Gulf of Mexico."

He sighed. "Just be careful, okay? Don't hang out there too long. Call me anytime if you need to. I wish I could get in touch with my uncle."

I assured Dave everything would be just fine. We would stay one night and come back to New Orleans the next day. He still looked worried. But why?

We got onto Highway 23 South, the only road along the last strip of the Mississippi. It was not the official Great River Road, which ended in New Orleans, but the air smelled more of the Mississippi. The houses along the highway sprawled and crouched low to the ground, as if dodging wind blows. Some had crumbled, half buried in the sand.

I had studied the map before and during the trip. This road was the main highway for hurricanes as well as for cars and trucks. Venice was called the end of the Bird's Foot because Highway 23 ended there and so did the main channel of the Mississippi. After Venice, the river bloomed into a flower, forking into three branches like a bird's foot, hence the nickname. To my eyes, the foot also resembled a bird's head, a young eagle, with its beak and wings spread wide and still forming, with Lake Pontchartrain being its heart, full of blue blood, and the Mississippi as its artery, and now we were driving along this artery feeling the pulse of the giant river pumping its blue blood from its heart up to its brain into the gulf.

The air smelled saltier and saltier as we drove. My heart started racing. Something was waiting there for us, something magical and terrible.

We entered Venice. Its short main street littered with abandoned grocery stores, bank, motels. I experienced déjà vu, as if I were back at Cairo, the ghostly towns and cities along the Three Gorges before the dam, buildings with black gaping windows, crumbling into garbage.

I was hungry, but there was no sign for a restaurant or hotel.

After the main street, the road became narrow, zigzagging along a thin strip of land. On our right hand, the scenery took away my breath: vast shallow water filled with reeds along the shore and bald cypress trees with singing birds, schools of mullets gathering and scattering like quick sand. I remembered Al's remark: they jump because they're happy.

I looked to the driver's side and almost screamed at what I saw: oil rigs, pipelines, and refineries, billowy smoke from the chimneys, mountains of huge black tires, rusty pipes and carts, schools of crows and vultures circling and cawing above.

Our narrow road became the divider between Paradise and Hell, one painted by God, the other by humans.

The road forked. Immanuel veered to the left, and we almost ran into a wall with a giant sign: HALLIBURTON. NO TRESPASSING.

Immanuel braked then backed off.

"Wait. Let me get out."

"Are you insane?"

I opened the door and jumped out. No time to reason with him. He would never understand. I didn't even understand myself. I just had the urge to say something to the wall. A gust of chemical odor hit me, almost knocking me out. So this was what it felt like in the heart of a beast. Halliburton. Didn't they supply the concrete to seal the wells in the deep sea? Didn't their concrete fail and cause the well to erupt? Halliburton with the BP spill. Halliburton with the Iraq war. Halliburton with the former vice president, with all the catastrophes and wars. Halliburton. The letters were painted with such large neon red they threatened to burst through the wall and engulf me if I dared go forward another inch. I made a step forward, then another. The air was thick, as if I were pushing into a sea of oil.

The wall rumbled with waves of warning.

"I am not afraid of you, Hal-li-bur-ton." I uttered the name, syllable by syllable. "You have no business in this paradise, our paradise. Leave the marsh alone, leave the river alone, leave the fish, trees, birds alone, leave the earth and sky alone. Just leave us, just let us be." I said slowly, my eyes wet as I thought of all the drillings in the sea, swamps, mountains, prairies, all the oil-stained animals, birds, all the dying trees, all the dams choking rivers, all the cars on the highways and streets, including my own. How could we stop this?

The wall swelled with anger. The letters opened their scarlet mouths. I stood firm. *Swallow me if you can. I'll fight you from inside.*

"Get into the car, right now!" Immanuel hissed. "Someone is coming. You don't want to get arrested, right? We need to hang our flags, remember?"

I looked up. An armed man in uniform was walking fast toward us. I waved at him, flashed a smile, and got into the car. Immanuel was right. We had things to do here: install the river flags at the end of the Bird's Foot and send a thousand wishes into the Gulf of Mexico. Our imagination and love would prevail. Our river flags could transform the dark energy into something positive.

We got back to the main road and kept going until it ended. So this was the end of the Bird's Foot? The place looked abandoned. A small storage house with tires leaned against its door, a rusty structure with a pulley, and a rusty ship leaning against the shore. I climbed on the ship. This would be a perfect place for the flag installation. The distance between the ship and the pulley was far, but I could tie three banners together to make it work. The noon sky was overcast. I had a feeling the sun would come out soon. I would wait until the sunset to let the twilight ignite the flags flying over the marsh and river. I looked around and saw a forest of sailboats.

"There's a harbor over there," I shouted. "Let's go and find someone with a boat. Perhaps we can even find something to eat."

We found the gravel path that forked off the main road. The harbor was a well-paved, well-maintained place. Hundreds of million-dollar boats parked along the dock. It was quiet and clean and white, but the air smelled uneasy. At the far end, a group of drunken men were loading the boat with beer coolers and fishing gear. Someone said something, and the group burst out laughing. I walked toward them hesitantly. I didn't want to talk to them, but I had to find someone with a boat, someone willing to take me out into the sea. I knew these men would not, but perhaps they could lead me to someone they knew. One man turned in my direction, fixing his bleary eyes on me for a minute and going back to his group. He didn't see me in his stupor. Perhaps they were just ghosts, in this ghost harbor with the ghost ships.

A cough from my right. I stopped. Not Immanuel. He stayed in the car, waiting. I resumed walking. Another cough, more forceful this time, enough to make me turn. A man on the dock, mending a fish net next to a small shabby fishing boat, sticking out like a rusty nail, without shame or apology, in the white marble wall of million-dollar boats. I walked toward him, thinking of Mr. Ran's nail house sticking out of the ruins by the Three Gorges Dam. The sun had come out, shining on his face, red, blue veins pulsing on his temple, sweat dripping down his neck, soaking his T-shirt. He was burning in the sun, burning with anger, and I felt the dock tremble under my feet. If I lit a match, the whole harbor and gulf would explode. But his anger and his shabby fishing boat felt a lot more real than all the boats in the harbor.

"Hello," I extended my hand. "My name is Ping. I'm from Shanghai, China, the mouth of the Yangtze River, but now I live in St. Paul, Minnesota, near the headwaters of the Mississippi."

He fixed his blue eyes on me, first steely, smoldering, suspicious, then softened. The pulsing veins calmed down, and the redness receded from his cheeks like a tide. He gave me his hand, mouth open with a smile.

"Mike, Mike Waddle. Welcome to Venice, the end of the Bird's Foot."

Lili walks in with a giant tray of chicken, brats, hamburger patties, lamb shish kebabs, all perfectly smoked on the small grill in the back of their trailer. Even though I met her an hour ago and chatted with her about Vietnam, I'm still startled to see how beautiful and calm she looks and how light and steady she walks. How could a seventy-year-old move like a young girl? How could she stay up all night long working on the shrimp boat, not just one night, but weeks, months, years? She can outdo every man in Venice, even me, says Mike, his laughing full of admiration and affection. Lili speaks fluent Mandarin, 100 percent Chinese, born and grew up in Vietnam, had three children with an American soldier, and left her beloved country with her children by hanging onto the last fleeing American helicopter.

Lili is my key into Venice.

On the dock, my conversation with Mike was difficult. After the initial greeting, he went back to his old self and grunted one-syllable answers to my questions.

"All these beautiful boats on this beautiful day, Mr. Waddle. But where's everyone?"

"God knows!"

"Is this your boat? Are you a fisherman? What do you catch?"

"Shrimp."

"How's the fishing business?"

"Sucks!"

"Why?"

"BP." Spat.

The dock shook with the force of his spitting. I waited for an explosion, but only silence and his trembling hands over the broken net.

"I was looking for, ehhh, a boat to take me into the gulf, Mr. Waddle. Do you know anyone?"

"Nope!"

He looked up and saw my face in despair. His steely eyes softened. "Why?" he asked, almost tenderly. "You don't look like one of those crazy, stupid sport fishing pussies."

I laughed. He was referring to the drunk fishing men on the dock.

"No, sir," I said and told him about my Kinship of Rivers, how it started in Tibet and snowballed along the Mississippi, and why I brought the flags to the gulf. His eyes opened wider as I talked, his hands stopped moving in the tangled net. His eyes twinkled.

"I could have taken you in my boat, but I'm planning to go shrimping tonight, and I'll stay out all night in the gulf, unless you want to do that. Ever tried that?"

"I'd love to, Mr. Waddle," I shouted, jumping up and down. "I grew up on the biggest fishing island in China, on the East China Sea. I grew up eating seafood, every day, but never went out in a fishing boat. Chinese fishermen never allow a woman on their boat, for fear of bad luck."

"No, we won't, Ping!" said Immanuel.

When did he get out of the car?

The smile on Mr. Waddle's face receded. I wanted to seal Immanuel's mouth with masking tape. *Just keep your mouth shut please, as usual! Please don't say a word. Please let's go to the gulf in the fishing boat. We'll never have another chance like this.*

"There's no time, Ping. We have to install river flags along the shore this afternoon, and tomorrow, we have to go back to New Orleans for the big party Dave is preparing for us. We can't go out all night chasing shrimp. No way we can do that."

"Yes way, Immanuel. This is what we came all the way from St. Paul for, to go fishing in a real fishing boat with a real fisherman in the gulf."

"Oh yeah? How come you never discussed this with me? Did I count for something in your eyes, ever?"

I watched his fluttering eyelids. He was right. I never told him about my desire to go fishing with a real fisherman. But I didn't know it myself until now, when the opportunity came up, a minute ago. So how could I have discussed the possibility? Immanuel's anger was real, and it was not the first time. He wanted to be a man, a king, who could make and carry out executive decisions. But I constantly foiled his plans with my willfulness.

"Never mind!" grunted Mike. "I don't want to cause no trouble."

A heavy silence fell upon us. I looked at Mike. He was back to mending his net. The volcano opened for only a minute, now sealed again. I looked at Immanuel, reeling in his mental maze again. Pleading with him would be useless. Crap. I wish I hadn't brought him along. What about going fishing with Mike just by myself? But where would Immanuel sleep tonight? What would he eat? There was no motel or restaurant in this place. Perhaps he could just camp on the side of the road? Sleep in the car? And make his own damn food? Be his own king? Take care of himself like a real man?

"My wife is Chinese, you know," said Mike out of the impossible silence, his head bent over the net, his words leaping like mullets' joyful jumps. "She was born and lived in Vietnam, then came to America when the war was over."

"Does she speak Chinese?" I asked, almost whispering, my heart jumping high like an Asian carp.

He looked up, his eyes full of tenderness. "I think she does. I think she misses speaking her mother tongue. Her folks live in Seattle. All her Asian friends here are Vietnamese."

"I would love to meet her and talk to her. I miss speaking my mother tongue too."

He looked into my eyes for a long time then dropped the net around his feet. "Come with me. I'll take you home."

≈≈≈

"Time for lunch," Lili says, her voice sweet and moist like the perfectly steamed sticky rice. She sets the tray down on the table, the only one in the trailer, on which a MacBook flickers and a giant TV blasts a Vietnamese soap opera. It is used as a desk, a dining table, and TV holder, just like the central space of the trailer used for the living room, dining room, and kitchen. Every piece of furniture is tightly packed into the small place: a couch at the entrance, a table against the window, a giant refrigerator that occupies half of the wall in the kitchen area, a small countertop and a sink, then a recliner by the door, where two tiny terriers look up at Mike with adoring eyes, begging him to sit down so they can jump on his lap. It is a typical trailer home in America, practical and masculine, softened by Lili's hand, its walls, door handles, and windows charmed by ancient coins, peace knots, figurines of Asian gods for money and safety.

Lili pushes the paper away to clear a space for her spread.

"Don't touch them," Mike shouts and dashes over to stack the paper together. "Almost forgot this," he waves an envelope at me. "I wrote to the governor of Louisiana, the federal agency for the environment, and many other places I could think of about the BP spill and what it's done to our place. I told them about the dispersants causing permanent damage to all the lives in the sea, on the land, in the air. Even flies won't lay larvae because the flies know how toxic the seafood has become. I sent them tons of pictures. I wish I could send them my shrimp samples. I wish they would send somebody to see what's going on here. The president did show up, and our governor, but we couldn't get near them. Nope ma'am, we small people couldn't get close to voice our concerns. The Coast Guard, paid by my tax money, shoved me out of the town hall as far as God allowed them. If they could shove me straight to hell, they would, just to get my big mouth out of the hall of lies. Yes, ma'am, they have their pretty lies and rosy reports for the president and governor, and they don't want to hear no truth from Mike Waddle. This is what they finally sent me, out of hundreds of letters. This is all they've got to say to my pleas."

He tries to pull the letter out, but his hands shake so much that he nearly tears the envelope in half.

"Damn hands," he cusses, holding his right hand out in front of his chest, opening and closing as if the tremor would go away. But it only shakes like a netted fish gasping for air. He drops it in despair. "The day the gulf burst into fire, my hands started shaking like this, as if they got a life of their own. My little brain couldn't fathom what was coming at that time, but my hands knew. They've touched every inch of the gulf, every living creature. They know the pulse of the sea, and they've been crying."

I want to tell him that the shaking comes from the liver wind. According to Chinese medicine, the liver is the general, commanding and distributing qi and blood to the whole body. This general is courageous but also hot tempered. When he is angry, his liver fire rises to his head and hands, causing red eyes, red face, ringing ears, shaking hands, and vertigo. But I keep quiet. I like Mike's theory better. His hands know what's coming to the gulf, and they are angry.

The letter has two pages. The first page is actually the letter that Mike wrote to the governor on February 2, 2012:

Dear ones, I write this because of what I have seen on the sea after the Mississippi Canyon 252 incident. Just because of the visible fish feeding frenzy on a substance that others and I witnessed and never noticed before the BP incident.

If you would view a time-lapsed photograph study using shrimp caught in this region, you can see when a species, that has been inflected with a visible inflection are less, that the "Flys" will not lay larvae on their carcass and you will see that these insects will come but they will soon fly away. No matter how you handle the specimens or where you place them under any normal condition the flies will act the same.

I found if I mix the shrimp with other species that this has similar effects just as in blending and mixing.

Hopefully you will be able to show cause why some of the dead foul odor around my home shows similar events are taking place. Not asking for help will likely jeopardize the Gulf Coast fishing industry and future generations.

May God Bless you in my Jesus name I ask this.

Respectfully
Mr. Jan Michael Waddle

Mike notarized his letter on February 25. So he waited three weeks before he sent it out. I turn to the governor's response from his constituent service office:

Dear Mr. Waddle:

Thank you for contacting the Governor's office regarding marine life and the Gulf Coast. Rest assured that your concerns are of great importance of the Governor.

As you may know, this matter falls under the jurisdiction of the Louisiana Department of Wildlife and Fisheries. I have forwarded your information to them for further review, and you should be receiving a response from them in the near future.

Holding the letters in my hand, I feel dizzy with déjà vu again. I read so many petitions from the Yangtze, heard so many angry, tearful pleas from the men and women displaced by the Three Gorges Dam. Not in a million years would I have dreamed of reading a petition at the end of the Mississippi River. The Chinese petitioners asked me to tell their stories to the world, especially America, the symbol of democracy and freedom. What would they think when they heard Mike's story? True, Mike did receive a letter from the governor's constituency's office, but it offered nothing. They just kicked him to another department.

“Did the Wildlife and Fisheries department send someone to investigate?” I ask Mike, just to make sure.

He stares at me, red eyes bulging.

“Nope! This letter is the only thing I’ve got. The governor’s office responded because they wanted my vote. Hahaha!” He laughs loudly, but it sounds like sobbing.

“Let’s eat, babe. Food is getting cold, and our guests are hungry,” says Lili, her hand on Mike’s sleeve so gentle that for a moment he seems to stop shaking, his breathing back to normal.

“Go ahead and eat.” He waves and sips the Coke he has been holding in his hand. “I’m not hungry.”

I survey the colorful and fragrant spread of meat grilled to perfection. Mike has no appetite. Lili doesn’t seem like a meat eater. So she prepared this feast for us. I am hungry, but I can’t take my eyes away from her hands, scarred, wrinkled, speckled with brown spots. Her face and body have made peace with all the tragedies in her life, but not those hands. Like Oskar Kokoschka’s painting where hands take the central stage, her hands scream her stories.

“What are you waiting for?” Mike scolds. “I thought you were hungry. The food is clean, and Lili is an incredible cook. She used to run a restaurant in Venice, the best Vietnamese food in Louisiana. I say this because it’s truth not because she’s my wife.”

“I believe you,” I say, still mesmerized by Lili’s hands. She notices my gaze and tucks them under her apron.

“Oh, oh, forgot the bitters!” She jumps and brings a plate of mint from the counter. “You need them to digest all the meat.”

How do you know the Chinese medicine and its five-taste theory, I want to ask. But of course she knows, being Chinese and Vietnamese. The knowledge of five tastes for balance runs in our DNA. Sweet, sour, bitter, hot, salty, five tastes correspond to our five organs. We need them all to make food tasty and our bodies healthy. My grandmas battered this into my memory: Without bitterness, how do you know sweet? Without pain, how do you know joy? Many ancient civilizations know this secret too: parsley for Greeks, Arabs, Jews, Romans, mint for Southeast Asians, turmeric for Indians, dandelion and shepherd’s purse for Chinese. Americans push out bitters, only keep salt and sweet, causing obesity, hypertension, acid reflux, putrid.

Immanuel waves away Lili’s mint and picks up a brat. “Not the hotdog by NYC Mafias, right?” he jokes, alluding to Mike’s earlier comments about the Mafia hotdogs. I laugh, happy for his effort at humor, though it is a bit ill-timed.

"Maybe yes, maybe no," smiles Mike cunningly.

Immanuel turns ashen. He stops chewing.

"Just kidding. It's clean. It's venison. My brother is a hunter."

Immanuel sighs with a relief and goes back to his plate.

The food is truly delicious, but I feel full quickly. It's hard for me to eat under Mike's watchful eyes while Lili darts around cleaning, washing, bringing us drinks as if she were serving in a restaurant. I want them to sit down and eat with us, but that doesn't seem likely.

My cell rings. Captain Morgan is returning our inquiry about hiring his fishing boat. I found him on the Internet, among hundreds of ads boasting their records of catching the biggest marlins and swordfish for their clients. Of all the messages I left, only Captain Morgan has called back.

"It's too late to go out now. You need to spend a whole day out there to catch something decent. So 6:00 a.m. tomorrow? I'll give you a discount. Six hundred dollars."

"What about this afternoon for two or three hours?"

"I can't guarantee that you'll catch anything."

"I'm not interested in catching. I just want to be in the gulf for an hour or two."

I could hear Captain Morgan's muffled voice: "Oh nothing, just some crazy foreign gal. I'll be with you in a second." From the Internet search, I discover that Venice is a fishing and birding village for commerce and tourism. If one comes to the gulf, the only purpose is to fish or capture a glimpse of birds, nothing else. I can explain to Captain Morgan why I want to go to the gulf, but it will make him even more confused. Captain Morgan is already intoxicated, judging from his slurry speech. Immanuel eyes me with his question: *I thought you wanted to catch shrimp with Mike.* I remain silent. There was a difference between experiencing fishing with a real fisherman and catching fish for trophies. I don't need a trophy. Already got one two years ago: a forty-five-inch muskie in my first fishing trip to Battle Lake in Minnesota.

"Well, how much would it be for a short trip?" I ask.

"Well, ma'am, it won't be much cheaper than the whole-day trip. Four hundred dollars."

"Four hundred dollars for two hours!"

"Yessum."

"May I call you back later, Captain Morgan?" I turn off the phone.

Mike puts down his Coke.

"Well, if you want, I can take you there in the morning. Don't worry about the fee. Just cover my gas, which seems to increase every day."

I can't believe my ears. Is he giving up his shrimp for us? That is a gift too big and heavy for me to accept.

He waves his hand. "My net is messed up. I was hoping to fix it today, but there's not enough time. So I'll go shrimping tomorrow night. I know you want to go out there today, but it's too rushed. Tomorrow morning is better. Captain Morgan is no fool. He knows he's in no condition to go today. And you never want to rush into the gulf. Have to make sure all the equipment is in good condition and the man in charge. You never know what can happen in the sea. So I'll go get ready for tomorrow and try to fix my damn fish net. By the way, where are you staying tonight?" He asks as he walks to the door.

"Ehhh, I was thinking perhaps we could find someone's backyard to set up our tent?" I say hopefully, looking at Mike. I already surveyed his yard. It is small but big enough for our tent.

"Mosquitoes will eat you alive. Stay with us. Lili will prepare the guest room. Don't argue with me. I know you Asian people have to put up a fight to show your politeness. It doesn't work with me. Lili will also prepare a dinner for us all. She's excited already, I can tell. You know, she's a great cook. But I'm still used to my daily burgers and hotdogs. Can't eat Asian food all the time. But tonight is special. We don't have guests like you every night. What time do you want to go to the gulf tomorrow?"

It takes me a while to find my breath and answer his question. "I'd, I'd like to catch the sunrise, if we could."

"That's fine. We'll need to get up at 3:00 a.m. then." He closes the door before I can say anything.

"Wow!" I turn to Immanuel. He looks dazed. Such hospitality is unheard of in the North, where personal space is guarded as sacred. If I get too close, people would get flustered, embarrassed, even indignant. For me, it's all so familiar. I have encountered many strangers who fed and sheltered me as I traveled along the Yangtze River, even at the risk of being arrested by the police. The deeper I went into the South along the Mississippi, the more familiar the scenes become: BMW, Quapaw Canoe, Dave Brink, and now Mike Waddle and Lili Liang. Is it the river? The bigger the water becomes, the bigger the heart grows? Didn't Ranger Bob say that river people are a different species? And who am I to receive such gifts? How could I ever repay so many cups of kindness?

"Let's hang river flags in their yard and save some for the roadside when the sun goes down," I say to Immanuel when he is done eating.

Soon hundreds of flags hug the fence, around the trailer, and flutter between the trailer and fence. The wind picks up, sending them up and down in the afternoon sun like school children. Lili comes out to help, her eyes shining as I tell her where and how each flag was made, and stories pour out of her mouth like a song bird. She is a twelve-year-old girl again, going to the Chinese school with her sisters and brothers in Saigon, her parents strict and loving, her nanny keeping a close eye on her every move. She was the flower of the Liang family, the beauty queen, groomed to marry into a richer and nobler family, to bring honor to her mother and father. But the war came. Everything shattered, no mother, no father, no fiancé, no siblings, no hope, only fire, bullets, bombs, hunger, fear, and surviving at any cost, bar girl, dance girl, children by GI Joes, beatings, fleeing from Vietnam to Thailand, from Thailand to America, fleeing, always fleeing, more abusive men, more cheating business partners, until she met Mike, and together, they bought the old shrimp boat from Mike's brother. Her children want her to move to Seattle, to retire in their mansions facing the Pacific, facing home.

"But Mike won't go. He will never leave Venice," whispers Lili. "He belongs to the water here, his bone and spirits. I am torn. I want to be with my kids, but Mike needs me. He's had a hard life. He won't last long on his own if I move to Seattle. He won't last long either if he moves to the West Coast with me. That's why I'm still here, stuck." She gazes at the image of the Buddha from the Three Gorges. I took the photo in a temple that is now under the water after the dam completion. The Buddha comes alive as the fabric flutters in the wind, his half-closed eyes fixing on Lili with compassion.

"Mike may talk and act tough, but inside, he's as soft as a lamb. Just look at how he plays with his dogs. They're his children. He has a son, thirty-five years old, but he hasn't seen him since his wife shot herself, and her family took custody of the boy."

"How could they take the boy from his father?"

Lili looks pensive. "Well, anything is possible if one has money. It's true everywhere, right? His wife's family is wealthy. They didn't want her to marry Mike in the first place. But she was a rebel, I guess, and manic depressive, from what Mike described about her. Mike was working on the drilling rig when she shot herself. That same night, he broke his back. You can imagine the pain. He had to take lots of drugs, including morphine. And her family used it to take the boy away. Mike rarely mentions his son, but I know he thinks about him every day, every night."

Tears fill Lili's eyes. "Did you say these flags will travel to Everest? Did you say the prayers will come true if they are sent from the roof of the world?"

"Yes, we'll bring them to Everest. And yes, Tibetans do believe their prayers, if sincere and pure, will come true. The mountains will lift them close to the sky, then the rivers will bring them to the right place at the right time."

She looks around the yard, crowded with her papaya tree, her vines of melons, beans, tomatoes, and the little bush where she put her tiny grill. "I wish for a little more land to grow vegetables," she says, giggling and blushing. "Well, I do have a wish. My old home in Saigon, if I could set my feet on it again before I die." Her lips tremble.

"Would you like to make a flag?" I ask gently. "I promise I'll bring it to Everest."

She nods. "Mike would like to make a flag, too. Can we make it together?"

The sun is setting on the paradise side of the road, painting the lagoon with a sheen of gold, pink, purple, lilac, blue, gray. The colors take my breath away. No human hand could possibly paint such a spectacular canvas. Mullets go crazy with their twilight feeding, and the lagoon trembles with rings of joy. The birds join in with their last dance for the day, flying between cypress and reeds, sky and earth, feeding, singing . . .

I take out three rolls of flags and tie them together to form a long banner. No tree on the roadside, having retreated into the deep of the marsh, as if trying to get away from the dump and oil pipes on the other side of the road. In fact, the trees close to the road are all dead. Even light won't cross over. While the paradise side is awash with brilliant colors, sounds, and movements, the hell side is gray, static, silent. Vultures circle above the garbage mountain silently, as if dark forces swallowed their cawing.

I shudder and turn my back. There is an electricity pole next to a pile of rocks littered with Coke and beer cans. Two men were fishing there but left soon after our arrival. I can use the pole and my car for the installation. I tie the rope as high as I can reach, and Immanuel brings the other end toward the car. I raise my camera as he tries to loop it around the antenna.

"Wait, the antenna will snap. Besides, it's too low. Could you just hold it up?"

The banner loops between the pole and Immanuel, cupping the entire lagoon in the middle, with all its birds, trees, and water, and the pink sun resting on top of a cypress skeleton. Everything is in the shadow, the flags, road, water, Immanuel. The sun casts a thin gold pink path upon the water, all the way to the banner. My heart is ablaze.

I lift my camera and click away. When it is done, we move the banner toward the shipyard. By the time we reach the end of the road, we have covered the entire Mississippi River with our flags, from Itasca to the end of the Bird's Foot, 2,320 miles and 3,734 kilometers long, not including the tributaries I paddled and traveled to in the past two years: the entire St. Croix, the Minnesota, the Missouri, the Ohio. Words and art, music and food, all come together in the river flags. Do our words count as matter? And love? If not, then why are they as indestructible as the matter itself, spreading like wild fire and expanding like the universe?

We almost reach the abandoned shipyard, the very end of the Bird's Foot. We are going to wrap the entire place with the flags. I was folding the banner when Immanuel said:

"Wait. Let's hang the flags across the road."

What? Flags on the dark side? No! Absolutely not! Then I see his eyes, the light I never noticed before. He is right. Our river flag banner can bridge day and night, water and land, truths and lies, hope and despair. I hug him, the banner between our chests. The way is open between us.

In the twilight, the dead cypresses awaken from the deep of the lagoon.

So this is it, I tell myself, my heart pumping as Mike fires the engine, and the rusty boat inches away from the dock. *We're going into the gulf. We are entering the bird's foot, into its brain. My dream is coming true. Our mission is half complete.*

I remember the times my heart leapt like this: my first travel on my father's navy ship to visit Grandma in Shanghai, my admission into Beijing University, my flight to NYC, starting a new life beyond my imagination, my first book lying in my hands like a dream, my PhD diploma, births of my two sons, their first steps, first words.

Somehow, this is different, something immensely joyful and heavy at the same time, something larger than myself yet personal and emotional. Dave's words come to me again: be careful, Ping, be careful. I put my hand on my heart. It beats in sync with the engine, batum, batum, batum, furious and steady. Mike gazes at the water, his hands light and firm on the steering wheel. They are not trembling at all, and his eyes are no longer bloodshot. I bet his blood pressure is down to normal. *He belongs to the gulf*, Lili's words echo in my ears. Droplets of mist rush to the windshield then trickle down like tears. On both sides, shores with thick reeds and oil rigs recede quickly. Immanuel sits in the back, a fish net hanging over his head. Above the windshield, a heavy-duty GPS shows the Mississippi's three branches in the shape of a bird's foot, and we are sailing through its central fork, the end of North America's artery.

Boats pass by, five times bigger than ours. One of them belongs to the Vietnamese fishermen I just met at the dock this morning.

At 3:30 a.m., Lili woke us up apologetically. Mike was waiting outside the trailer. I rushed out of the door without using the bathroom. By the time we got the boat ready for departure, I had to pee. There was no bathroom on Mike's boat. You could use a Coke can, he said, half joking, half serious. Or pee into the gulf from the end of the boat, like us when we're fishing. I shook my head. Mike sighed and gestured me to follow him. He took me to a group of Asians picking shrimp in the twilight, a giant boat parked at the dock. The men all looked young, laughing and shouting "Hey, Bug Man" when we approached them. At the head of the table stood a beautiful middle-aged woman. She smiled as she watched Mike pick up a shrimp and examine its head.

"What can I do for you, Mike?" she asked. She never looked at me once, but I knew she had already sized me up from head to toe the moment we started walking to them.

Mike greeted her then asked if I could use the bathroom upstairs. She frowned and continued chatting about the weather. My bladder was about to burst, when she nodded, "Okay, she can use it, but no photos."

I ran upstairs and entered a spacious office decorated with ink paintings and gobs of money. They must be doing well if they could afford such a big fishing boat plus the two-storied office building. Did they catch shrimp better than Mike? It didn't seem so. The pile of shrimp on the table looked emaciated. Mike showed me the black spots in the head as the young fishermen watched and laughed, imitating his words while decapitating the heads to make the shrimp look "normal." I asked a friendly looking man if they planned to go out shrimping that day.

"Nope," he shook his head, "not much to catch in the gulf. Seafood is not coming in like the old days. It took us three days to get this much," he pointed to the pile on the table. "It won't even cover the fuel."

I was aghast. Three days for this? How much could they sell? Definitely not enough for gas, let alone to pay all the workers. And why did they wait three days to process the shrimp? No wonder it looked on the verge of rotting. Well, they must have lost interest in processing their catch because there was no money.

I locked the bathroom, sat down on the toilet. Such relief! I looked up in gratitude. Before me, next to the toilet paper, was a file box full of manila folders. Some of them were open, revealing copies of checks. The first sheet had three checks copied together, in the amount of $21,000, $50,000, and $19,750. They were all paid for shipping goods from Louisiana to Texas. I picked up that folder, and flipped through the sheets, each with three or four checks, starting from $15,000 to $75,000, each folder containing at least forty sheets. I counted the folders. Fifteen in total, each bulging with checks, some paid, some past due.

Mike said the Vietnamese ran a multimillion-dollar fishing business every year. If it was true, then it was nothing compared to the transportation business.

What did they transport?

No wonder the woman forbade me to photograph. Did she know her file box was open? I jumped up, flushed, and ran out. If she suspected I was a Peeping Tom in her bathroom, who knows what would happen!

I wave at the passing boat. The woman stands at the end of the deck, looking at me without blinking. Oh God, she's coming after me for her files. But how would she know that I peeked? Is she going to shoot me? Mike cranks up the engine. His boat roars and speeds up. The young fisherman behind the steering wheel laughs and speeds up his engine too. For a minute, we race neck and neck, and the woman never takes her eyes off me. My hair stands on end, and I hold my breath until the woman and her boat pass by, leaving us in the huge wakes.

"Son of a gun!" Mike laughs like a child. He is having fun racing. My shirt is soaked with cold sweat. The woman still hasn't moved an inch, standing like a statue on the deck. With her back to us, I can still feel her beautiful, melancholy eyes. It occurs to me, now that the boat has passed us, that she was not looking at me but through me into a distance place, in search of something.

Is she looking for her old home she had left behind? Is it why she looks so sad despite her big boat and big money?

And where are they going? The young fisherman told me they are not going out fishing today.

"They must be hunting for some work," Mike says, reading the question in my eyes. "They don't really need to since their boats are all paid for. These

Asians have tight family ties. They pool their money together to buy boats, in cash. They don't like to owe money to banks and become their slaves. And they like to work. It's in their blood. I've never seen anyone work harder. That's why I have no qualms about their big boats and big earnings; they earned every goddamn penny with their sweat and brain."

Should I tell him what I saw in the bathroom? Probably not. Mike is right. They work hard for every penny they make. It's not my place to question or judge.

Mike kicks a small stool toward me. "If you want to sit. It's Lili's. But she rarely uses it. She just squats all night cleaning and sorting shrimp I catch." He points to the metal boxes and a bag of brine on the deck. "The catch goes into this box. Lili soaks them in the brine water to keep it fresh and shiny, then she sorts. The shrimp stays, and the rest, fish, crab, eels, have to go back to the sea, dead or alive. We are licensed only to catch shrimp, and that's what we are allowed to keep. We can't even eat the fish or crab, even if they are dead. It used to bug me to no end. What a waste! And how absurd! How humiliating! I, a fisherman all my life, can't eat the seafood I catch with my own hands and have to buy it from a fish dealer. But the law is the law. If I get caught, we lose the license."

He sighs, his eyes pooling with tears. "But it doesn't matter anymore. Everything from the gulf is poisoned anyway. It has poisoned Lili. She got cancer, now spreading from her breasts to her lungs."

I remember her hands. That explains the shocking brown spots along her lung meridians. But how does she still move like a sixteen-year-old?

"Is she getting treatment? Surgery? Chemo? Radiation?"

He shakes his head. "No insurance. Medicare covers some, but still too much for us. Besides, Lili doesn't want to go through the torture. She doesn't want to put more toxins in her body. She wants to leave the world clean, as she came to the world clean."

No wonder she wants to visit Vietnam.

"I wish I had money to take her home to Vietnam. I wish I could move to Seattle with her. But I wouldn't make it there. If I die, Lili would die. If Lili dies, I'll die. So Lili is holding off her cancer for me."

I want to say her love and willpower are stronger than chemo and radiation, but I can only ask, "Do you miss seafood, Mr. Waddle?"

"Do I miss seafood?" he repeats, syllable by syllable, his eyeballs almost bursting out of his sockets. "Are you asking if I miss the air, water, and earth? I am the sea. The sea is me. I was born here, grew up here, and will die here. When I die, I want my ashes scattered in the gulf, my womb and grave. They say you are what you eat. How true! Sometimes, I believe I'm a fish, a shrimp, a crab, a bird, a reed, things I have lived on from the day I was born. My parents, my grandparents, my great-grandparents, all lived off the sea since they crossed the ocean from Ireland and settled in the gulf. We have owned the land, lost it in the floods, then owned more, and lost it again, back and forth, back and forth, like the moon cycles. But we live on happily as long as the gulf lives, as long as life comes in and out with the tides. It's a circle, rings of circle connected and connecting, things we see and can't see, hear and can't hear, touch and can't touch . . . our genes mixed, after our daily exchanges. Two years without seafood, and I'm starved, not just here," he pounds his stomach, where his guts spilled in Katrina, then his chest, held together by a steel rod in his spine. "My heart is also starving. Ask Lili, she knows. She's also a sea creature, a mermaid. All the Vietnamese are, coming from the Mekong and the Pacific coast. There's a reason why so many of them live in Louisiana as fishermen. And I have to say they're the best fishermen I've ever known. They speak the fish language, sing their songs, move with their rhythms. That's why they do so well here, with their fishing fleets. Other fishermen are jealous, but not me."

The sun is coming out of the shoreline, gilding the reeds and water with its metallic light. Somehow it makes the river look darker, like the ink sky before dawn. The GPS shows we are at the end of the river's plume, and soon, we will enter the Gulf of Mexico.

As the channel becomes wider, more and more pipes appear in the reeds and waterways, each with a sign warning against trespassing.

"Spaghetti fields," Mike points at the pipelines.

"What?" I know what he is saying, but I have to make sure. It's too poetic to be true. Too visual not to be true. Spaghetti fields.

"The whole gulf and delta is rigged like a plate of spaghetti. What you see here is nothing to what is really going on. Twenty-eight thousand wells along the coast, five thousand feet into the sea. Imagine the constant leaking. Yes, the wells leak all the time, small and big, because the cement that seals them doesn't last long, even without the constant drillings and shaking and breaking. Twenty-eight thousand wells, twenty-eight thousand holes punched into the gulf. And let me tell you something you may not know. Our sea floor is fragile because it's filled with salt, gas, oil, and radioactive minerals. The reserve is huge, the size of Everest, held together by a thin crust. You punch a hole into the crust, you change the pressure, and the whole structure could collapse, just like the lungs. That's why it took BP eighty-eight days to seal the damn well of the Deepwater Horizon. It's not the first time and won't be the last. We're sitting on the mound of hell, with twenty-eight thousand bombs ticking."

His hands are shaking again. No wheel or water can extinguish the storm in his brain. I start shaking too. I could see, hear, and smell the hell Mike just described. I glance at Immanuel, stiff like a statue, tears filling his eyes. He truly believes the world will end, already filled our basement with water, beans, and rice for emergency.

"I'm leaving, Ping," he cries, tears streaming down his face. "I love you, but I am a king, an eagle, and I need my own kingdom and sky."

He covers his eyes with his hands. I say nothing. His decision comes without a warning. I'm not surprised, though, only disturbed: Why am I not feeling sad or upset?

"Why are you crying?" shouts Mike. "She's supposed to cry, not you, damn it!"

Immanuel sobs louder, covering his head with his hands, as if afraid of the dangling fish net snatching his neck. I want to laugh, put my hand on his shoulder, tell him that the kingdom he imagines is a lonely one, and the sky won't be real unless it is open for all the birds to fly. But I look beyond him. The Mississippi is about to end and the gulf about to begin. All the shores and borders will disappear. The gulf will be one body of water, one world, where we are all set free.

Immanuel is setting himself free, setting me free too.

"Just shut up," screams Mike. "You've been planning the breakup for a while, haven't you? You didn't just come up with the idea now. So why on Earth are you here?"

Immanuel winces and stops sobbing. The only sounds are the roaring engine and the seagulls crying in the wake.

Good question! Why are we here? And why are you here, Mr. Waddle, despite your anger and love? I want to ask but don't know how to start. Why do we travel all the way here, from the headwaters to its very end, hanging flags along the way, camping, paddling, talking to people, hosting workshops for poetry and making new flags, searching for food, shelter, getting lost, finding new paths? This is not the typical vacation for most people. There are no five-star hotels or restaurants, no fenced-in beach or golf course, and there is nothing glorious about the project but working late into the night after night in my basement, cutting, dyeing, and ironing fabric, scanning, photoshopping, and updating the website and Facebook, spending days and weeks on proposals, letters, workshops, and installations at river communities, bringing people in, by tens, hundreds, thousands—what is it that sustains me and the core group of people? What force draws so many people in, including Immanuel? He insists this is my project, not his, and the trip is his vacation and nothing else, and yet, he helps along the way.

What force has kept us together?

Our capacity to hope?

Is hope a matter? If yes, why does it have no physical substance to occupy space, for people to see, feel, touch, hear, smell, or taste? If not, why does it permeate and persist with such force and last as long as life permits? Why can't it be destroyed? If hope is matter, where does it originate? Our heart? Our mind? Our soul? If our body serves as a temple for this force, then where will it go when the body dies?

"Look, the gulf!" shouts Mike, eyes clear as if lights have switched on from inside.

And I smell it. The scent of the ocean tides mixing with fresh water, salty, fishy, sweet, pungent. My lungs contract first, as if hit by a fist, then open hard and wide. The air rushes in, filling my alveolar sacs with oxygen, filling my brain with light. I open my mouth, inhaling and exhaling like a newborn.

I am home. The sea, origin of life, destination of all rivers. Tears fill my eyes as déjà vu floods me with its tidal waves. I am in Shanghai again, the mouth of the Yangtze, the East China Sea, where I was born, then grew up on an island fed by the mighty river, the Adam's apple of the blue dragon at the mouth of the Yellow River. And I am also here, at the end of the Mississippi, a rising phoenix, fueled by the oil and minerals underneath.

Mike takes something out of his chest pocket and opens it. Two flags. One with "Love from Little Dick, Jan, Mike Waddle," the other with "Please give back our river, our Gulf, Lili Liang." They made the flags in the middle of the night. These lovely people. They could have wished for his son's return, her going home in Vietnam, a better fishing boat, a cure for cancer . . . Yet, all they want is love for the gulf.

The sun is leaping out of the horizon, lighting up the flags, the words and flowers on the fabric, the hands that hold them, the wind that blows them up, and the sparks in Mike's eyes. I open the flags from the upper Mississippi, the St. Croix, the Yangtze, all humming with the spirits of the makers, people who love rivers and Earth, who put their energy and blessing into the flags. The wind whips the banners, sending them up into the sky, joining in with Mike's flags.

And inch by inch, the gulf lights up from the top down, the bottom up. It reveals the twenty-eight thousand rigs in the sea floor, crude oil flowing up along the pipelines forming the spaghetti fields into a giant bird, feathers and scales in neon green, red, and yellow, eyes gleaming with hunger, beak and claws poised to snatch, snatch, snatch, cancerous veins sucking the essence from the sea and Earth and sky. The Piasa! I shudder and am about to close my eyes when something comes alive in the deep water: blue fins, croakers, marlins, swordfish, tilefish, shrimp, crab, oysters, plants, deformed and sick from the polluted sea, yet living, stubbornly. One by one, they light up like stars in the deep sky, forming constellations around the Piasa, the spaghetti fields, setting fire on them. The gulf is rerigged into a new galaxy, a phoenix. I listen to its hum, and the flags in our hands start humming too, along with the flags from Mike and Lili's yard, from the confluences along the Mississippi and its tributaries, along the Yangtze River, and all the rivers on Earth. When the flags reach Everest, the phoenix from the gulf will pull the blue dragon out of its muck, and the dance will begin, creating an energy field that will cut through money, war, suffering.

The phoenix is rising.

"That's why we are here, Mr. Waddle," I announce loudly, lifting the banners higher into the air. "It is the wish from the sky and earth, rivers and mountains, and all the sentient beings under the stars, the wish to live in peace and harmony. This is matter, our matter."

My cell phone dings. Dave Brink just sent me a video clip: "Issa sends a blessing from the water dragon." I press the play button, and hold it high to the sky. Kneeling between a wooden xylophone and Indian drum on the family's mahogany table, Issa, Dave's one-year-old daughter, is singing her blessing to the world, her green dress open like a lotus.

The Green Tara is dancing.

VI

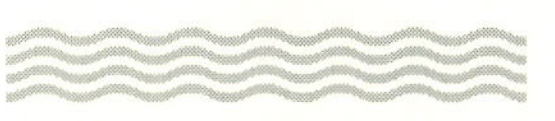

We Are Water

29

We Are Water

"Walk through the checkpoint, Ping, and don't look back," says Tashi, our Tibetan guide. "Pass the soldiers as if they don't exist. If they shout to stop you, keep walking as if you didn't hear them. If you hear a gun clicking, stop. Do not run. Do not move your arms or turn around. They'll for sure shoot if you do. Just wait till they come."

"You're kidding me, right, Tashi? Tell me you're just kidding," I whisper.

"Ping, in the heart of a storm, there's stillness and peace," Tashi replies.

I glance at him, his sleepy eyes now lit with a mysterious light. Behind us, the military tent used as the checkpoint for the Everest Base Camp is bulging with tourists waiting to have their permits verified. Before us, a gravel road leads to Mount Everest, guarded by soldiers on both sides of the checkpoint. If something happens, a whole battalion of them will rush out from their camouflage tents along the mountain path. On the right of the road is an open field dotted with yak dung, Coca-Cola cans, Budweiser bottles, plastic bags. The soldiers can see any moving object, as small as a mole or a roach, in one glance.

And Tashi wants me to walk through this death field.

"You slipped through two checkpoints already. You know what to do," he says.

This is different, I want to shout. Those two checkpoints had a much bigger crowd, and a public bathroom nearby. Had I gotten caught, I would have told the soldiers that I was using the toilet, and all they could have done was shoo me back. But here, the other side is our final destination, the Everest Base Camp. If the soldiers catch me, I can say nothing but admit that I've slipped through the first and second checkpoints, am now crossing the last one without a permit, and they'll interrogate how I got here, in what car, and everybody will be in deep trouble.

I remain silent. Tashi has warned me many times about the consequences.

"Ma Jinhua?" shouts a soldier in the tent. He sounds young, about the same age as my sixteen-year-old son.

"She's outside, officer," says a girl. "She's sick."

"I need to see her face. Bring her in."

"She's vomiting. Altitude sickness. I'm her sister. See my permit? Ma Yinhua. We're twins. We look exactly the same on the photo and in person. Please, let us pass. She's too weak to walk, let alone push through this crowd."

"She must show her face here. No face, no pass. Next?"

I hear sobbing from the tent, then shouting from the crowd outside the tent. "She's fainting. Yinhua, come quick. Your sister is fainting!"

I run toward the chaos. "I'm a doctor, Tashi. Let me take care of the girl first."

Outside the tent, a crowd has gathered. I push in. A girl in a fake Mountainaire coat lies in a pool of foamy vomit. Her eyes are closed, her face is white, but she's breathing. I check her pulse. Feeble and quick but relatively regular, no fluttering, no sudden surging or stopping. That's a good sign. I pick up the oxygen bottle hanging around her neck.

"It's empty," says her twin sister, tears in her eyes. "She used it up long before we got here. I told her to use it sparingly, but she wouldn't listen."

"Get another one, quick." I order. A man hands me a bottle. It seems every Chinese here carries oxygen supplies. I hook it to her nose.

"Breathe, Jinhua, in, out, in, out," I whisper, breathing in sync with her.

Color returns to her face, and she opens her eyes.

I feel like weeping. I wish I could lie on the ground like Jinhua, in the fetal position, so I don't have to run through the checkpoint alone.

"Time to go," Tashi whispers, taking me out of the crowd by my hand and leading me to the back of the tent again. "This is your best chance to get through, and your last. It's going to be dark soon. No more delay, if you want to see the peak. Summon your lion spirit, Ping!"

I look at the sky. It's gray and cloudy. I won't see the peak even if I sneak through the checkpoint. Is it worth the risk of being shot at? I look at the road, deadly silent. No rumbling trucks or milling tourists to make myself inconspicuous. No sunlight to blind the soldiers' eyes nor heat wave forming one mirage after another to hide my presence as it did when I slipped through Dingri checkpoint and walked two miles on the Dingri Highway. Here, I'll be an open target once I step away from the tent.

I feel Tashi's hand on my elbow. I glance at him. How bright his eyes are, his body taut and alert like a snow leopard on the prowl.

Since I met Tashi at the Lhasa train station, I debate with myself constantly if he's the best or the worst, if not the laziest guide, I've ever met. Well, I've only met two so far, Helen from Qinghai Province, and Tashi from Lhasa, both assigned to us by Bean, a Sichuan travel agent I found online. There are hundreds of them, all promising the best service and lowest price. I spent many hours interviewing the agents, negotiating costs, and discussing routes. Finally, I picked Bean. She sounded the most rational and sincere, and her fee seemed the most reasonable compared to others. Still, it was $10,000 for five of us to travel through the Tibet Plateau for thirteen days. We didn't have a choice, since foreigners are not allowed to travel alone in this region. We must get a permit to enter Tibet, and another one to visit Everest. A licensed tour guide must accompany us from the moment we arrive in Lhasa until the last minute of our departure.

When we first arrived at Lhasa, nobody came to meet us. Twenty minutes passed, and we were sweating profusely, not just from the unforgiving sun and heat from the concrete square but also from the soldiers patrolling around us. We looked suspicious, four foreigners and a Chinese, with musical instruments and heavy bags of flags. In the station and on the train, our passports and permit had been checked and rechecked at least twenty times. Now in Lhasa, the security seemed even tighter. A troop of soldiers approached us. The leader saluted and said, "Ruzangzheng."

Our permit to enter Tibet had been confiscated by the security guard at the Lhasa station. I tried to yank it back from his hand. Helen had instructed me repeatedly to keep the permit, at any cost. "No permit, no Tibet!"

"This is no longer valid," the guard said sternly. Seeing the despair in my eyes, he added, "Your guide should be waiting outside with the original permit."

Where was our damn guide? What was I supposed to say to the soldier? I wish Lao Han were here to meet us, the way he used to welcome me to Tibet. But he disappeared after his wife caught him fooling around with their babysitter. Besides, he was always drunk, and I was not sure if he could handle a group of five plus installation of river flags along the way. Bean assured me that she would assign her best guide to take us around Tibet. Yet the soldiers were about to arrest us, and the guide was nowhere to be seen.

"Welcome, Tashidelek!" A brown man appeared out of nowhere and started throwing hada scarves around our necks, shouting in English and

Tibetan. He waved away the soldiers with his tour guide licence then turned to us with a big smile. "I'm Tashi, your guide. And this is your driver. He's Tibetan, like me."

Tashi's smile had magic. A few seconds ago, we were annoyed, sweaty, and terrified, but now, we were in good spirits. He looked to be in his midthirties, with spiky black hair, dark brown skin, and a belly pushing from under his T-shirt. He was about my height, short for a Tibetan, and he looked dreamy with his sleepy eyes, but I had a feeling that no one would mess with him. The driver smiled and waved at us, then helped us carry our baggage into the van.

We drove into Lhasa in silence. Tashi gave the driver directions in Tibetan then dozed off in the front seat. He was very different from Helen, who would have given us a detailed plan for the day and the entire trip. For some reason, I trusted Tashi right away, even though he was twenty minutes late and seemed to ignore his "duty" as a guide. Soon, we reached the edge of Barkhor Market in the center of Lhasa. The driver stopped. Tashi told us to get out.

"Your hotel is inside," he said, pointing to the deep of the bazaar. "No car is allowed beyond this point. We have to walk in."

He led the way without looking back. We tried to keep up as we dragged our trunks through the cobbled streets and throbbing crowd. Soon we lost him.

"I want Helen back," cried Alex, the musician from LA.

I looked at him with great sympathy. His face was burning in the sun, his beard drenched by sweat. He had been the rock star of our group as we traveled along the Yangtze, charming Chinese girls and men with his steel guitar, blue eyes, and red beard. Alex, the filmmaker, and my son Wei remained silent as usual. They looked sleepy and pale. The midsummer sun hadn't tanned their skin at all. Oliver looked around with his ear-to-ear smile, clicking away with his camera. Thank God I brought him on board at the last minute. He had been so helpful with hanging flags and carrying baggage and cheering us up. He was the easiest to please and most adventurous when it came to food. Anything delighted him, even cow penis, which he tried in Chongqing when we passed through the Three Gorges.

"Let's wait here till he finds us," I said to my group. "Let's be patient. Tashi is not a doting 'mother' like Helen, but he may be something else, something greater."

I was right about the first prediction. When Tashi finally found us wilting away under the glaring sun, he just said, "Oh, you're here," and motioned us to follow him again. No apology, no help with the baggage. As soon as we registered in the hotel, he said good night and dashed out.

I grabbed his sleeve. "Wait. Do we have all the papers for tomorrow?"

He looked at me sleepily. "Papers?" Then he slapped his head. "Yes, the permit to Everest! You guys have no problem," he pointed to my four American teammates.

"It's all here," he patted his pouch around his waist. "But I need your *shenfenzheng*, Ping, your residential ID, to get a permit for you to visit Everest."

I smiled, handing him my passport. "This is my shenfenzheng."

He shook his head. "Passport no longer works. For this year, we need your ID issued by the Chinese government."

"My passport is issued by the central police station in Beijing, the highest in the Chinese government. You want to know how many bloody hoops I had to jump through to get this in 1986?"

He shook his head again. "It has to be a residence ID that shows where you live in China, the province, the city, the street, issued by the local police, like this," he took out a small laminated one, similar to a student ID. "If you're Chinese, you must have one like this. No?"

"I *am* Chinese," I pointed to my dark brown passport that has been renewed three times over twenty-eight years by the Chinese consulates in NYC and Chicago.

"Then we can't go to Everest," he said, whipping out his cell phone. "I'll see if you can get some refund from the travel agency."

I heard a silent moan in unison. I turned to my group and saw their pinched faces. We had traveled for two weeks, from the mouth of the Yangtze through the hot, flooded Three Gorges to the no-man's land of the Qinghai-Tibet plateau, enduring diarrhea, flu, hunger, constipation, altitude sickness, and sleep deprivation, just for a peek of the highest mountain on Earth. "You'll forget all the pain once we get there," I told them repeatedly as I prodded them on. "It's worth every penny and pain."

"We shall go," I turned to Tashi, stone-faced, "with or without the permit."

His eyes opened. My words awoke him from his sleep mode. We stared at each other.

"Hello, hello, this is Bean. Speak up, Tashi. What's up now? Are you even there?" A woman's voice rushed from Tashi's phone, fast and hard like bullets. Bean, our travel agent? I had spoken with her a dozen times from the United States when I tried to negotiate fees with her. She sounded nothing like this shrew. In fact, I picked her because of her sweet voice.

Tashi covered the cell phone between his palms. "We have to go through six checkpoints: Dingri entrance and midway and the Everest Base Camp and three more on the way back. We can beg and bribe the soldiers to let us through. The chances are slim. I tried for a couple from Australia. Same thing: only passports but no ID. Actually they got a temporary residence ID through our agency, but the soldiers wouldn't acknowledge them. They saved ten years for this trip, flew all the way from Melbourne, spent three days in a car to Dingri, enduring headaches, nausea, insomnia . . . and the soldiers refused to hear their story or take their money. They cried all the way back to Lhasa."

He looked at me ponderously. "Are you willing to take that risk?"

"Yes," I said without hesitation.

A flicker of light animated his dark brown eyes. He was fully awake now. Bean was shouting profanities, her voice muffled between his palms. My eyes opened wide. I would never have imagined such dirty words coming out of Bean's mouth. Tashi picked up the phone with his thumb and forefinger, as if picking up a dried piece of turd, then shut it with a flip of his wrist.

"Very well, then. I shall see you tomorrow at 9:00 a.m."

He disappeared as suddenly as he had appeared. I tried to recall his facial features, the clothes and shoes he wore, but all I could get was the light flickering from his sleepy eyes then vanishing into a dark brown face.

I turned to my group. "Guys, we may have found a snow leopard."

"This is a suicide walk. Can't we think of a better solution?" I look at Tashi in despair. At the bottom of my heart, I know there's no other way.

"We can still return to Lhasa," he says. "We'll be driving in the dark."

I shake my head. We've climbed over two humongous mountains to get here, along a treacherous road filled with potholes made by streams of water rushing down from the cliff on the left, washing over the road, then over the cliff on the right. The road is too narrow for two cars. When our tire popped and the driver spent twenty-five minutes changing the tire, we created a huge traffic jam. Tashi woke up from his doze and helped for the first time. He worked intensely, never looking up at the honking trucks or shouting drivers until they fixed the tire. The potholes rattled our bones, and our heads hurt as if hammered by mallets. We were held together only by the promise that we would see the summit and hang our flags on the roof of the Earth. Even Wei, who's been sick and sleeping in his seat for the past eight days since we entered the Tibet Plateau, has woken up. The summit is calling him too. I can't let them down. Not here, not now, not after I slipped through the heavily guarded Dingri checkpoint, walking two miles alone in the sizzling sun, my heart racing at my throat, ready to be shot down by the guards with each step. We are already here, at the base camp. We can see the summit, almost, if the clouds clear up, if I would just walk through the checkpoint, through the death field.

"Hat and jacket, please," whispers Tashi. "Your white hat was the most conspicuous thing on the Dingri Highway. I could see it miles away, almost died from holding my breath."

So he was worried. Would I have felt less terrified and abandoned had he let me know? Will he be watching me perform this third miracle?

I peel off the knock-off Mountainaire hat I bought in Lhasa for the Everest trip. I'm not going to argue with him about the hat, but the jacket? "I'll be frozen to death without it," I murmur as I unzip it slowly. The temperature is dropping fast as night approaches the base camp. Why on Earth did I buy the flaming red fleece instead of the brown one from Patagonia on Grand Avenue in St. Paul? Ah yes, I wanted something light for the 3,915-mile journey along the Yangtze, something warm and flashy at the same time for the frigid air at the 17,060-foot altitude of Everest. The six-foot-four red-haired salesman picked it off the rack and handed it to me with a big smile: "You won't regret having this."

"Camera," Tashi reaches out his other hand.

"Shouldn't it help, if I say I'm a tourist?"

"Not unless you want to lose your Canon 5D and the photos."

I am shivering. My head feels light, my body weightless without my Canon.

"Your purse."

"No!" I clutch it to my chest. It holds my passport, green card, driver's licence, and my sons' photos. "I need them, just in case I get . . ."

"No, you don't. If they catch you, you'll tell them you're alone. You don't know me or anybody in our group. Our paper doesn't even have your name, see?" He lifts the permits for my son, Oliver, Alex, and Alex. "If they shoot you, you don't want to bring us down together with you, right?"

I can't believe my ears. Is this for real? This sounds too much like those illegal Chinese charging through U.S. customs at the airport to declare political asylum. Before their crossing, the snakehead, their ringleader, strips them of all documents and IDs, so the U.S. government can't send them back to where they are from. I've helped them appeal their cases to the judges from local to federal courts. I've written many poems to broadcast their stories. Now, it's my turn to be nameless. And what an irony, considering how I've sneaked Americans into Tibet since 1994! I've remained a Chinese citizen all these years so that I can travel here without the need of a permit!

"Tell me why I don't know you?" I ask. I just want to hear him confirm the answer I already know.

"Because I don't want to go to jail for ten years, or if I'm lucky, lose my licence and never find a job again as a guide. I can wash dishes if I were ten years younger without a family, but my daughter is growing up fast. I want her to go to a boarding school in the mainland, like the rest of the Tibetan kids, to get a better education and perhaps a better chance to go to college in America, like you. But she'll get citizenship, unlike you."

He gazes at the bare mountains under the gray sky and the military tents along the roadside. "Everyone is looking for a way out. The ice is melting. The leopard is gone. There's nothing left for us anymore." He turns to me, eyes red. "Why do you keep coming back, Ping? Why still cling to the brown passport so long, so stubborn?"

I am speechless. I wish I could answer this question myself. Since my first book, *American Visa*, my publisher pleads with me often to become an American citizen so they can nominate my books for awards. My friends worry that my big mouth may lead to my deportation back to China someday. My family, my ex-family? Aiden is married now with his ideal woman: a blond who worships the ground his feet touch. They live in the house I redesigned and renovated, the garden I built on my hands and knees, but we pass each other on the street as if we were strangers. My sons, my half-Chinese and half-Jewish sons, do they know their mother is still a Chinese citizen? Wei turned sixteen on the day we entered Tibet and told his father on the phone that it was his worst birthday ever, and when he gets back home, he only wants to enjoy American life: video games, pizza, and burgers.

I look at the sky, so low and wet that I could grab it and wring water out of the clouds. I look at the mountains, tall and naked like newborn giants, streams gushing down their brown cheeks like tears. Nothing seems to have changed since I stepped on the plateau in 1992, 1994, 1996, 2001, 2004, 2006, 2007, 2008, 2009, 2013. I've come here whenever I had money and time, by myself, with Lewis, Aiden, and now this group. I know nothing ever remains the same, even for the tallest mountain on Earth. As India keeps pushing it up from below, Everest continues to grow, 2.6 inches a year. Yet, this strange familiar sense of coming home, of belonging, has never changed.

"I was born here, many times," I whisper to Tashi. "This is your home, also mine. There's something for us as long as the mountain stands and the water runs."

Tashi says nothing, but his sparkling eyes say everything. He cups my elbow in his palm. Heat enters my heart meridian along my inner arm. He's blessing me, his brown face red and sweaty from the transfer of energy. Blood surges through my heart, now beating at a steadier, slower pace, like the hearts of Tibetans and Sherpas, who know how to extract oxygen from the thin air and use it at the maximum efficiency.

I hand over my purse to Tashi and look back to the other side of the checkpoint. Our gray van waits at the end of the line. May angels blindfold Wei's eyes so that he won't see my crossing. Would they also blindfold the soldiers?

"Do not fear, Ping, you've got Tara's hand over the evil eye." Tashi whispers as he puts a bottle in my hand. "Sometimes, the most dangerous place is the safest."

With a gentle push, he delivers me into the field.

≈

How thin is the air at Everest?

At the base camp, 5,400 meters (17,500 feet), the air has about 50 percent oxygen. You feel dizzy, nauseous, sleepy. Your head hurts like being pounded by hammers. You gasp for air. You vomit everything you eat, then vomit your guts. At Camp One, 6,100 meters (20,000 feet), the oxygen level drops further, then 40 percent at Camp Three, 7,400 meters (24,000 feet). You hallucinate. You hurt everywhere. You can't breathe, eat, or sleep. But you keep walking, one step at a time, after long, painful gasps. You go on with sheer willpower. When you are near the summit, 8,850 meters (29,035 feet), the air has less than one-third oxygen, and it can drop as low as 14 percent, as recorded in the 1996 snowstorm that killed twenty climbers. You should have dropped dead, but you keep going.

Above eight thousand meters (twenty-six thousand feet), the mountain is an open graveyard where one hundred bodies have mummified in fetal positions, face up, face down, sitting, hanging upside down. Among them is George Mallory, who disappeared into the clouds in 1924. Those who tried to take the bodies down never returned themselves. Above eight thousand meters, you use far more oxygen than you breathe in. Every step you take, you need five minutes to rest. Your body is so starved of air that it eats itself for survival.

First, it cuts off the blood to your hands and feet, causing frostbite then gangrene, even though you need them desperately to hang onto the rope as you climb the vertical ice in the jet stream wind. After the extremities go, your blood stops flowing to your guts and liver, just so your lungs can keep grabbing for air, your heart pumping blood to the brain to keep it nimble in the haze of hallucination. Any mistake—a wrong step in the ice, a missed buckle of your rope, a hesitation of your will to keep moving—you'll die, and you should have been dead long ago, with so little oxygen in your blood, PO2 at the level 3.5, about one-tenth of the normal and less than half than the patients in intensive care. Above eight thousand meters, Mount Everest is a death zone.

"Breathe, breathe, breathe . . . step . . . breathe, breathe, breathe . . . step," I chant silently as I baby-walk past the guards, into the naked field, my back wide open to their QBZ-95 rifles. Tashi says they have a much greater accuracy. My knees buckle with each step. The entire Everest is sitting on my shoulders. My heart beats madly to send some blood, now blue from lack of oxygen, to my brain. My brain has become a sea of sticky phlegm. How do I cough the phlegm out of my eyes? My mouth is raw, stuffed with burning sand from the Golmud Desert, the giant sand dune we tried to climb barefoot, three days ago. Pain seeps through my soles and heels, reaching all the way to my scalp. My organs are on fire. I jump like a bean, trying to get away from the boiling dune, but I'm stuck in the middle. Going up or going down, I'll be boiled alive in the sand. I need water, but my hands shake too much to open the thermos. Why did Tashi give me this? He didn't allow me to carry water when I trekked two miles on the Dingri Highway in the afternoon sun, when the temperature in the valley reached over 110°F. Here at 5,200 meters higher, where the temperature has dropped to -30°F, my neon-red fleece would have kept me alive, not this damn thermos, cold and slick and steely like the oxygen tanks scattered among rocks and corpses in the death zone. I am cradling the bottle I can't open. *Freeze, Ping, freeze*, a voice screams from below, inside, above. *Another step, they'll see you. Go back to the checkpoint, back to your son, before they shoot you down in front of his eyes. He just turned sixteen, and your younger one is about to turn fourteen, waiting for your call to say happy birthday. Turn around, Ping! You can't die, not yet.*

"I know exactly what you want," the Sea Witch rasps, her voice far and near. "It is very foolish of you . . . for it will bring nothing but grief, pain, loneliness . . . Are you willing to suffer all this?"

"Keep going," yells the guard at the Potala Palace, shoving me across the threshold. "No loiter or return beyond this point."

"The longest and most painful journey is to know yourself," whispers Tashi, his sleepy eyes wide open under the stupa of the fifth Dalai Lama, which contains twenty thousand diamonds and gems, and a thumb of Sakyamuni, the Supreme Buddha. "You'll die many deaths along the way, but it's the only way for your rebirth, away from the wheel of desire and attachment."

Feet sticky, as if the ground were paved with magic glue. A miracle I'm still walking, after so many deaths. Mother's wrath, sister's tongue, my awkward stubbornness, loneliness, the Cultural Revolution, exile on a farm at fourteen, first love, marriage falling apart during the honeymoon, NYC with twenty-six dollars in my pocket, ten homes during the first eight months, Allen's yelling for Buddha, poetry, first book, PhD, first son, first loft overlooking the Mississippi, second son, full-time teaching three weeks after labor, torn birth canal.

"Just be quiet and do it," says the chair. "We've all gone through this, in silence."

"And what's the fuss about sleeping with girls in Amsterdam? It's just a handshake, a business transaction," says the father.

"No, you are not good enough for promotion," says the provost, "just not good enough for us."

The mountain looms like a tower, underneath bones, fossils, molten rocks, temperature reaching 1,300°C.

In the death zone, the mind enters another space and time.

Thumb in my belt, unbuckled. If the soldiers see me, I'll squat and tell them I have to pee and there's no bathroom around. This is the land Aiden walked with me seventeen years ago, with our tent and sleeping bags, with the beautiful Sherpa we met at the base camp. He carried our bags, singing, laughing, chain-smoking, and leaping ahead of us like a mountain goat, and we watched from behind, gasping, stumbling forward inch by inch. We hitchhiked our way to the base camp in a military jeep, sharing our beef jerky with the officers.

No permit was needed then. We could walk and photograph freely. Aiden was jealous. The Sherpa was too friendly with me. We had a fight in NYC, and we didn't know if the trip would be our first or last. The Living Buddha from Lhasa blessed us: "Everything will be okay upon your return." And soon Wei was born, then Di. Now, I'm on the same path again, alone, with my group on the other side of the checkpoint, my son waiting to follow our path to Everest.

Keep walking, Ping, do not look back.

≈

"You're lying, Ping," said Aiden's father. The room was silent like a grave. The whole clan had gathered there in the family's condo, father, step-mother, sisters, brother, and in-laws, gathering to make peace and harmony. No one said a word.

I looked at him in disbelief. I had rushed here for this meeting. The family counselor promised that it would heal the family nicely. Aiden's father complained he had spent a fortune to fly his children from east and west. I had told Aiden I would be an hour late. I had an appointment with INS in St. Paul to do my fingerprints, scheduled a year ahead of time. All went smoothly, but I left the office with a heavy heart. Soon, they would call me in for the pledge, and I would no longer be Chinese.

"I called the college. It's closed for Good Friday. No class."

"Yes?" I said, blood receding from my head as anger gathered in my liver.

"So why are you an hour late?" he asked. His wife beamed as she anticipated a drama.

I shot a glance at Aiden, then at the counselor, who got paid to put this family together through healing. Aiden hung his head. The counselor's eyes were glazed over. Both had chosen not to hear or see.

I lifted my ink-smeared hands. "I did my fingerprints at the immigration office. I told Aiden to tell you that I would be an hour late for the meeting."

"Aha," Aiden's father smiled, exchanging a look with his wife. "I knew you would say it. So we called the immigration office. The phone rang and rang, and nobody picked it up, which could only mean one thing: CLOSED for Good Friday!"

I laughed. INS doesn't observe Good Friday. Did he know phone calls to INS are never answered? Not enough staff to handle the incoming calls. But, of course, how would he know, three generations away from his great-grandparents who sailed to NYC from Russia? Did he know how many circles lined around the INS building at 26 Federal Plaza? Did he ever stand twenty-four hours in line just to pick up an application form?

Aiden's father and step-mother beamed at each other as if they had just caught a petty thief red-handed, and from now on, the thief would never dare to show her annoying face again.

I took out an envelope from my bag. It had an American flag stamp on the right upper corner. Inside was the citizenship application. Everything was ready: proof of my immigration status, history, jobs, property, physical exams, fingerprints. It took two years to put all the documents together, to wait for the INS stamps, to wait for the quota. Everything was ready except for the photo of my face, which I had delayed for no reason. Had I had the photo ready, the immigration bureau would have kept the paperwork, and in a month, I would be a U.S. citizen. The paper had today's date and stamp. This would prove my innocence.

Then, it dawned on me. He and his wife had called both my college and the immigration office to catch me as a liar in front of the whole "family," which was not mine. No words or paperwork would change their conviction.

I looked at Aiden. For ten years, I served him as girlfriend, wife, mother, chef, travel guide, cleaner, gardener, house remodel designer. Would he say a word to lift me out of this hole?

"Why did you wait so long, girl?" chided the agent, pressing my inked fingers one by one on the paper. "You've been eligible for citizenship for fifteen years. What kept you?"

"I've been busy and moved around a lot," I murmured.

I scanned the room. It smelled rancid. It smelled of fear. Fear of what? The alien invasion? I lifted my chest. I was the tallest in the room. My sons, nine and seven, already showed signs that they would be over six feet, towering over their father, grandfather, aunts, and uncles.

I'm an intruder, with the tall-man genes from my mother's side.

Aiden buried his head between his knees. Was he reciting the prayer from the Torah that he would never be born as a woman?

I smiled, the smile Aiden wanted for his father's monthly family gathering.

"Would you smile, Ping, please? It would make things so much easier. You don't have to carry the world on your shoulders all the time."

I raised the envelope and tore it into pieces. Scraps of white paper fell around my feet like confetti. Some had my black fingerprints, some bore the red ink from the INS.

Who am I?

A question I've been asking since my first memory.

"You're a girl, and please, act like one," said Grandma, her deformed feet bound in bandages.

"You're a ghost," said Mother, still dreaming of college at age seventy.

"Wish you were a boy," sighed Father in his bed, alcoholic liver rotting with cancer.

"You want to write poetry with your sixth-grade English and get published?" said Danny from McGill. "Well, you have a better chance to win the lottery or go to heaven or get hit by lightning."

"You got the NEA because you're Chinese," said Larry, when I told him about my National Endowment for the Arts award.

"Look at me, Ping," said Soek-Fang, coming to my dreams during my suit against the college where I had taught since 1999. "You must not die like me, in silence, alone. Too many bones lie under the ivory tower. Bring it down, and lift us out of the white dust."

"Do you know, Ping, when we were in China, how many Chinese men pulled me to the side and warned me about you?" said Evan. "They assure me that you're not a woman, definitely not a Chinese woman."

"狂," said John Li, who guided our international seminar in Shanghai. He gave us seal chops as souvenirs. Everyone's had a nice word: wisdom, peace, beauty. I was given *kuang*: crazed, arrogant, maverick—the worst insult a Chinese person could unleash on another Chinese.

"Fly, Ping, fly," said Professor Xi, the legendary gymnastic coach from Beijing University, as she threw me onto the uneven bars without warning. "If your heart sees the stars, your body will grow wings." When I got off the bars, she invited me to join her team. After one month's crash training, I earned my first gold medal for the Beijing University gymnastic team.

Professor Xi opened my wings at age twenty-one, and I've been flying since.

"Fierce and fearless," said Louise Erdrich, securing a porcupine pin to my hair at her Birchbark bookstore.

It's drizzling. Everything is gray, cold, wet. *If your heart sees the stars, your body will grow wings.* I set my eyes on Rongbuk Monastery, the highest temple on Earth. Behind the stupa and prayer flags, Everest looms in the rain. My eyes can't see, but my heart feels its pull, my ears hear its call, and my nose smells its scent. People are pulled to Everest, over and over again, at great pains and costs, including their lives, by the scent of mountains and water in the thin air, the scent of stardust from the big bang.

Is this why I am here, why *we* are here? Is this why I hang onto my Chinese passport? For this smell, invisible, inaudible, untouchable, and unspeakable, yet stuck in my skin and blood since I stepped on this land?

No word can describe what's passing through my mind and flesh.

For every step, you gasp fifteen breaths to squeeze some oxygen from the air.

Of every fifteen people who reach the summit, one of them never returns.

How have you lived, Ping, all these years? You're not supposed to be alive with so little oxygen in your blood, so few nutrients in your stomach, while carrying so much on your back. Aiden is right. You do carry the world on your shoulders, and it's too much for him. He wants a wife, who cleans and cooks and keeps her mouth shut, not a fighter with a chip on her shoulder.

Keep walking, Ping, said Tashi. *Once you pass the line, there's no return.*

Rongbuk Monastery is only forty yards away. I'll be safe in a few more steps.

≈

"Hey, you," says a voice, "what are you doing here? Where's your guide? Your permit?"

I freeze. The voice seems to come from all directions, front, back, right, left, above. It's firm and authoritative but not vicious. Is he pointing his rifle at me? Can I turn my head to look? Then, I'll have to turn my whole body because my neck is stiff as if it were fused with a steel rod.

Stand still, or they'll shoot.

"What's your name?" he asks gently.

I open my eyes. He's been right in front of me, the whole time. I didn't see him because my eyes were closed. He's still in his teens, a hint of moustache on his upper lip, a shiny rifle on his shoulder. He inspects me with more curiosity than ferocity, like a scientist inspecting an alien from another star.

I point to the monastery with my shaking hand, teeth clattering. "My guide and friends are inside praying. I have to pee, but the toilet is too gross, so I came here."

How grateful I am to Tashi for stripping my jacket and purse! Now I look like a normal tourist sneaking out for a clean toilet. That explains why I don't have my jacket, camera, or purse with me.

"Oh, no, I'm sorry," I slap my head. "My guide told me I'm not supposed to pee outside, especially at the sacred ground. Am I in trouble?"

He smiles. "Yeah, the toilet does stink beyond tolerance. What's this?" He points to my metal bottle.

I turn pale. The bottle looks like a bomb and feels cold like a bomb.

"It's a bottle." I hand it to him. "My guide gave me this."

He takes it, weighs it in his hand, then brings it to his nose.

"It's just water," I say, suddenly remembering the scene. "We got it from a spring on the way here. It's hidden under the road and rocks. Our tire popped there and we had to stop and change it. That's how we discovered the hidden spring." I smile as I remember how excited Tashi was. "Our guide emptied our bottles and containers then filled them with the water. He said it's sacred water from the Rongbuk glacier. Tibetans and Sherpa travel far to fetch the water for special events, ceremonies."

I check myself. Tashi also said the government ordered the soldiers to seal the spring with concrete and steel because they don't want too many pilgrims near the base camp. That's also why they won't repair the road.

The soldier has opened the bottle, face red from the effort. He's inhaling its scent.

"Please, help yourself," I say. "I haven't touched it. I couldn't open it."

He takes a sip, nods, then hands back the bottle, as if he were passing weed.

"You," he says, making a drinking gesture with his hand.

I take a sip. It glides down my throat like an ice cube coated with honey, soothing my inflamed lungs, heart, and liver. For the first time since I entered Tibet, I can breathe. I will bring a bottle back to America, I tell myself, if I can survive this.

Survive? No, we're sharing water from the same bottle like friends. I look at the solider in disbelief. He's supposed to interrogate me, arrest me; yet, he's taking my bottle for the second time, drinking the liquid contaminated with my saliva.

Suddenly, I understand why Tashi handed me the bottle, why he closed the cover so tightly. He wanted the "soldier" to have the first taste.

"What's your name?" I ask.

"Tashi," he says. "From Nagqu."

I laugh. "Tashi, good fortune from the Black River. I've been there, in 2007 and 2008. I was following the train, to find out what the railroad brings to the nomads, and the winter worm trade. I almost died from the altitude sickness in Nagqu. Actually, I was weakened by diarrhea from the contaminated water.

Floods broke into the sewage system. Why *Black* River? It's more brown with angry currents, like a mad dragon."

What am I doing? Why are words pouring out of me like a spring? This man is supposed to be my enemy. He's supposed to check my permit, my ID, then arrest me. Yet, he's smiling and nodding as if he agrees with everything I said.

"How long have you been away from home?" I ask.

"A year, too long." He looks beyond the looming mountains, to the north, where his home is, Nagqu, Qiangtang Highland. Surrounded by the Kunlun, the Tanggula, and Ganddis Mountains, the highest grassland on Earth spreads six hundred thousand square kilometers, four thousand meters above sea level, frozen in wind and snow for eight or nine months of the year. It's a no-man's zone, except for the wandering Tibetan nomads, and because of that, it is a paradise for animals: wild donkeys, yaks, white-lipped deer, and, most beloved of all, chiru, Tibetan antelopes. There used to be over a million of them running wild in the grass, giving birth at the same time, blood turning lakes red, sky darkened by birds snatching up placentas. But the train brought poachers hunting Tibetan antelopes for their underwool to weave *shahtoosh*, shawls that sell for thousands of dollars each, symbolizing wealth, luxury, and class, shawls that have driven chiru into near extinction. The train also brings nomads digging for winter worms, followed by hui merchants, the herb believed to increase men's sex power; yet, its harvesting is turning the grassland into a desert. The train awakens the plateau with desire, changing it deeper and faster than guns, cannons, and laws: mountains bought and blown up for mining, houses and buildings rising, roads extending, oil, gold, and minerals taken out of Tibet daily, and thousands of tourists and migrants pouring in. Nomads can no longer roam with their cattle. The government nails them to one lot, easier to manage, easier to control. Grass becomes thinner each year, as the land gets no rest from grazing. Cattle shrink. Rodents thrive. Land becomes desert. Cattle die. Nomads starve. They dig winter worm herbs for a living, turning more grassland into desert.

Is that why he's here, guarding Everest, the nomad's son from Black River?

I know the story, his and others. I've visited their homes, drunk their yak butter tea.

He knows. That's why he's not demanding my permit. That's why he's not pointing his rifle at me. That's why we're chatting like humans.

"Why so many Chinese at the base camp?" I ask. "Last time I was here, it was mainly Sherpa and mountain climbers from Europe."

He smiles mischievously like Tashi the guide. "Chinese pay big money to see the summit, but very few got to see it because of the monsoon. You see the summit in fall and winter. That's when the foreigners come. They pay attention. But Chinese? They are worms: stay in holes in winter and crawl out in summer."

We laugh. I'm supposed to be mad, being Chinese, being called a "worm," but truth is exhilarating if you let go of the ego. I am a worm, a laughing worm.

The sun comes out. In the immense blue, Everest shows its white face.

We stare at the sublime. It blinds our eyes. But we don't care. We don't have a choice but to gaze.

"You bring the light," says Tashi the soldier, looking at me, the peak, me again. "The sun is not supposed to shine. No one has seen the peak for six weeks. Nobody expects to see it in the monsoon season."

He pauses, then asks, "Who are you?"

I am a worm, I want to say, jokingly, but my tongue is tied.

Then I hear her, from the summit 8,848 meters above sea level, from the 37,000 glaciers, tumbling, dancing, laughing, and screaming her way into the Indus, Ganges, Brahmaputra, Yangtze, Mekong, Yellow, into the mouths of the Arabian Sea, Bengal Bay, East and South China Sea, Gulf of Yellow Sea . . . I hear her meandering out of the snow and wild rice from Lake Itasca, through the most fertile land of North America, into the gulf, nursing billions of people, nursing trees, plants, fish, birds, animals, rains, snow, wind along her paths.

She is the matrix of life, dissolving, balancing, transporting nutrients.

She is equalizer, solvent, conductor, cleanser, life and death all at once.

She wraps 75 percent of the Earth.

She makes 75 percent of us: bones, muscles, blood, organs, tendons, hair, brain.

She's a trickster, forever moving and shifting, up, down, circle, gas, liquid, ice.

She welcomes everything with open arms, no judgment or grudge.

No border, dam, or politics can stop her flowing to the sea.

Nobody can own her: money, power, greed.

Nothing can destroy her: herbicide, pesticide, fracking.

This precious thing, most abundant on Earth, so old and young, so abused . . .

If we're careless, she drowns a few, to remind us of our origin.

She makes us. She is us.

"I am water," I want to say, but my tongue is tied, my mouth dry. I am weak.

Tashi hands me the bottle. I reach. Our hands touch. The bottle is open like an O. O is for oxygen, cradled in our hands. Hands are for hydrogen.

Two hydrogen molecules hold one oxygen; two rivers—the Yangtze and Mississippi—hug the Pacific under Everest, keeping this world together. One drop of water may be nothing. But two, two hundred, two million, two trillion drops of water make a stream, a river, a sea, a planet.

"We're water," I whisper.

Tashi laughs. His laughter roars with the glaciers gushing down Everest. In the thunder of joy, I see my people start crossing the checkpoint, Alex with his National guitar, Alex with his camera, Oliver with his sketch pad and pen, and my son Wei, who has been sick from the altitude and cold, lifts his camera for the first time since he entered Tibet, his eyes sparkling, his nostrils flaring with excitement.

Everest lights up every soul who lays eyes on her.

I hear Allen Ginsberg fly across the mountains, uttering cries half-human, half-bird.

Coda *My Kintsugi*

Five o'clock in the morning, March 3, 2014, Marquette Hotel, Minneapolis.

Jamyang Tashi ushers me into a big room, my sons Di and Wei follow, carrying two thousand river flags from the Mississippi, Yangtze, and many other rivers. In the center, His Holiness Dalai Lama. He reaches out, grabs my hands, holds them against his heart, and laughs.

I laugh with him, my hands between his palms, against his enormous heart that thaws my frozen heart. It's been a harsh winter, one snowstorm after another, one cold front after another, one bad news after another. My body is riddled with pain and doubts.

Never give up, develop the heart.

Never give up, no matter what is happening.

His words hang on the walls of my office and home as my daily mirror.

I have a million thoughts to share with him, a million questions to ask. I want to tell him how I've tried to calm a storm with a storm, to soothe anger with anger, to combat hatred with hatred, to ward off evil with bleeding eyes, to pay tooth for tooth, hand for hand, ash for ash. I want to show him how I've pleaded for a kind gesture to ease our daily grind, how I've made hundreds of banquets for peace, each morsel prepared with prayers.

Yet, I'm charred like a Joshua tree, radioactive across the desert.

I want to ask him how to put a broken heart back together.

All I can do is laugh with him, feeling the warmth of his chest, feeling his heartbeat, blessings flowing from his palms into my hands, heart, and soul.

What's a blessing? A transfer of energy from one being to another.

The world stands still. A space opens in me, a void cleared of noise and dust, a bud with infinite potential. I stop thrashing against the glass wall begging to get inside. I stop sobbing for mercy in the sea of lies, insults, and silence. I stand still, as the river of blessings flows from His Holiness into my hands, along my arms, into my lungs, filling up.

A new heart is made from the shards, sturdier, stronger, and more beautiful, with veins of gold filling cracks and over scars, the art of kintsugi.

How far have I traveled to get here, to stand so close with His Holiness, blessing Kinship of Rivers, blessing my sons?

I pick up a banner of river flags from the boxes and unroll it. The first flag reveals a glacier river running down snowcapped mountains so high that the child's little hand almost touches the sky. "Love and peace for my river, my land, and my people." I recognize the flag, made by a Tibetan girl born and raised in Minneapolis, who came to All My Relations, a Native American art gallery, for the first installation of Kinship of Rivers.

His Holiness bows, eyes wet with emotions. The flag contains a picture of Tibet and the title of his book *My Land and My People.*

It's been fifty-five years since His Holiness left Tibet in the night of March 17, 1959. All he wants is to go home.

The flag, opened by chance, brings him back to his land and people.

I've come to the hotel with a prepared speech about Kinship of Rivers, my travels in Tibet . . . all said by the child's words, in her painting, on her flag.

Tashi brings a bowl of raw rice. His Holiness sprinkles it over the flags, chanting, blessing, laughing.

And I laugh with him. Tashi joins in. Wei and Di join in.

This is life—a journey to reach home, each step a gift, a faith, a miracle of love, spiced with five tastes.